FASTER NEW PRODUCT DEVELOPMENT

MILTON D. ROSENAU, Jr.

FASTER NEW PRODUCT DEVELOPMENT

GETTING THE **RIGHT** PRODUCT TO MARKET **QUICKLY**

amacom

AMERICAN MANAGEMENT ASSOCIATION

Library of Congress Cataloging-in-Publication Data

Rosenau, Milton D., 1931–
   Faster new product development : getting the right product to
market quickly / Milton D. Rosenau, Jr.
      p. cm.
      Includes bibliographical references.
      ISBN 0-8144-5942-0
      1. New products—Management. 2. Product management. I. Title.
   HF5415.153.R67 1990   *89-81027*
   658.5'75—dc20   *CIP*

Printing number

10 9 8 7 6 5 4 3 2 1

Contents

Preface

WHO THIS BOOK IS FOR

Staying competitive in a fast-changing marketplace is today's challenge. To quote one observer, "The subject is a hot button today." While this book's central focus is on high technology products for industrial markets, it will be valuable for you if you have any involvement with the development of new products or services. The intended audience are those executives and managers who are trying to improve their company's competitive position through new products and services. It will also be valuable for other senior personnel in the marketing, engineering, manufacturing engineering, manufacturing, and research and development functions who are developing products, especially when these are technology-based products. Others involved, such as persons in quality assurance, technical service, finance, procurement, and similar functions, will also find much that is useful.

The intent of this book is to provide you with practical help to shorten the time required to develop a new product or service. While several other books outline systematic procedures for the development of new products, most do not stress speed. This time reduction is increasingly imperative because product life cycles have already shortened and are becoming still shorter. You can earn higher profits, both earlier and for a longer duration, if you get to market before the competition. In addition, a shorter development effort is normally less costly. And if you complete your new product quickly, your market research will be more accurate because there is less likelihood that the market at which you are aiming will have changed or that technological improvements will have bypassed you. Finally, and perhaps most importantly, if you can introduce new products more quickly than your competitors, you can make use of newer technology, which offers a variety of potential advantages.

Thus, faster development has a big payoff. However, there is no single "best way" to achieve faster new product development. Consequently, I do not provide a magic template that you can blindly trace nor do I offer a "silver bullet." Conversely, there are many very helpful approaches you can adopt and actions you can take, which I liken to many "platinum BBs." This book provides specific guidance on how to reduce the time from conception of the need or idea for a new product or service to market introduction. In fact, merely avoiding proven pitfalls, which I identify, is an obviously valuable first step.

Although most of the detailed discussion in the book is explicitly applicable to industrial products, the general principles are also applicable to consumer products and all new services. While the concentration is on new product development in larger organizations (more than a few dozen persons), the central ideas will also benefit smaller companies and start-ups.

There is another reason this book can be helpful to you. Corporate restructuring has diverted both management attention and limited corporate resources (especially capital) from producing new products and services. Many large corporations now prefer to purchase existing product lines rather than develop new products and build new businesses. This trend is due, in part, to the comparatively long time it now takes to develop a new product. Thus, if the time-to-market can be reduced, more corporations can emulate the successful few that grow in both size and profitability from a stream of new products. Finally, however, even the very largest corporations in the world have limited resources, only some of which can be applied to the development of new products and services. Thus, it is crucial that you use your firm's resources that are dedicated to developing new products and services as effectively as possible for the highest possible productivity.

AN APPROACH TO FASTER NEW PRODUCT DEVELOPMENT

Very little systematic attention has been given to the increasingly urgent need to produce new products faster. To date, the subject has been discussed briefly, if at all, and published information is fragmented. Recently, my clients, some prospective clients, and many participants in my seminars on new product development have been asking for help to complete new product development projects more quickly. Everyone wants new product development to be more productive. Curiously, the lessons of what works are generally well known but often not practiced with urgency or otherwise fully exploited. As a result, I have pulled together much of the available material, added techniques that I have developed or honed, and organized this into a coherent and practical summary.

All of the approaches, structural forms, and tools and techniques that I describe are used by one or more companies, but no company that I know uses all of them. Thus, I believe most companies can improve their performance by practicing more of these proven methods. This book provides a framework that each company can adapt to its own needs, market dynamics, and corporate culture. That is, no single prescription is universally applicable because the circumstance of each company is different.

The goal of this book is to provide both a general approach and some specific techniques to help you shorten the time your company spends developing a new product. The core of my faster approach makes use of:

1. Commencing the time-critical new product development activity with optimized specifications that are agreed to by a multifunctional (interdepartmental) team and then cast in concrete
2. Separation of feasibility projects and maintenance efforts, both of which can be very important to new product development and both of which often use many of the same human and physical resources, from the time-critical new product developmental activity itself
3. Utilizing short, very fast phases, each of which has specific requirements and a clear end point
4. Adopting an organizational structure to foster multifunctional teamwork and concentrating your corporation's limited resources on a manageable number of promising new product development efforts
5. Using a variety of tools and techniques, such as time efficiency, appropriate project management techniques, installation of productivity enhancements, schedule focus, incentives, and other adaptive methods, to make the entire process as fast as possible

Some advocates today debunk phased approaches as inherently slow. This is not correct. Properly arranged and managed, such an approach can be fast and low risk, and may help ensure management commitment. Further, the use of a phased approach does not inherently preclude the use of alluring new techniques such as quality function deployment (the so-called house of quality) or simultaneous engineering, which may also be helpful.

For simplicity, I replace the phrase "new products and/or services" with "new products" throughout the book, unless the distinction is important. (I discuss the explicit issues in developing new services in Chapter 18.) Further, "new products" includes a diversity of products that:

- Perform a totally new function (for example, a deep diving manned submersible);
- Provide enhanced performance of an existing function (for example, a digital timepiece replacing analog);
- Serve new applications (for instance, pump-action for toothpaste); or
- Offer increased features (for instance, telephones with autodial).

Much of what I discuss will also apply to situations in which the "new product" serves a new market, is offered at a significantly lower price, is amalgamated or combined with another, or is otherwise significantly reconfigured. Given this wide diversity of what constitutes a new product, a single company may logically use different approaches for these different new product situations. Finally, there are some new product situations, such as automobile air bags, in which slow-moving cultural and political changes are the pacing factor; nevertheless, a company can still use a faster approach within the constraints of that environment.

USEFUL AND UNIQUE FEATURES OF THIS BOOK

This is a practical, "how-to" book. Therefore, I stress multifunctional teamwork throughout—and this is crucial in any corporate situation. Fast, successful new product development results from harmonious cooperation among three primary functions—marketing, technology, and manufacturing—and the multiple ancillary functions such as quality assurance, technical service and procurement. I call this multifunctional team of marketing, technology, and manufacturing personnel the triad, because it involves three groups. (However, I know of one company that calls the triad a delta team, naming it after the shape of the Greek letter.) I identify suggested roles for triad members at each phase of the new product development process.

Also, I describe a general approach for fast new product development that you can adopt or modify. Finally, I present numerous specific accelerating actions that you can take regardless of the general approach you use.

HOW THIS BOOK IS ORGANIZED

This book is organized into six parts. Part I provides an overview, which the experienced practitioner may choose to skim. It provides detail on why shorter development durations are increasingly important.

Part II provides a description of a variety of *approaches* to developing new products as well as the phased approach that I favor. Chapter 2 reviews varied ways by which new products are conceived, developed, and introduced, and describes a specific fast, low-risk phased approach; Chapter 3 covers how and why to optimize and delineate specifications; Chapter 4 deals with converting the specifications into a product design that you can manufacture at low cost; Chapter 5 discusses issues in the manufacturing operation itself; Chapter 6 covers the impact of the often-overlooked necessity to maintain and support your company's prior products; and Chapter 7 deals with feasibility efforts, which are often required but cannot be rigidly scheduled. Although feasibility efforts normally *precede* a new product development activity, they are discussed *last* in Part II to emphasize that they must be separated from time-critical new product development, because you cannot ensure that a needed breakthrough will occur when you want or need it.

Part III deals with your choices for organizational *structure*, namely the issues in organizing your human resources. Chapter 8 reviews some organizational forms; Chapter 9 covers ways to improve the effectiveness of your human resources; and Chapter 10 discusses why harmonious interdepartmental relationships are crucial and describes several mechanisms to promote better harmony.

Part IV describes several *tools and techniques* you can use to shorten your new product development efforts (many of which you can adopt regardless of the specific way your company develops new products). Chapter 11 advocates reducing wasted time between new product development phases and using other shortcuts; Chapter 12 describes some available project management techniques that can be gainfully adopted; Chapter 13 covers the value of improved productivity; Chapter 14 reviews the benefits you will obtain from concentrating on the schedule; Chapter 15 reviews the value of incentives; and Chapter 16 covers a variety of other adaptive devices.

Part V provides implementing guidance. Chapter 17 reviews how you can install the fast phased approach described in Parts II, III, and IV in your company; Chapter 18 discusses the development of new services (in distinction to tangible products); and Chapter 19 covers some means by which you can stay current with new thinking, a topic so crucial because many new ideas are still evolving.

Part VI is a summary of my key points. Finally, six appendixes provide some historical background, specific detail on a tradeoff analysis to quantitatively translate market requirements into new product specifications, a new product development checklist, a way to conduct face-to-face or telephone interviews to improve market research underlying market-based specifications, a new product development audit, and illustrative extracts from procedures used by two companies.

Acknowledgments

Since this is a practical book, I am grateful to many past and present clients for insights into what works—and what doesn't; these people are not identified and many real-world examples are disguised to preserve confidentiality. Early versions of the manuscript were read by reviewers at AMACOM's request, and I am especially appreciative of the considerable effort and insightful comments by these people: William Dresher, Donald F. Hoeg, Mark Spivak, and Kurt M. Trampel. Any mistakes or confusion that remain are my responsibility, not theirs. I am also pleased to acknowledge helpful comments by and discussions with numerous participants in my executive and managerial training seminars. The generosity of all these practitioners in sharing their experiences enriches this book for all its readers.

Patricia S. Lucas of Symantec provided many of the illustrations of TimeLine, and Jeffrey Ford and Hal Miller of Computer Aided Management provided the illustrations of ViewPoint, all of which appear in Chapter 12. Finally, Lin R. Myerson worked and reworked the manuscripts with intelligence and cheerfulness and I am grateful for her support.

Part I

Overview

Part I reviews the reasons faster development of new products and services is increasingly crucial.

Chapter 1

The New Imperative: Faster Development

Today you must complete the development of a new product faster than ever before. This urgent need to shorten the time it takes to get from a new product idea to market introduction is caused primarily by increasingly shorter product life cycles. Three other considerations also demand that companies shorten their development durations:

1. The opportunity to both increase profits and reduce development costs
2. The advantage of aiming at a stationary target
3. The opportunity to employ more timely technology than your competitors

SHORTER PRODUCT LIFE CYCLES

Product life cycles are getting shorter. We can observe this trend everywhere; it affects undertakings as varied as consumer toys and high technology industrial products. Let's review the evidence and the reasons.

The Evidence

There are three kinds of evidence that product life cycles are getting shorter: (1) actions taken by practitioners, (2) the judgments of knowledgeable people, and (3) research data.

Actions Taken by Practitioners. Consumer product companies are omitting some previously sacrosanct test marketing to save time. Competition is forcing some outstanding marketing companies to use shortcuts to deal with shorter product life cycles. At the other end of the technology spectrum, Bobby Inman, the first head of Microelectronics and Computer Corporation (MCC, an advanced development consortium funded by major U.S. computer corporations), resigned to explore other means to move laboratory research to the market more quickly. Some of my clients are not merely developing new products to replace current ones, they are simultaneously developing the follow-on new product to replace the new product—all because product life cycles are shortening.

Actions by other corporations underscore the importance of timely new product development. For instance, in February 1986, Eastman Kodak reorganized its research and development operations in an effort to speed product development. Two years earlier, Xerox had gutted an overgrown bureaucratic structure to get the machines to market quickly and at lower cost. Historically, IBM introduced a new computer and leased it for five years before introducing a higher-capacity and lower-cost replacement; now it must introduce new products at shorter intervals because the cost of computing capacity is falling rapidly and competitors can (and do) introduce better devices quickly.

Finally, many of my corporate clients are stressing faster new product development. These corporations are altering procedures and introducing project management techniques for the specific purpose of shortening development time. Virtually all participants at my executive seminars cite isolated actions, such as installing computer-aided design tools, taken to shorten time-to-market. An article by another observer states: "In the current environment of intense international competition, a company lives or dies by its ability to develop products quickly and efficiently. But the product development process in most companies is in great need of improvement."

Judgments of Knowledgeable People. Virtually all current business and marketing publications have been commenting about how product life cycles are shortening every year. As one example, an article quotes Illinois Institute of Technology's dean of the business school: "I can't document it, but every industry we look at seems to be undergoing shorter cycles."

In addition, I ask participants at my executive programs and management seminars to forecast what they believe will occur in the next five years. Since 1986, 70 percent have expected product life cycles to become still shorter than they are now.

Research Data. Although the product life cycle is both important and popular, there are very few scientific studies of it. The data from one study, shown in Exhibit 1-1, reflect increasingly shorter product life cycles. While this study measures the life cycles of only thirty-seven household products, it is empirical, scientifically rigorous, and covers a span of nearly six decades.

At least four other research studies have drawn the same conclusions.

Reasons for Shorter Product Life Cycles

There are several causes of shorter product life cycles that have been cited. There is broad agreement that rapidly changing technology and improved mass communications are but two of the several causes of shorter product life cycles:

> Rapid development of new technology, aggressive marketing, and the willingness of buyers to try new products.

> The rapid rate of technological change, plus the easy availability of credit and the power of mass communications and advertising.

> The increasing pace of technological innovations and the rapid rate of new product introduction.

> The ever-increasing pace of technological change means these "windows [of opportunity]" are opening and closing at a faster rate. Not getting an early jump can mean missing an opportunity.

> Technology has forced the pace of change and sharply cut the effective lifetimes of all kinds of products.

Better Communications. There are two reasons for the impact improved communications has on product life cycles:

1. Information about the newest new product reaches the intended user or purchaser faster, which promotes an earlier switch away from the existing product.

Exhibit 1-1. Product life cycle data.

Period	Number of Household Products	Introductory Stage Duration (years)	Growth Stage Duration (years)
1922–1942	12	12.5	33.8
1945–1964	16	7.0	19.5
1965–1979	9	2.0	6.8

2. Information about your new product reaches actual and potential competitors quickly, which permits them to respond sooner.

Many durable products, such as videocassette recorders, are purchased only once (or a very few times) by each family, so market saturation marks the end of the product life cycle. Modern advertising (television or other) and more effective public relations effort provide faster communication of features and benefits, contributing, at least in part, to shortening the product life cycle.

Changing Technology. Rapidly changing technology also makes it easier to develop an innovative new product that offers advantages to users. This change can make the existing product obsolete.

Some companies have fallen into the "mature product trap," as illustrated in Exhibit 1-2, which makes it more likely that others will exploit changing technology. This trap can arise when a structure of the company inhibits new product development. The key point is that when technology is changing, you must make a choice:

1. Stick with the existing technology, in which case your company's cash cow will be made obsolete by a competitor who successfully exploits the new technology; or
2. Successfully embrace the newer technology first and make your own product obsolete sooner than you would otherwise wish.

Exhibit 1-2. Mature product trap.

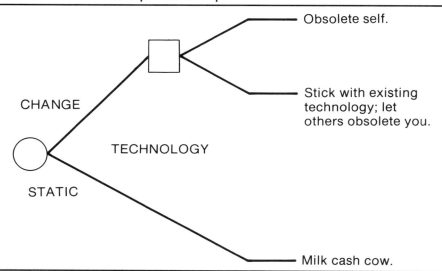

General Electric and RCA continued with vacuum tube technology long after Texas Instruments adopted and exploited transistor technology; neither of these dominant corporations in vacuum tubes ever became an important provider of transistors, and vacuum tubes are no longer a significant business. In the 1930s, many airlines successfully adopted emerging airplane technology to surpass the railroads in moving people; but now the airlines are about to lose some share of their business traveler market to improved teleconference and videoconference facilities, a new technology that they are not yet trying to exploit.

As another example, two managers from a major sugar company attended one of my new product development seminars in 1980. They doubted whether their industry was subject to shortening product life cycles or important changes. Since then, however, we have seen sugar consumption decrease with increasing rapidity. Corn sweeteners, saccharin, and, most recently, aspartame are all making inroads. Newer sweeteners are already threatening to replace these recent innovations.

If there is a profitable business available to a competitor exploiting some new technology, that same business opportunity is available to you. If the newer technology will render your investment in an existing technology obsolete, this process will occur regardless of whether you or a competitor exploit the new technology. Thus, in the long run, you are better off to inject the new technology into your own business. It is important to continually conduct critical objective reviews of how technology can produce an impact on the markets you serve. When this is done, it will often cause you to initiate a new product development effort sooner.

INCREASED PROFITS AND REDUCED COSTS

There are three financial reasons to carry out the new product development effort quickly: (1) You can earn more money; (2) the development effort is likely to be less expensive; and (3) it will be easier for you to persuade your management or others to provide development funding.

Increased Profits

If you can develop and introduce your new product quickly, there are two ways you can earn more money:

1. You can obtain more total sales, hence more profits.
2. If there is no initial competition, you can charge a premium price.

As soon as a competitor introduces a similar product or another way to fulfill the function of your product becomes available, some sales are lost. Thus, getting to the market before there is either direct or functional competition will increase your total sales.

Similarly, when competition exists, profit margins are always reduced, as illustrated in Exhibit 1-3. If you have no direct or functional competition, you may be able to charge a premium price, especially if you can promote your product on the basis of snob appeal or novelty to the initial purchasers, so-called first nighters. Without that prestige premium, the price you can charge is limited solely by your product's economic value to the buyer. When there is competition, your price can eventually be driven down to your product cost; however, if you have volume or other cost-saving efficiencies, you may still remain profitable in an absolute sense. It is possible, of course, to sell your product at less than your cost, as a loss leader, but this is always risky.

Reduced Costs

Exhibit 1-4 illustrates some of the financial consequences of developing a new product. Shown is a typical financial pattern during a product's life cycle, showing expense, sales, income or profits, and the cumulative net loss or gain. The expense line illustrates low expenses during the period of initial exploration and development activities. There is a significant increase in expense when you purchase tooling or start introductory promotion efforts for the new product. These period expenses (which are typically calculated monthly) may continue to increase after sales commence because initial sales may themselves be unprofitable.

Exhibit 1-3. Sell price considerations.

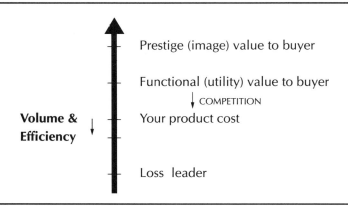

Exhibit 1-4. A typical financial pattern during a product's life cycle.

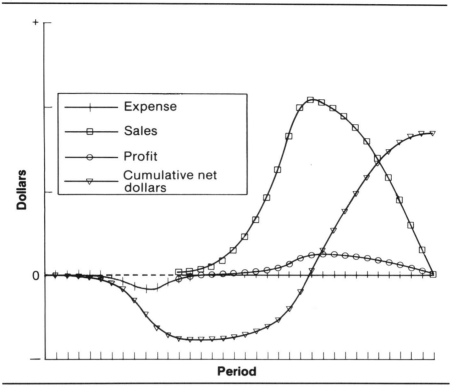

Eventually, sales start earning a profit, and period expense turns into period income. At the time period expense becomes income, the cumulative net income curve (which is the sum of all period income minus expense from inception of the development effort to the current time) reaches its lowest value. Usually, the peak in the profit curve (that is, the period income curve) occurs before the peak in the sales curve because of actual or threatened competition. Exhibit 1-5 shows both sales and period income ending at the same time; but it is possible to have a product for which the terminal sales are themselves unprofitable, creating a second period expense valley. It also shows the cumulative net is positive at the end, which is the desired outcome; however, it does not require much delay in the product's introduction to leave the cumulative net at a loss, as illustrated in Exhibit 1-5. In some cases, you will earn more money by spending extra money to shorten your time-to-market.

Consider the following specific case: You have planned a thirty-

Exhibit 1-5.   The result of early product introduction.

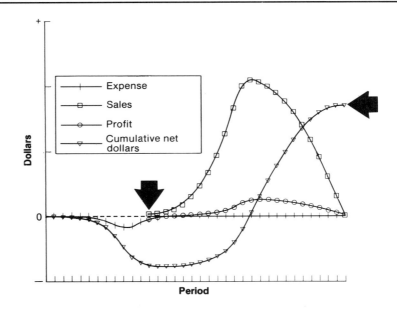

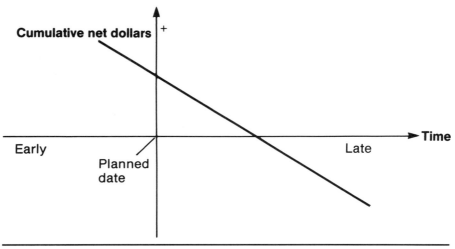

month duration new product development effort for which the period
expense is $100,000 a month (obviously an artificial uniformity, but
helpful to simplify numerical calculations). Assume that money costs
your company one percent per month so that at the end of the first
month, the interest expense will be $1,000. After the second month,
you will have added $2,010 more interest cost: The $100,000 expense

required for the second month will cost $1,000 at the end of the second month, and the $101,000 attributable to the first month (expense plus the $1,000 interest on that expense) will add a further $1,010. Thus, the cumulative interest expense at the end of the second month is $3,010, which is the sum of $1,000 for the first month and $2,010 for the second month. At the end of thirty months, the interest expense alone will be $513,270, as illustrated in Exhibit 1-6. An unplanned thirty-first month adds $36,130 interest and an additional $100,000 of period expense.

Even if you do not spend more than the planned $3 million for the development effort and merely spread it out over a longer period of time, the increased penalty attributable to the cost of money can be considerable. Exhibit 1-7 summarizes the value of one month's time reduction due to interest saving for a program costing $100,000 per month for various intended durations and costs of money. Exhibit 1-8 provides a graphic picture of the interest expense required to fund a $1

Exhibit 1-6.   Costs for a hypothetical new product development program.

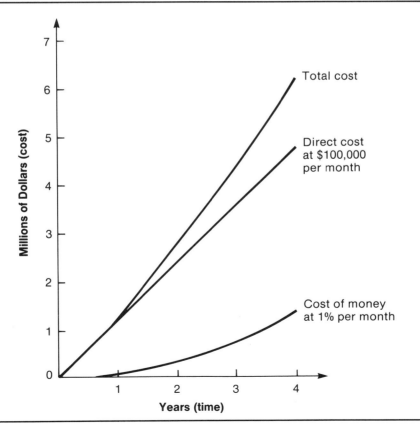

Exhibit 1-7. Interest expense saved (in thousands of dollars) by shortening a new product development one month, assuming program expense is $100,000 per month.

Intended Duration	Cost of Money (percentage per month)		
	0.5%	1.0%	1.5%
Year 1	6.16%	12.68%	19.56%
Year 2	12.72	26.97	42.95
Year 3	19.67	43.08	70.91
Year 4	27.05	61.22	104.35

Exhibit 1-8. Interest expense for a $1 million new product development program (at one percent interest per month) of various durations.

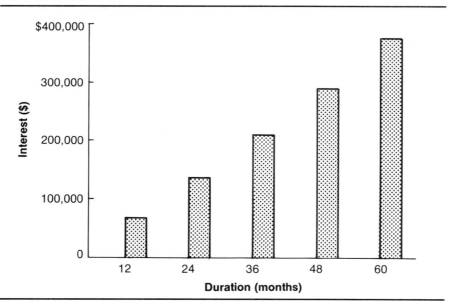

million new product development program; a fast development program is decidedly less costly than a long program.

Your company may be in the fortunate position of not having to borrow money to fund new product development efforts. Even so, the line of reasoning about the extra interest cost is still pertinent because your company is forgoing income that it could earn if the money were freely available for investment elsewhere.

You may also feel that a cost of money of one percent per month is too high or too low or that the uniform investment rate for every month throughout the life of the development effort is artificial. If so, you can make an exact calculation, which will change the details but not the central point.

The key point is that a longer new product development effort costs more than a short one and a shorter market life with attendant lower sales and income may also accompany this increased cost.

Capital Market Credibility

In large corporations, you must persuade your management to fund a new product development activity. Some large corporations, and most smaller ones, must obtain funding from external capital markets. If you can realistically promise to develop your new product quickly, you will have greater credibility and be more likely to obtain the financing. In fact, many start-up companies can only obtain (promised) incremental funds by meeting development milestones.

The converse is frequently illustrated. For instance, in mid-1988, Apollo's stock price dropped dramatically. This was due, in part, to being two years late getting a computer that could run a new operating system to market.

A STATIONARY TARGET

It is highly desirable to aim at a stationary target, as illustrated in Exhibit 1-9. That is, you don't want any big changes to occur in the market for which your new product is intended while you are still developing it. Since many markets and technologies are subject to rapid change, it is important to develop your new product before these changes render it obsolete or irrelevant. Fast new product development increases the likelihood that your market research (which should support all new product development) will still be valid when your product is introduced.

Consider the rapidly changing market for personal computers. Osborne Computer Corporation had a very successful product when the market was first emerging. However, frequent competitive introductions of improved models rapidly pushed Osborne out of this growing market. Unfortunately, Osborne announced its forthcoming improved product far in advance of its availability for shipment. After the new product announcement, dealers stopped buying the original Osborne computer. The dealers wanted the newer model. Perhaps a faster new

Exhibit 1-9. Aiming at a stationary target.

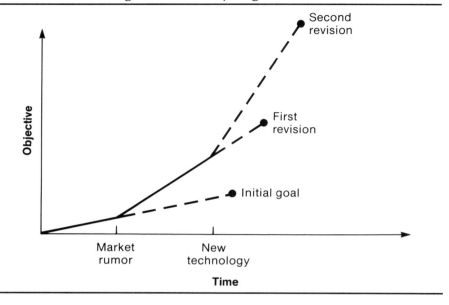

product development effort could have saved Osborne from its eventual bankruptcy.

Producing a new model of automobile currently requires several years. The 1987 models of General Motors' luxury cars became available for consumer purchase when gasoline was selling for less than $1 per gallon. However, the models had been specified and designed years earlier, when gasoline prices were forecasted to be $2 per gallon for the period in which the models would be sold. Thus, the downsized models sold very poorly because the new product development time was—and still is—too long. Today's challenge is to be both fast and to have the right product specifications (discussed in Chapter 3), as illustrated in Exhibit 1-10. Faster new product development, for the sale of speed alone, is not the answer.

MORE TIMELY TECHNOLOGY

Exhibit 1-11 illustrates how the company that can start its new product development later, because it can complete it more quickly than its competitor, can make use of later technology. If your product embodies new technology of the sort that is likely to change rapidly, being faster can produce a substantial competitive advantage. Since easily changed

Exhibit 1-10. Speed of new product development.

Specifications	Faster	Normal	Slower
Optimum	Goal	May be a better product, but too late.	Very risky
Normal	Acceptable improvement on current situation	Current situation	Not tolerable
Wrong	Not helpful	Not tolerable	Not tolerable

Exhibit 1-11. The result of more timely technology.

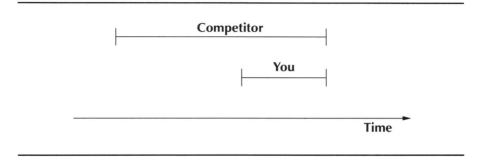

and improved technology is a part of more and more products, this may be a decisive consideration.

HIGHLIGHTS

Shorter product life cycles, caused by better communications and changing technology, have created an increasing need for faster new product development.

Companies must respond to this need for faster new product development—and many are—by changing how they develop new products. These faster companies gain several financial benefits, such as:

- Increased profits
- Reduced costs
- Improved credibility in capital markets

Faster new product development also offers two other advantages:

1. A stationary development target, that is, one that does not change during development
2. The opportunity to employ more timely technology and more current market research than your slower competitors

Part II

Approaches to Faster New Product Development

Chapters 2–7 describe the elements of a fast-phased approach for new product development. The key concepts of setting firm specifications and separating feasibility and maintenance activities from the time-critical development activity are universal; you will want to make use of these whether you choose this particular phased approach, a variant of it, or a more revolutionary approach that you believe will shorten your time-to-market (such as new product rugby or simultaneous engineering).

Chapter 2

A Fast, Low-Risk Phased Approach to Product Development

Companies introduce new products in a variety of ways, ranging from the chaotic to systematic. While successful results are obviously the payoff, it is unwise to rely on luck to salvage an unorganized procedure. Although you can also obtain your new products from external resources, usually you must share some of the expected profits.

UNSTRUCTURED APPROACHES

Unquestionably, any new product development effort must be preceded by or initiated with an idea for a new product. This idea may range anywhere from a vague notion to a specific and detailed construction. Exhibit 2-1 reveals two sources of ideas: A real need and technological capability. When the idea for a new product is generated because someone has devised a solution to a market problem (market pull), you are more likely to have a commercial success. In this case, you find or create a solution to a sharply targeted goal. For example, many products created in response to market pull are incremental improvements over existing products. Ideas derived from a technological capability (technology push) are less likely to be commercially successful. In this case, you have a solution looking for a problem, and you must search for potential users whose unmet needs can be satisfied at acceptable cost. If you can find or create such an unmet need, your technology push product can sometimes have great market success, as demonstrated by 3M's Post-its.

Generating this idea may require time and effort, but I only intend

Exhibit 2-1.   Two different idea sources.

A Real Problem	Technological Capability
Market driven	Technology driven
External orientation	Inward orientation
Better success rate	More failures

to deal with the process and time following the articulation of an idea. Actually, as one expert, Theodore Levitt, has said, "The fact that you can put a dozen inexperienced people into a room and conduct a brainstorming session that produces exciting new ideas shows how little relative importance ideas themselves actually have." Nevertheless, there are companies that mistakenly believe that an idea will easily become a successful new product. Thus, once a superficially attractive idea has been articulated, such a company pushes ahead, but forgets or overlooks required steps and slips from its desired schedule. Sometimes unstructured development leads to seizing the opportunity to demonstrate an early prototype at an important trade show; later, the company is unable to manufacture production quantities quickly, which can invite a more nimble competitor to beat them to the market.

Another problem with the chaotic or random approach is that it fosters changes in the new product's specifications every time anyone has an embellishment. Without a formal structure in which to freeze specifications and evaluate changes, creeping elegance often runs amok and nothing is ever introduced because the far-off hills always look greener.

NEW PRODUCTS FROM EXTERNAL SOURCES

You can introduce a new product quickly if another company (or individual) has already completed its development and will sell it to you. You might use licensing, a joint venture, outright purchase, or some subcontracting arrangement to obtain the rights or the product itself. However, there are two problems with this.

First, the other party must have already spent time on the development. That time is still a part of the limited window of opportunity in which the product is feasible. Although your own involvement may be short, this does not necessarily speed up the entire process.

Second, the most important reason to introduce new products is to increase your company's profits. When you obtain the new product from an external resource, you'll have to share some of the profits, so unless the procured new product offers you some synergistic leverage, you're unlikely to make as much profit as you would with an internally developed new product.

In the development partner approach, the other company may have people you lack, its people may have pertinent experience, or it may have faster equipment. Conversely, it requires time to locate a development partner, and using one will not increase your own capability. Even with a strong internal new product development, you should not forgo this external route entirely. In fact, a proactive search for products that you can acquire is normally worthwhile.

GENERAL CHARACTERISTICS OF PHASED APPROACHES

Phased approaches are widely advocated for the development of new products, although these approaches differ in detail. A phased approach can improve comprehension, provide a sharp focus for the work, improve speed, and reduce risk. It can also help maintain challenge and motivation in an inherently lengthy new product development effort, since there may be several major intermediate milestones on which to focus. Nevertheless, it is important that the phased approach you adopt be tailored to your business to avoid problems such as excessive detail. Any new product development process should include some intermediate reviews to try to ensure that the corporation's resources are being deployed in the most effective manner.

Most phased approaches to new product development (such as those reviewed in Appendix A) have time sequences as depicted in Exhibit 2-2, under (a) and (b). In these illustrations, there is a time gap between phases (whatever their specific content). Exhibit 2-2, (a) illustrates the so-called relay race, in which a baton is passed from one runner to the next. Here, the transfer is from one department to another, which exacerbates the cross-functional conflict. The other four situations depict the use of multifunctional teams from beginning to end, which I will stress in more detail later. It is clear that eliminating dead time between long phases, as shown in Exhibit 2-2 under (c) is an improvement over the first two approaches.

Recently, even overlap of several phases has been advocated, as shown in Exhibit 2-2 (d). In this new product rugby simultaneous work is carried on by several departments (such as marketing, engineering, and manufacturing). It is claimed that this approach is much faster than other approaches. This is probably true in the special case where the new product is similar to a previously developed product and where the same experienced team is available. However, that is a rare situation.

Exhibit 2-2.   Five phased new product development concepts.

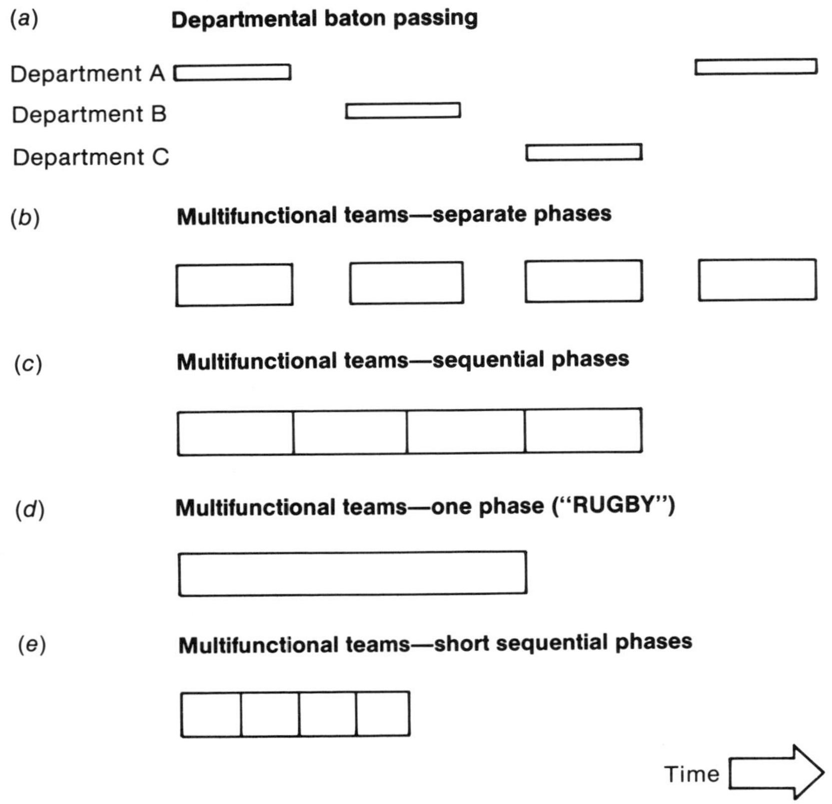

(a)   **Departmental baton passing**

Department A ▭

Department B   ▭

Department C   ▭

(b)   **Multifunctional teams—separate phases**

▭   ▭   ▭   ▭

(c)   **Multifunctional teams—sequential phases**

▭▭▭▭

(d)   **Multifunctional teams—one phase ("RUGBY")**

▭

(e)   **Multifunctional teams—short sequential phases**

▭▭▭▭

Time ⇨

No rapidly growing company can afford to dedicate its most experienced people to working on only one new product at a time; in fact, these people are likely to desire career growth, in which case they would subsequently want to head their own new product development efforts. If the experienced team is not available or if the product being developed is unique, there is greater risk that activities will be overlooked in the mad scramble to finish. As one bumper sticker puts it, GIVE BLOOD—PLAY RUGBY. The cost of correcting a runaway new product development project can be enormous.

Part of the alleged attraction of new product rugby is the absence of strangulating procedural obstacles that sometimes accompanies a phased new product development procedure. However, no one has to erect unnecessary paperwork hurdles, and it is possible to have a simple phased new product development policy.

Any new product development project (or any other corporate activity) will be delayed by the need to prepare an elaborate presentation, conduct a lengthy review, or await a tardy decision. The problem is with the elaboration and tardiness, not with the phased approach. Reviews have to be thorough not elaborate, and the resultant decision has to be made promptly. Despite the allure of new product rugby, especially the cooperative teamwork (which I strongly support), I am not aware of anyone who favors unsystematic, unmonitored, unchecked, unplanned, or undirected new product development; quite the reverse. As a practical matter, if you must play new product rugby, be sure to have some brief intermissions in which to review the effort to lessen the risk.

In distinction from the first four concepts illustrated in Exhibit 2-2, I propose shortening the total new product development process by having short, sequential phases as illustrated in Exhibit 2-2 (*e*). By analogy to rugby, this can be thought of as a soccer or a basketball game (without a half-time recess) in which a cooperative team moves together toward the goal. This offers lower risk than overlapped phases. I eliminate (or minimize) dead time between phases to shorten the total process. The shorter phases, in which the required work is completed very quickly, are realistically achievable by using the varied approaches, organizational structures, and tools and techniques that I describe in this book.

Finally, I propose, as will become clearer in Chapter 3, separating the feasibility work and the maintenance work from the time-critical new product development process. These two activities are important, but the first, feasibility, cannot be rigidly scheduled. The latter, maintenance, cannot start until the new product is introduced.

The specific practices in different companies with which I am familiar apply various portions of phased procedures. In one industrial product company, the steps or phases are: (1) idea; (2) feasibility phase; (3) specification phase; (4) breadboard phase; (5) engineering prototype phase; (6) pilot lot phase; (7) production; and (8) follow-up. In one customer product company, the approach is as shown in Exhibit 2-3. A process business might use laboratory feasibility, process development, pilot plant, semi-commercial or mid-size batch, and full-scale commercial production phases.

I believe the more successful companies have simple, easily understood procedures that are well known to all the key personnel doing new product development work. One company summarizes the key steps and guiding principles of its new product development procedure on a 3¼-by-5½-inch laminated card, which easily fits into each person's pocket.

Beckman provides a successful industrial product case:

From Idea to Market:
Completing the Product Development Picture

Exhibit 2-3. Five-stage approach used by a consumer product company.

Stage 1: Ideation
- Idea generation
- Preliminary criteria screening
- File search and secondary data investigation

Stage 2: Concept testing
- Concept and alternative product positioning
- Concept evaluation

Stage 3: Product testing
- Prototype development
- Consumer product testing

Stage 4: Test market
- Marketing plan
- Test marketing and evaluation

Stage 5: Commercialization
- Market expansion

Starting with input from customers, who need to do something faster, cheaper, easier, or more precisely, a Beckman product comes to life. The wheels begin to turn. As many as fifty departments, 500 people, five years, and 250,000 manhours are involved in a product's venture from idea to shipment.

Take SYNCHRON CX3 as an example of a product in the development cycle. It is one of the newest instrument systems to approach shipment out of the Diagnostic Systems Group in Brea. SYNCHRON CX3 is a STAT/Routine clinical analyzer, part of a new family of analyzers for the diagnostic marketplace. SHHH!!!—Its code-name is S-4000. [See Exhibit 2-4, showing eight major milestones marking the progression of a major instrument system from input to customer use. In the timeline, steps may overlap or expand, but the overall process usually takes between two and three years.]

Milestone I—Concept/Product Definition

"We have a dream"

Basically the concept/product definition stage is pinning down dreams and making them realities.

In the case of S-4000, customers dreamed of a new clinical analyzer more in line with changing cost constraints and clinical test throughput needs.

Says Mike Whelan, then Marketing Manager for the Clinical Instruments Division, "In visits to clinical labs, customers told us that basically they have limited funds and they need a versatile, flexible instrument."

Adds Mary Beth Armstrong, Clinical Chemistry New Products Marketing, "We listened very carefully. They wanted a product that was fast, economical, low maintenance, labor efficient, and extremely reliable. The entire product concept was geared to these needs."

After many meetings of a New Product Screening Committee, the final product concept was formulated: Take the best technologies in AS-TRA and System E4A and develop a system that performs the nine most frequently run critical tests in a clinical lab (glucose, creatinine, BUN, electrolytes, and calcium). Make it FAST, under a minute for all nine tests. Develop concentrated reagent formulas for customer convenience and cost containment. And, make the instrument modular in design to interface with later instrument systems.

Project S-4000 was born.

Milestone II—Feasibility

"Great concept! Now, can it be done?"

Feasibility shows that the concept can be carried out and actually become a Beckman product. According to Francis Yim, hardware design project engineer, hardware engineering begins feasibility by defining, building and testing each subassembly—and piece that will be needed to build the system—to see if it can perform the job it was designed to do.

Exhibit 2-4. Beckman's product development cycle.

Customer input		
Milestone I:	Concept	2 months
Milestone II:	Feasibility	6 months
Milestone III:	Breadboard	3 months
Milestone IV:	Prototype	9 months
Milestone V:	Pilot Manufacturing Units	2 months
Milestone VI:	Reliability Qualification Testing	3 months
Milestone VII:	FDA Product Approval	1.5 months
Milestone VIII:	First Production	3 months
Customer use		

Says Yim, "If things don't work out in the feasibility stage, you have to rethink the entire concept."

Frank Shu, Senior Project Scientist, worked on the chemistry feasibility and development on S-4000. Says Shu, "For this particular system we modified the existing Beckman chemistries. The big feasibility challenge was to make a concentrated reagent formula." After nine months, the glucose and BUN, reagents, electrolyte buffer and the CO_2 acid reagent concentrate formulas were developed.

Gayle Nobbs, Senior Software Engineer, was in charge of the software feasibility and development on S-4000. Says Gayle, "The software makes it go. Without it you have no motion, no reading of values, no calculations, and no operator interface."

On S-4000, Software Development started with a Master Feature List of tasks the instrument is going to perform. In the feasibility stage, the programs were written to guide the operation of the instrument. According to Francis Yim, feasibility was established in six months and the breadboards were begun.

Milestone III—Breadboard Development

"It's not pretty, but it works!"

The breadboard is the first attempt to put all the pieces together and run them as a whole system. According to Wing Pang, Project Leader on S-4000, breadboards are a major step in proving that the system concept will work. "Breadboards may be twice the size of the end product," says Pang. Adds Francis Yim, "The first one is very messy, but it does what it is supposed to do. The second one is more refined."

Breadboards are used to test small lots of new reagent formulas. Also, preliminary testing is done with the software—does it make the hardware perform all the right functions?

Randy Mills, Industrial Designer, was instrumental in the total look of the S-4000 system. During the breadboard stage, Industrial Design prepared detailed drawing and concept sketches of the final design.

"We help establish the size, shape, materials, methods, colors and graphics for the finished products," says Mills. "After sketches are approved, full-scale models are first made out of lightweight foam board, which permits us to quickly explore and evaluate the design options."

With the data from the breadboards, sketches, and foam board models, major refinements begin.

Milestone IV—Prototype Evaluation

"If it looks like a product, and works like a product—then it's a prototype."

A prototype is an integrated system. Components are in place, the software runs the system, the chemistries supply correct test results, and the covers are on the instrument.

According to Wing Pang, "Most people looking at a good prototype would think it was a manufactured, finished product; that's how complete they are. They do the job, look like the real thing, but almost all of the parts are handmade—hand machined molded parts, handmade covers, hand wired components.

"The finished prototype should be trade show quality. In fact, two of the S-4000 prototypes went to AACC (American Association of Clinical Chemists) in July!" says Pang.

Prototypes are built from the knowledge gained from the breadboard and are reviewed for design, performance, serviceability, reliability, and overall cost. A total of eight prototypes were built for S-4000.

Prototype refinements typically take from nine months to a year. The capability to make a totally integrated system at the prototype stage will make or break the project.

An army of professionals becomes involved in evaluating prototypes once they are completed. Departments include test engineering, manufacturing engineering, applications and quality assurance. They ensure that the product definition is met and that the product is reliable and able to be manufactured in large quantities.

Prototypes move the product concept one giant step closer to becoming a reality.

Milestone V—Pilot Manufactured Units

"Manufacture a few to be sure they're right."

In pilot production, manufacturing builds between ten and fifteen units based on the final prototype design and documentation. Called pilots, these first few manufactured units allow manufacturing to fine-tune the process of assembling instruments on a large scale. According to Vince Smith, Manufacturing Engineer Project Coordinator, twelve pilot units of S-4000 have been built. "We have the parts made, assemble them, and then review the process. From this first assembly we establish suppliers, arrange the assembly area, develop tooling, and evaluate test equipment requirements."

Typically these pilot units never make it into a customer's lab. They are primarily used for in-house evaluation, manufacturing, and service and sales training, but some do end up at trade shows and special customer previews.

Milestone VI—Reliability Qualification Testing (RQT)

"Yes, but will it rotate 180 degrees 10,000 times in a row?"

"Essentially RQT determines if the product, manufactured in large lots, will meet requirements listed in the original product definition," says Bob Weinstein, Quality Assurance Engineer.

During RQT, various system parameters such as reagent consumption, sample throughput, system diagnostics, metering systems, calibration, software, chemistry performance, and component reliability are checked.

"We will run pilot instrument and/or critical subassemblies all day and all night for weeks to watch for system or component failure. It has to be reliable and meet specifications in the customer's lab," says Weinstein. Overall, RQT validates the design and manufacturing process of the system.

RQT takes from one to three months. S-4000 is scheduled to complete RQT by November.

Milestone VII—FDA/Product Approval

"Getting 'Big Brother's' Approval"

Before a diagnostic product goes on the market, it needs approvals from the U.S. government watchdog agency, the Food and Drug Administration (FDA). The Applications Department prepares extensive documentation on the product and chemistries.

Mike Williams and Debbie Cote, Applications Chemists, will spend eight weeks preparing data on S-4000 for product approval. Says Mike, "We evaluate the prototype, gather the data, and send the documents to our Legal Department who submit them to the FDA. In the documents, we must prove that the S-4000 is substantially equivalent to other analyzers on the market. Thus, the test results obtained from S-4000 have to be comparable to results obtained from ASTRA and E4A."

Approval is usually received within ninety days. Besides FDA approval for diagnostic instruments, there are other product approvals necessary before products are shipped. They may include electrical safety, radiation safety, and communication frequency interference. These approvals are handled by Beckman Corporate Product Assurance.

Milestone VIII—First Production

"Let's get the assembly line rolling."

All components for the new product are made to exact specifications supplied by Engineering Services Documentation. Parts are made and supplied by the Central Fabrication and Central Plastics Facilities in Fullerton, Central Manufacturing Facilities in Porterville and Paso Robles, California, and various outside manufacturers.

With the pieces in Brea, first production units are assembled by hand. One by one they roll off the assembly line and are tested again for reliability. With a final stamp of approval, systems are packaged and crated for shipment.

"Out the door and into laboratories around the world"

Shipment, the final step in the movement from idea to customer use, is only two months away for S-4000. A three-year odyssey from concept to market is almost over. When it emerges, the S-4000 will be known as the SYNCHRON CX3. The customer's dreams will be fulfilled.

Today, the rest of the products in the SYNCHRON family of clinical systems are just a few milestones behind S-4000. And many other bioanalytical and diagnostic instrument systems are completing the product development cycle, some slated for introduction in 1987, some as far off as 1989.

Beckman's products of the 1990s and beyond will go through roughly the same product development process as S-4000. Essentially, they are only an idea, a few years and eight milestones away.[1]

THREE REASONS FOR USING PHASED APPROACH

There are three important reasons why you should use a phased approach for your new product development efforts: (1) improved understanding; (2) greater urgency; and (3) reduced risk.

1. *Improved Understanding.* Comprehension of the participants is improved. It is much easier to understand a short-term program and the involved steps in it than to understand a much longer and necessarily more complex program. In a short phase it is possible to start out with all the steps you will have to undertake explicitly articulated and identified. In addition, you can easily list the required steps that comprise the new product development process in their time sequence. Then, your development team is not likely to suddenly be surprised by the requirement to undertake some development activity for which they had not made allowance. Exhibit 2-5 illustrates that an ambitious new product development goal must necessarily have some initial uncertainty about the exact objective and when it will be achieved. In a single phase, however, you only have to accomplish certain things, not the entire totality of steps required to introduce a new product. Distraction is reduced because you don't have to deal with unrelated future activities. Thus, a short phase is easier to understand than the entire new product development process. To put this differently, a specific near-term goal is easier for people to understand than a long-term, and thus somewhat imperfectly defined, goal. The target is both more precise and less remote.

2. *Greater Urgency.* Not only are the participants more likely to have a better schedule plan for a fairly short phase, but they are also less likely to let the clock run without making progress. There is a

1. Copyright 1986 Beckman Instruments, Inc. Reprinted by permission.

Exhibit 2-5.   Phases of a new product.

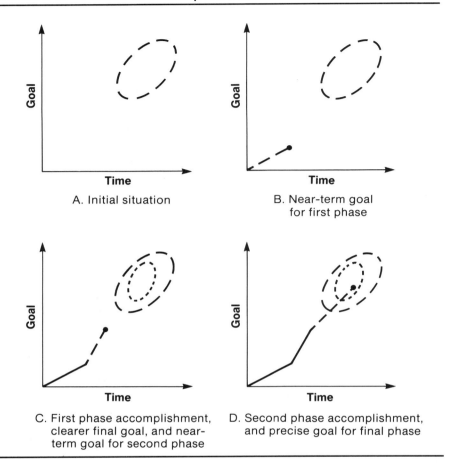

A. Initial situation

B. Near-term goal
for first phase

C. First phase accomplishment,
clearer final goal, and near-
term goal for second phase

D. Second phase accomplishment,
and precise goal for final phase

greater sense of urgency. It is hard to let the first month of a three- or six-month phase slip by without making progress. Conversely, participants can all too often exhibit low schedule urgency at the start of a three-year new product development effort.

3. *Reduced Risk.* Short phases have lower risk. Not only is the schedule risk less, but the financial risk is also less. You only approve small development increments at any given time, so these are inherently less costly than the entire development effort. This obviously limits risk. (Also, you have approved only a limited, specific effort, so there is less temptation to change specifications during a short phase.)

Approving a phase does not guarantee that anyone must approve the subsequent phases. Clearly, one does not approve a phase without an expectation that he will approve subsequent phases. However, if the goals of an approved phase cannot be achieved, then you do not have to approve subsequent phases. The goals of a specific phase on a particular new product development effort might in fact be achieved satisfactorily, but approval of the next phase can still be withheld to reallocate resources onto a higher priority or more promising new product development effort. In approving the entire development project at the beginning there is both a long period of time for the entire development cycle as well as a large amount of money. Consequently, management has less assurance that the time and money will be efficiently used.

Conversely, in a phased approach, where each incremental work package is itself relatively small, there is less opportunity to aimlessly use resources ineffectively, especially since the approval for additional, subsequent work is made only after milestones are successfully achieved. You can stop work in the middle of a phase if an unexpected revolting development occurs. Similarly, one of the benefits of any phased approach is that you can discontinue less promising efforts even if they are progressing in a fully satisfactory way. This allows your corporation to concentrate its limited resources on the few most promising new product development efforts. It is much better to produce a few successful new products than to work with great energy on many and produce none.

OVERVIEW OF APPROACH

The general phased approach that I favor is neither a rigid straight-jacket nor a magical solution to the complex process of developing a new product, but it does avoid many of the common pitfalls that can needlessly delay the new product development process.

In broadest overview, there may be three activities involved with the introduction of a new product: feasibility, development, and maintenance. Obviously, an idea for a new product, which may range anywhere from a vague notion to a specific and detailed construction, must precede or initiate this sequence of activities.

Exhibit 2-6 lists these three activities and also shows four development phases: optimization, design, preproduction, and production. These four are illustrative, not prescriptive. You must have optimization to establish firm specifications; and this can be followed with one or more phases leading to routine new product shipment. These four phases, or others better suited to your business, divide the total development activity, which is often lengthy, into short periods, each of which has a specific, limited goal, as the table shows. Thus, each phase involves only a portion of the work required to introduce a successful new product. The total budget for all development activities in the company is its new product development budget less those amounts reserved for

(*text continued on page 35*)

Exhibit 2-6. Activities and development phases involved with the introduction of a new product.

Activity = Phase =	FEASIBILITY		DEVELOPMENT			MAINTENANCE
		Optimization	Design	Preproduction	Production	
Start point	Start with possibility.	Start with product idea and proven technology.	Start with specification.	Start with complete documentation and breadboard.	Start with prototypes and debugged documentation.	Start with problem.
Goal	Goal is proof of technology.	Goal is to put specifications in "concrete."	Goal is to prove specifications can be met.	Goal is to prove documentation is complete and accurate.	Goal is routine shipment of product.	Goal is to solve problem.
Some typical activities	*Technology critical* Laboratory experiments, breadboards, analysis *Process critical* Bench & pilot scale trials *Market critical* Exploratory market research	Secondary market research and test marketing or primary market research completed. Musts and wants clearly defined. Market segments and competition understood. Technical tradeoff studies, including crude production cost estimates	Product's promotion basis developed. Preproduction prototypes built or pilot line operated. Production cost estimates and schedule completed. Discounted cash flow analysis	Final product name selected. Advertising to trade and users planned. Sales and distribution plans completed. Completion of designs, parts list, scale up, formulas, quality assurance plan, technical service requirements, test specifications, and vendor qualifications Obtain final regulatory compliance, if required. Order long-lead tooling.	Initiate production. Complete service and training manuals. Complete all sales support materials, advertising, and other promotion.	Limited quick fixes where cost or quality justified

Key decisions	Continue to invest in or drop exploration.	Select most attractive combination of product attributes for initial market introduction of product.	Whether production is justified.	Production methods, tooling design, and vendor selections	Production rates, inventory levels, and similar issues	Authorization of a new product (improvement) development program, when justified
End point	Output is report plus model, bench chemistry, analysis, software module, or similar conclusive demonstration.	Output is approved specification and critical path schedule for development.	Output is complete production documentation, working breadboards, and critical path schedule for preproduction.	Output is production of prototypes, final production documentation, and production schedule.	Output is product.	Output is minor revision and/or new idea.
Schedule	Typically 1–24 months	Typically 1 week–3 months	← From critical path network diagrams →			Typically 1 day–6 weeks
Management authorization	Approve only 3 months at a time.	Approve entire phase.	Approve entire phase, review quarterly.	Approve entire phase, review quarterly.	Approve entire phase.	Approve entire project.
Market introduction	No product plan, but efforts must support strategy.	Product introduction date only approximate.	Product introduction quarter set.	Product introduction month set.	Product introduction date set.	
Budget	Total budget perhaps 5–10% of NPD budget.	← Total budget is 100% of NPD budget less amounts dedicated to feasibility and maintenance. →			Standard factory cost	Requires 10–25% of NPD budget.

Exhibit 2-6. (continued)

Schedule vs. cost-risk trade-off options	Can authorize procurement of long-lead items for design without commitment to undertake design.	Can authorize procurement of long-lead tooling and other items for preproduction without commitment to undertake preproduction.	Can authorize procurement of long-lead tooling and other items for production without commitment to undertake production.

GENERAL NOTES ON THE PHASED APPROACH:

1. Some products may not fit the normal procedure, and must be exempted from the details (but not the spirit).
2. The start of any phase is not a commitment to initiate the next phase.
3. For every production phase project, there might be:
   - 1.1 Preproduction phase projects
   - 3 Design phase projects
   - 10 Optimization phase projects
4. Maintenance phase work should be assigned to a separate sustaining engineering group or else the people working on new products should not be scheduled for more than 75–90 percent time effort.
5. Feasibility phase projects should be limited to some preset fraction of the new product development budget. The reports on each project must be circulated widely within the corporation.
6. Reviews between and within phases must be prompt, and "go/stop" decisions must be rendered promptly.
7. The approval authorization levels to initiate phases must be established to be consistent with other assigned responsibilities.
8. Checklists for specification ingredients should be established for use in optimization phase projects.
9. If the specifications are obvious, the optimization phase can be shortened to a one-day meeting of the triad team for approving it and creating the critical path schedule for the design phase.

feasibility and maintenance activities. (The new product development budget is often called the research and development [R&D] budget, even if very little research is truly included.) I elaborate on each activity and phase in Chapters 3 through 7.

A more general view is shown in Exhibit 2-7 (in which the specific numbers at the bottom depicting the number of ideas and relative cost are meant to be conceptual rather than exact). This highlights four other aspects of my phased approach:

1. While it should be easy to initiate a development activity, you filter out less promising efforts as you move progressively through the phases, which helps you concentrate your company's limited resources on the better opportunities (or, to put it differently, you have to kiss a lot of frogs to find one prince).
2. You can afford this selectivity because the earlier phases have much lower costs than the later phases.
3. All departments or functions should be involved in each phase.
4. Approvals require higher levels of management as the cost risk increases, which often induces companies to search (unsuccessfully as far as I know) for algorithms and quantitative devices to try to replace qualitative judgments.

Three other points are also illustrated:

1. Ideas can arise anywhere.
2. You might (although rarely) kill a new product effort that was in the production phase.
3. There can be a short (or long) gap after the development activity ends and a maintenance project starts.

A fast new product development effort is one in which the allowable schedule for each of the four development activity phases is as short as possible and where there is no (or a very short) time gap between the end of one phase and the start of a successor, as previously illustrated in Exhibit 2-2(*e*). To put this somewhat differently, one of the activities during a phase is to ensure that appropriate management personnel are suitably aware of the project's status. It then requires only one management meeting to both approve the end of one phase and authorize the initiation of the successor.

Exhibit 2-8 provides a partial picture of the new product development work that might be under way in a corporation during an interval of time. Authorization of a feasibility activity is not a commitment to launch a new product or even to undertake any development activity, as illustrated by many feasibility activities that end without any direct

(*text continued on page 38*)

Exhibit 2-7. Overview of the phased concept.

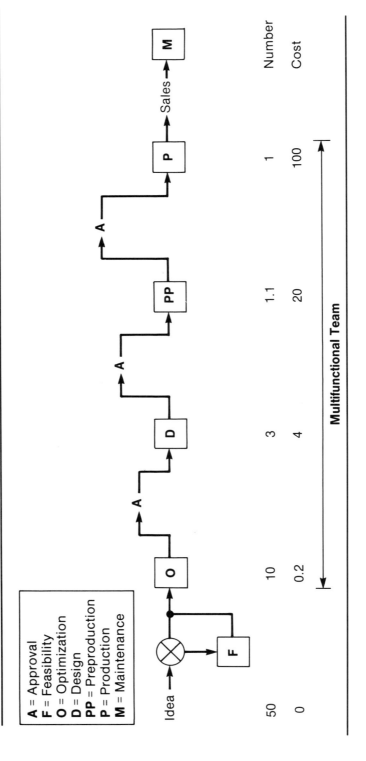

Exhibit 2-8. An illustrative workload situation.

Feasibility

M = Marketing

Development

O = Optimization

D = Design

PP = Preproduction

P = Production

Maintenance

Time

follow-on effort. While feasibility activity work is normally done by a technology department (such as engineering, research and development, or software), sometimes it might be done by the marketing department to investigate a totally new market, as suggested by the "M" in one feasibility activity bar in Exhibit 2-8. In other situations, feasibility work might be done by the manufacturing department to investigate a new production process.

The optimization phase must be separate from and precede the design phase because it is impractical, if not impossible, to make a schedule or budget for the design phase until the product specifications have been set, as illustrated in the five situations in Exhibit 2-8. It is clearly possible to omit the optimization phase if the product specifications are obvious and you do not require market research before initiating the design phase, as illustrated by one project that commences with the design phase. Undertaking the optimization phase is normally, but not necessarily, a commitment to undertake the design phase. However, undertaking design phase does not constitute a commitment to produce the new product, even though there may be a schedule for a proposed market introduction. The preproduction activity normally is a commitment to produce; however, you can stop a development activity in the preproduction phase (or even in the production phase). You might do this, for instance, if you learn that a competitor has just introduced a similar or better product at a selling price lower than your intended price.

You will have a better track record meeting your new product development objectives if you recognize that feasibility efforts and maintenance efforts must be allowed for but made separate from the time-critical new product development efforts themselves. These two activities commonly require the same human and physical resources that the new product development activity requires. The three new product development activities in Exhibit 2-8 that reach completion all illustrate subsequent maintenance activity. If your company does not recognize that reality, then you will find that schedules for new product development efforts are not met. There are two reasons for this and they are different depending on whether you look at feasibility or maintenance.

If there are no separate feasibility efforts allowed for, then new products that require new technology or move into totally new markets will require inventing on schedule, which, in fact, does not occur on schedule. The feasibility activity, as important as it may be, may require an invention or technical breakthrough that cannot be scheduled; thus, the most that can be done here is to identify that requirement, provide resources, and develop a sense of urgency. To put this differently, the goal of feasibility efforts is to give you a stockpile of proven technologies in the form of breadboards, bench-scale chemistry demonstrations, completed analyses, or, perhaps, new debugged software algorithms. Or, you may have feasibility activity efforts to evaluate unknown markets or to experiment with new manufacturing technology.

After you start to sell a product, maintenance activity may be required. Typically, a user, a customer, or perhaps the sales department, discovers that there is some problem. When this happens, you must solve the problem immediately. In many cases, the people who did the original product design can solve the problem most quickly. Unfortunately, this is especially true when the problem arises due to a software defect (or bug), because the documentation is often defective or nonexistent. If you have not allowed for this reality, then your next new product development effort will suffer because the people who work on it must go back to firefighting on the prior product's maintenance problems. Realistically, therefore, you must either have a separate maintenance group (commonly called sustaining or continuing engineering) or you must not schedule the development effort of subsequent new products on the assumption of 100 percent availability. You should examine your own company's historical record, but, as a guideline, only about three-fourths to four-fifths of the time of your development people will be available for development if they must also do maintenance work.

Finally, when you establish a phased approach such as this, you must always permit an escape clause if the new product itself can't fit this exact procedure. For instance, you can extend or recycle any phase, although, as a general rule, this may be a danger signal suggesting that the new product development effort is seriously off track. Similarly, you can omit any phase. In your own company, because of your market position, competition, or corporate culture, you can combine or divide these phases differently to provide a procedure which is most useful in your own organization. There is no single right way to carry out new product development. In fact, you may want to have different procedures for different kinds of new product development efforts (for example, totally new-to-the-world, minor revision, and so on). You can create a summary table (such as Exhibit 2-6) for whatever procedure(s) you do adopt, but you will have to decide which characteristics and phases to define. From time to time specific cases may require a deviation from your company's general procedure, and this is acceptable as long as the key people understand clearly why it is happening. As an example, you can exempt some very small projects from many of the detailed reviews normally given to a larger new product development effort. Obviously, the risk of lack of control for exempted projects is much greater, but that risk may result in less expected cost than the certain cost of subjecting very small projects to even a simplified new product development procedure.

AVOIDING UNNECESSARY DELAYS

There are three frequent problems with new product development, as it is commonly practiced, that result in delayed market introduction. By adopting the phased approach that I outlined generally in the previous section, you can avoid all three of these.

1. Where they exist, unphased efforts tend to wander, and upper management is invariably surprised that the resulting new product is both later than and not the same as their original expectation. Exhibit 2-9(*a*) illustrates this unfortunate result.

Obviously, if you install a phased procedure, but the product specification is not rigid, the same type of surprise is common. I have heard many senior executives complain that products are frequently introduced late and some key attributes (for instance, the factory standard cost) are not what they were previously led to expect. One of the reasons this happens is that the specifications are changed during the development effort. However, in a typical case where this occurs, top management is not aware of the changes in the specifications because no flag went up. Thus, there is no visible signal that the development project now has a different goal than it had when it was originally authorized. Therefore, my approach starts with clear specifications that are cast in concrete during the optimization phase. If it is necessary or desirable to change the specifications at some later time during the development effort, then the development team should stop (or kill) the initial devel-

Exhibit 2-9. Three unnecessary delays.

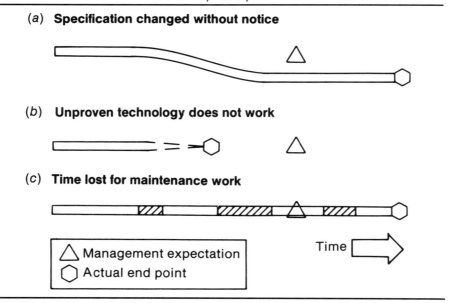

(*a*) **Specification changed without notice**

(*b*) **Unproven technology does not work**

(*c*) **Time lost for maintenance work**

△ Management expectation
◯ Actual end point

Time

opment effort. This requires the concurrence of top management. You can then start a new effort, preferably with a new title. The new effort might start at a later phase of development effort, because good work should not be thrown away when you discontinue the original effort. However, unless the specifications at which the effort is aimed are clearly understood, many people will lose time by working in counter-productive ways.

2. New product development efforts sometimes take much longer than anyone wishes because the effort depends on an invention. Unfortunately, inventions cannot be produced on schedule. In some cases, the inventions just don't occur at all, as illustrated in Exhibit 2-9(*b*). Although the work within any feasibility activity effort is scheduled, successful results are not guaranteed. That is, you authorize people to do laboratory or market research work for short periods of time (typically three months) consistent with and in support of corporate strategy, but you do not rely upon success. New product development activity may be difficult, challenging, and even lengthy, but it starts only when there is a belief that no problems having unknown solutions will arise. If there are significant unknowns, however, the schedule becomes unpredictable and feasibility work should be undertaken rather than development.

3. You may have established a reasonable phased schedule for the new product effort. Then, an urgent maintenance problem on a previously introduced product requires work by some of the development team. Exhibit 2-9(*c*) illustrates the delay caused by this fire-fighting, which unfortunately is a common occurrence in many companies.

COMPRESSING THE SCHEDULE OF THE PHASED APPROACH

Phased approaches for new product development have existed for many years. In an era where product life cycles were long, these were adequate. Today, we have to salvage and make productive use of the good ideas available in a phased new product development concept, but we must eliminate unnecessary lost time. How do we do that?

To start, we strip away the three worst features that delay the conventional approach. That is, we first eliminate lost time between phases, as shown in Exhibits 2-10(*a*) and 2-10(*b*). I propose the following ground rule to overcome this problem:

1. The multifunctional triad leading the development team must schedule the end of phase review one month before phase completion; normally, the marketing function's member of the leadership triad is primarily responsible for this. Then, management has one day to render

a go or stop decision; the absence of a stop decision is to be taken by the development team as a go decision. The advantage of this ground rule is that it focuses attention on a success-oriented program, but it gives management the right to redirect or terminate the new product development effort if appropriate.

2. Each phase is itself made as short as possible. Exhibits 2-10(*b*) and 2-10(*c*) illustrate this. Parts III and IV of the book cover the variety of means by which this can realistically be done.

3. We preclude the traditional baton passing problem that occurs when phases are organized to be run like a relay race. This classic problem with phased new product development arises when one department is responsible for one phase of work. When that department is finished, it hands off its completed work package to the next department, which is then responsible for the following phase of work. The second department naturally blames the first department for doing an incomplete job (whether or not this is the case). Similarly, the first department criticizes the second department for either failing to appreciate the good work that they did or for destroying it. This approach, baton passing, diminishes interdepartmental harmony rather than promoting it. This is a very serious and unfortunately prevalent problem in many companies that have phased new product development procedures. However, it is not inherent in any phased approach and can be entirely avoided by involving every functional department in each phase.

Exhibit 2-10. Avoiding wasted time.

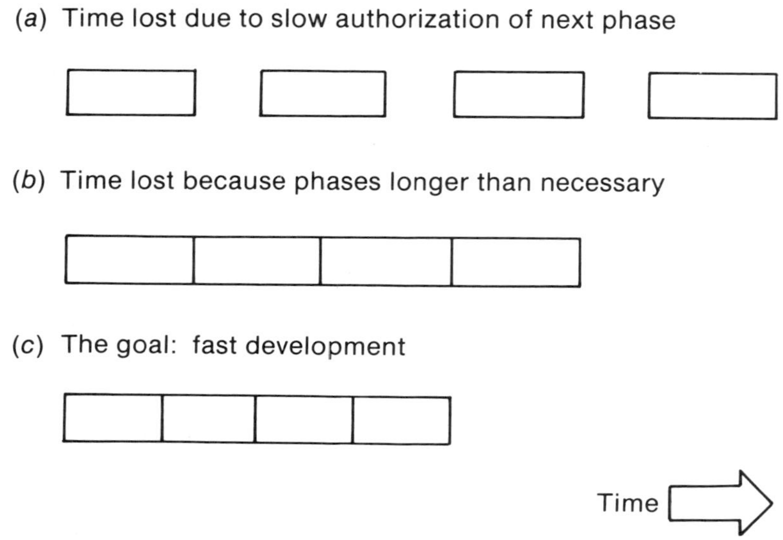

(*a*) Time lost due to slow authorization of next phase

(*b*) Time lost because phases longer than necessary

(*c*) The goal: fast development

Time

LEADERSHIP BY A MULTIFUNCTIONAL TRIAD

Because of the problems with baton passing and interdepartmental disharmony, I advocate that a multifunctional triad consisting of a key person from each of the marketing, technology (which includes research and development and engineering), and manufacturing departments manage each new product development effort; the first among equals should normally be the person from the marketing function. She must have superb people skills to ensure that the other two triad team members are proactively cooperative.

Although a multifunctional triad provides the leadership for all work, the amount of work done by a particular department does tend to vary from one phase to another. For example, most feasibility activity work is done entirely by the research and development department (or the research department if it is separate from the development department). However, the feasibility investigation of an entirely new market could be primarily a marketing department effort, and the investigation of a totally new manufacturing process or technology could be primarily a manufacturing department effort.

Unfortunately, there is a practical problem, as one observer puts it: "My experience with manufacturing causes me to doubt how useful they can be in traditional business organizations in feasibility activities, including evaluating new manufacturing processes or technology. Typically, manufacturing doesn't want to do anything that will divert attention from on-going production." This attitude is prevalent. In one company, manufacturing personnel said: "We don't want to spend time working on new product development activities that aren't going to get to manufacturing." The result, of course, is that they also do not work on nor contribute to those others that eventually do reach manufacturing. This normally causes the designs to be difficult to manufacture or of high factory (standard) cost. In many cases the design has to be done again, causing a painful delay. There is a solution, which is to treat manufacturing engineering work as a development expense (which is really what it is on a new product development effort), rather than a manufacturing (overhead) cost. If you do this, you will be able to hire more manufacturing engineers to participate in the early phases of new product development, thus saving a lot of subsequent waste.

The most crucial phase for equal participation by all functional departments is optimization. Even market research, a primary responsibility of the marketing function, will be of better quality if both the technology and manufacturing functions also participate. Conversely, the technology departments, especially engineering, do most of the work in the design phase; however, extensive participation by manufacturing engineering helps, as I amplify in Chapter 4. In the preproduction phase, manufacturing engineering is the department most actively involved, and, obviously, the manufacturing department is primarily involved in the production phase. Nevertheless, the entire development is led by a multifunctional triad to ensure that nothing is done to create avoidable problems.

Maintenance activity is similar to feasibility activity in that one department may be almost entirely responsible. This is obvious if a separate sustaining engineering department is established. However, some maintenance problems can be most quickly solved by another department. For instance, the marketing department could change advertising claims or lower the product's price if several buyers complained that some feature was not as specified. This might be a quick fix until engineering and manufacturing introduce a product modification to overcome the shortfall.

Thus, every phase of the new product development effort involves the participation of all the key departments and it becomes a joint responsibility.

HIGHLIGHTS

Unstructured approaches, which some people advocate to unleash creativity or reduce restrictions, are risky and not necessarily fast.

It may be helpful to use external sources (using licensing, joint venture, purchasing, or sub-contracting arrangements), although you may have to share some potential profits.

Feasibility and maintenance activities should be separate from development activity.

Development activity should start with an optimization phase in which you establish specifications that are consistent with the desired schedule.

You can choose the other specific development activity phases, which might be design, preproduction, or production, to satisfy your own market and business needs.

A phased approach promotes improved understanding and increased urgency and reduces risk.

Fast new product efforts require multifunctional teamwork and should be led by a triad.

Chapter 3

Optimization of Specifications

In the sense that everything depends on the specification, this initial phase of the development activity is the most important phase. If the triad team does a good job of trading off product attributes, the development schedule, and the development budget, then the development activity has a good chance of being successful. The converse is also usually true, that is, a bad specification trade-off leads to disappointment.

The commercial success of your new product depends on market acceptance. Therefore, market research is normally an essential optimization phrase activity, the sine qua non of ultimate success. Effective market research translates market requirements into development specifications relevant to the technical and manufacturing members of the triad. The key to a good specification is precision or measurability: If you cannot define a characteristic quantitatively, you probably do not understand it. Ways to perform the crucial primary market research include interviews and mail, which should be done in conjunction with thorough secondary market research.

THE CRITICALITY OF SPECIFICATIONS

Exhibit 3-1 contains some quotes from practitioners who were asked to identify their key problems in achieving faster new product development. It is clear that the specification optimization phase is a major challenge. What can you do to overcome this challenge? Here are three actions:

1. Form a triad to decide what specifications are realistically achievable. If a trade show or seasonal sales opportunity is a *crucial* schedule goal, then you have to settle on a product performance goal (or level)

that can be accomplished by the required date, as shown in Exhibit 3-2. Naturally, this is often less than what could be done if more time were available. The involvement of a triad can eliminate cross-functional finger-pointing (such as engineering or manufacturing personnel accusing marketing of inventing trade shows to get the product finished on their schedule). This also can eliminate the time-consuming ping pong game in which one department sends its contribution to another and awaits the moment when the ball returns to swat it back again. An optimized specification for a family of products is one that the triad knows how to achieve or schedule.

2. You may (and often should) involve the other functions, such as sales, service, and quality, even if their role will be relatively small. It's a lot easier to react to and take advantage of their useful input early than when the new product is being assembled. This multifunctional involvement also reduces the likelihood that your customer(s) will be disappointed and reject your new product, as illustrated in Exhibit 3-3. Broad multifunctional participation based on solid market knowledge, which I will discuss later in this chapter, is a way to ensure that the voice of the customer is considered early in setting specifications; and checkpoints during the development work can help assure that the product meets the specification. To put this differently, there are three possible customer reactions to your new product: dissatisfaction, satis-

Exhibit 3-1. Quotations from practitioners: some cited challenges for faster new product development.

"Defining right product at right price."
"Defining full requirements and constraints."
"Getting a good product definition."
"Maintaining direction to get NPD done fast."
"Establishing 'firm' specifications."
"Finding features to add true product distinction."
"Getting the NPD group to focus on the objective."
"Setting requirements for finished product."
"Establishing the appropriate product to develop."
"Getting marketing to quickly firm up a product definition."
"Product definition prior to engineering start."
"Getting firm up-front definition of what the product is."
"Getting good specifications that meet requirements without overkill."
"We need fewer short-time specification changes."
"No enhancements or additions after a cutoff date."
"Avoid premature promises or demonstrations to customers."
"Incomplete and changing requirements or specifications."
"Product definition, ensuring that we are developing the right product."

Exhibit 3-2. A product performance goal schedule.

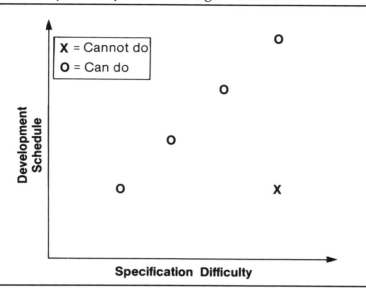

Exhibit 3-3. Product development's "ring of distress."

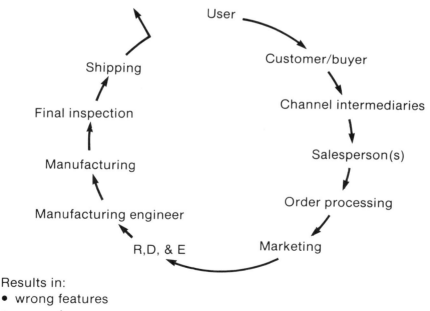

faction, or enthusiasm. Product (or service) defects are a nuisance and often can be a major trouble to a user or customer. The absence of defects does not necessarily cause satisfaction and certainly does not ensure enthusiasm. Your optimized specifications must aim at satisfying both rational an emotional needs of your target market to produce enthusiasm.

3. You start the optimization phase when you believe that solutions exist to all technical problems. Committing to and announcing a product introduction date that the triad does not know how to achieve may be stimulating and challenging, but also extremely costly and wasteful. What's the value of a specification that cannot be met? It is immaterial whether the genesis of the new product was market pull or technology push, although the former is more likely to be commercially successful. If there are major technical unknowns, it is impossible to provide a realistic market introduction date.

If your new product uses technology or manufacturing processes that are new to your company, or involves unfamiliar marketing, it is more likely there will be unknowns. As illustrated in Exhibit 3-4, if two or three of these are unfamiliar, the difficulty and your risk increase. In

Exhibit 3-4.   Increasing difficulty and risk as unknowns grow.

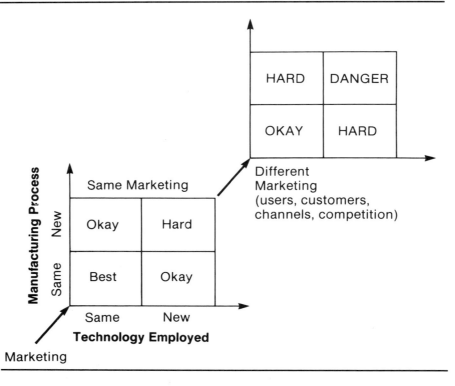

that case, the sensible course of action is to initiate a feasibility effort so that when you undertake the optimization phase, it is possible to have a schedule for product shipment. Obviously, the development activity may encounter unexpected technical problems or may just involve a lot of hard work, but the triad only sets the target product introduction date when they believe it can realistically be met. Thus, the goal of the optimization phase is an achievable specification upon which the subsequent design phase can be based.

However, the commitment to undertake the subsequent design phase is not, in fact, automatic. The reason to have separate optimization and design phases is to ensure that the much more expensive and time consuming design activity is focused on an optimum combination of product features. Product features, or attributes, include technical or performance characteristics *and* the selling price (which is frequently translated into an allowable factory cost). You initiate the optimization phase when there is a plausible idea for a new product that will satisfy an attractive market and for which there is no substantial unproven technology. One of the most important activities in the optimization phase is to define explicitly the *musts* and *wants* for the new product's attributes. Obviously, such an explicit definition requires a clear understanding of the market and competition. In some cases, you will complete the optimization phase work and decide that the subsequent design phase is not justified because there are more attractive uses for your company's scarce resources.

Your objective is to specify a product that is just right for both your marketplace and your bottom line. Product specification and direction emerge from thorough and complete interactive development, using the full capability of the triad's expertise. Tradeoffs and alternatives must be explored and choices made. This can assure you that the remainder of the development will be completed quickly. Compaq reportedly spent two years deciding on the specifications of the new Deskpro 386 computer, after which it only required nine months to build it. While that is still a total of thirty-three months from start to introduction, it illustrates an efficient and lower cost method, which I commend.

THE OPTIMIZATION PHASE

I now cover the considerations summarized in Exhibit 2-6.

    1. START POINT. This phase starts when there is both:

      A. A plausible idea for a product which satisfies a prospective unmet market need

B. Proven technology that leads you to believe the product can be
    produced without any requirement to invent on schedule

2. GOAL. The goal is to create an achievable specification that is
cast in concrete. Ideally, the specification will also include parameters
for the follow-on family of products, although these specifications may
be less firm (especially for those that are further into the future). There
are five advantages to considering entire families during the specification optimization phase:

A. You can start with a low-end, simple member of the family that
    can be introduced quickly;
B. This early entry provides you real market information to con-
    firm or adjust your market research;
C. You should be able to obtain lower costs by the use of common
    parts, modules, and processes;
D. The follow-on members should themselves reach the market
    more quickly, since large portions of them are already designed;
    and
E. Such a family can provide a "hook" to extend your product's
    lifetime.

3. SOME TYPICAL TASKS. These are listed in Appendix C.
While publishing a firm specification is clearly the key task, in general this is dependent upon market research. Normally, you must complete secondary market research during the optimization phase, if it has
not been completed previously. This is required so that test marketing
and other primary market research can be completed during this phase.
To facilitate market research, it may be necessary to have early crude
models, frequently called breadboards (or sometimes brassboards).
These might be made with paper, cardboard, or even an erector set to
help convey key working principles of the product and to ensure that
the market research is performed with insight. The market's *musts* and
wants have to be clear, which means that you must understand the market segments and competition.

In addition, you will perform technical trade-off studies, including
crude production cost estimates.

4. KEY DECISION. The challenge is to select the most attractive
combination of product and adjunct attributes for initial market introduction of product. The adjunct features (such as service, financing, and
training) may interact with the product features. Ease of access and part
replacement is an obvious example. Because different people, especially
when they come from different functional groups, may see different op-
tima, this decision can be difficult.

An optimum specification is one that allows your company to meet its strategic objectives. In some cases you will desire maximum profits for the near term; in other cases you might aim for long term growth of market share. Thus, you must understand what you are trying to achieve before setting a new product specification.

5. END POINT. The output is an approved specification and the critical path schedule for the design phase. A complete new product specification involves three different considerations, explained in Exhibit 3-5. Money appears in the specification in two different ways. First, it is a part of the product attributes, where it is used to specify the product's selling price or your own company's factory (or ongoing product) cost. What a customer will pay depends on the other performance features; greater speed and accuracy, for instance, may command a higher selling price. It also varies from one kind of customer to another, so you must have a clear market target. In one company, identifying the prime prospect is called the yellow pages test, because they target specific companies to assure that they will produce the right product at the right time. Second, the development budget is usually stated in terms of money; however, in some cases, the development team may work with a labor hours or headcount budget. (Obviously, such labor budgets are equivalent to money when labor and overhead rates are accounted for). In almost every case, product cost is more important than the development budget, since the former is incurred in every product and the latter is incurred only once.

Just as the performance features fundamentally determine the

Exhibit 3-5. Ingredients of a specification.

Product Attributes (as seen by the customer)

- *Performance features (such as speed, sensitivity, accuracy, efficiency, size, weight, or similar items)*
- *Nonprice aspects (such as the user interface, ease of use, training, reliability, warranty, maintenance, or similar items)*
- *Selling price*

Development Schedule

- *A critical path network for the design phase*
- *Best estimates for the preproduction and production phase schedules*
- *A target product introduction date*

Development Budget

- *Expenses (such as labor and supplies)*
- *Capital items (such as tooling)*

product's cost, the target date for the product's introduction depends on the agreed specifications. It is easy to set incompatible performance attributes and development schedules, so it requires the triad to make intelligent trade-offs. Obviously, you must also understand how rapidly the market is changing (or is likely to change); as with bird shooting, you must aim ahead to hit the target.

At the time the specifications are set in the optimization phase, the schedule for the design phase can be set by the multifunctional triad team. If the specification defines a complex product, the design phase will be much longer than required for a simple product. Nevertheless, the scheduled end of the design phase can be forecast with considerable accuracy after the specification is set and a critical path network diagram is constructed. Normally, the preproduction and production phases can be forecast even more accurately when the design phase is nearly complete.

At the same time the schedule is set for the first product, it is also important to plan for a family of follow-on products, perhaps in somewhat less accuracy and detail. When the design phase of the first product in the family is complete, the design team (typically mostly composed of engineering personnel) can start the design phase of the second product.

The optimization phase ends when the new product's specifications are cast in concrete. That is, the specifications (including the development schedule and budget) are embodied in some written document. This may be as little as one page or it may require many pages. One technique that is especially useful if the product requires any software is to write the entire operator's manual. The grammar, spelling, style, and similar aspects may not be final, but all the detailed features, display screens, user adjustments, operating instructions, and other key options are included.

Another technique is to wrote an advertisement for the product. Again, this is not meant to be in final form for publication in external media. Rather it is a detailed enumeration of the specifications that will attract the user or customer. You must plan to fulfill their real unmet needs, and you therefore must know which are *musts* and which are merely *wants*. Your advertisement (the triad's working specification) must be put in the customer's terms. You should also identify the media in which this advertisement might be placed, since this helps you clearly identify your market target.

Similarly, the advertisement may specify the entire family of new products, even though you do not intend to introduce them simultaneously, nor even mention the later products in the initial media publicity. This clarifies the overall goals and guides design and manufacturing personnel to strive for parts commonality, modular construction, and similar time and cost economies.

Working on an entire family can also avoid creeping featurism. Consider the lament from one of my clients when the development team made a change to a specification that was supposedly cast in concrete. Realizing the change would delay the new product's introduction, he said: "We do not now have the ability to establish a firm specification for what a customer requires. Either we are inefficient in our market research or we are trying to be all things to all people and thus reacting to the whims and desires of a possible minority." If this company had been working to develop an entire family, perhaps the change could have been introduced into later models, which would have avoided a one month delay.

6. SCHEDULE. As I state in Chapter 2, short phases have the virtue that their end point can be more clearly perceived and, thus, scheduled. The optimization phase need not be very long; it may only require one or a few days. I do encounter cases where the engineering or manufacturing members of the development team complain that they have been at work for many months and still do not have a complete specification. Everyone is at fault for letting this happen, especially since a prime cause is simply that the triad never blocked out a few days to work together to finish a complete specification.

The work for this phase can be scheduled quite precisely. If the phase will be longer than a few days, the triad should use the first day to create a critical path schedule for the balance of the optimization phase's work. This is very important because this phase typically involves highly interdependent work of all triad components and this ensures for quick completion.

7. MANAGEMENT AUTHORIZATION. Management should approve the entire phase. Optimization phase efforts are not very costly, even with extensive market research, compared to the work that will follow, so the approval to initiate this phase is not normally one for top management. In fact, you want to make it as easy to initiate this kind of work as reasonable control permits.

8. MARKET INTRODUCTION. At the start of this phase, the product introduction date is only a guess. After the specification is complete, a target date is set, but that remains only an approximate estimate. Or, a target date, typically a key industry trade show, can be set, and then the product's specification can be established at a level that allows the introduction date to be met.

9. BUDGET. Triad teams must have very easy access to enough budget so that they can carry out a few days work without seeking upper

management approval. Beyond that point, budget authority must conform to the normal corporate controls.

10. SCHEDULE VS. COST-RISK TRADE-OFF OPTIONS. Normally, optimization phase work is not a commitment to undertake any further development work. If your company is strongly committed to introducing this product quickly, you can authorize procurement of long-lead items that are required for the design or subsequent phases. But this is still not an irrevocable commitment to undertake the design phase.

11. TRIAD ROLES. The optimization phase may require as little as a few hours or it may require weeks or even months (especially if extensive market research and breadboarding are required). In the cases where it is short, all members of the triad may devote full time to the effort; in longer optimization phases, some members may not be intensively involved full time. For instance, market research might be carried out primarily by the marketing department or marketing consultants, and the triad would work together only at the beginning, during joint reviews, and at the conclusion. Similarly, most breadboarding work is done by the engineering part of the triad and the preliminary cost estimate for parts or processes is done primarily by manufacturing personnel.

INTERRELATIONSHIP WITH SUBSEQUENT PHASES

Because the company's profitability is critically dependent upon the product's gross margin, namely the difference between the selling price and the product's cost, it is clear that the triad team must be able to make some estimates of what a performance feature will cost. This must be done in the optimization phase, without benefit of a completed design phase. Exhibit 3-6 illustrates this interdependency, showing that later phases must be completed before the product's cost will be known with accuracy. Currently, analytic models to predict manufacturing cost are not very accurate. These will improve in the years ahead and expert systems may also be developed, so it is probably worthwhile to watch for such software.

The complexity of this interrelationship clearly reveals why it is so important to involve all three triad functions when attempting to optimize specifications. To put it differently, marketing personnel will often desire performance features and a selling price that engineering personnel feel will require a long time to design; engineering personnel may design the product in such a way that the production cost targets cannot be met by the manufacturing department; and the product's factory cost does not allow the selling price to be as low as the marketing depart-

Exhibit 3-6. Achieving your desired profit.

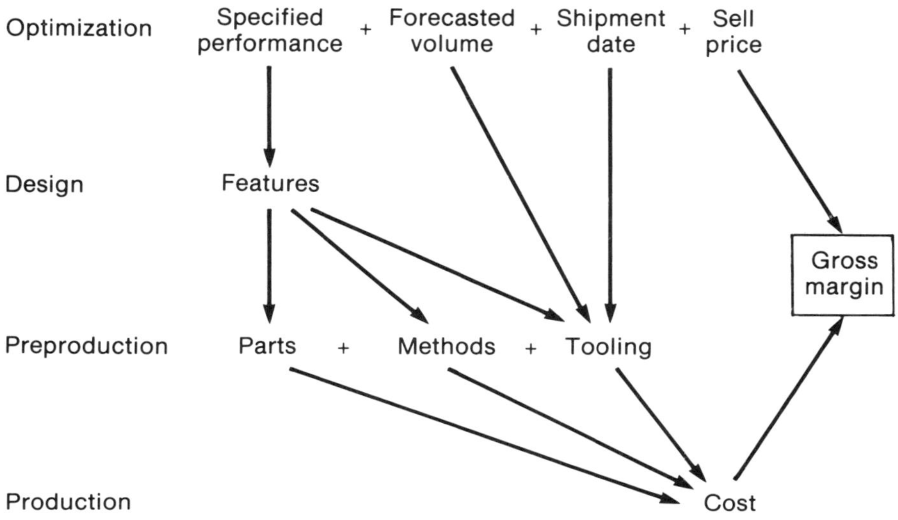

ment desired. This self-defeating cycle can be eliminated, or the problem can at least be diminished, when the specification is optimized by a triad.

When the product is intended for sale in international markets, through your own company's foreign business units or through separate intermediaries, these relationships are even more complex. Legal and cultural issues must also be given consideration, and you may have to convene group of people from many countries to assure the product's specifications are appropriate.

MARKET RESEARCH

It is easy to create ideas for possible new products and devise new products that cost more than people are willing to pay. Commercial success is crucially dependent on the existence of a real market need and your understanding of it. This must be reflected in your optimized specification.

The key to a good specification is an intimate knowledge of the intended market, which requires either having been a deeply involved participant in that market for a long time or conducting high quality market research. The key to market research is asking the right question. Data reduction, as important as it may be, is less important. The insightful question is likely to open up an entirely new way of viewing a market opportunity and this can give you an earlier start than anyone else.

Consider the following real (but disguised) case. A manufacturer believed their customers stressed reliability. Their design engineers usually satisfied this requirement by designing the product to have a long mean-time-between-failures (MTBF), which made the product very expensive. Preliminary market research confirmed the importance of reliability to customers, but it revealed that this could be accomplished more easily and inexpensively by providing responsive service to quickly repair the product when it did infrequently fail. Thus, it was more useful to design the product for ease of access and part interchangeability and to improve the service department's responsiveness.

Insightful market research requires a forecast of what people will do in the future. Unfortunately, however, this forecast depends on limited available information, such as shown in Exhibit 3-7. The further into the future you must project, the greater the difficulty. Thus, there is another benefit of fast new product development, since a short development duration implies that your forecast will not be too tenuous.

Kinds of Market Research

Market research activities are normally divided into secondary and primary sources. Secondary sources are usually examined first, so that the primary research can be more sharply focused. Secondary market research sources include published articles, reports, data, indices, and similar publicly available information. Primary market research is proprietary to your firm and is obtained by gathering information from sources such as customers, potential customers, users, or others who are knowledgeable about the market being considered. Data that are collected may be either qualitative or quantitative. Primary market re-

Exhibit 3-7. Market research forecasting using limited available information.

Available		Desired
What people have done	What people: • do • say	What people will do
Past	Now	Future
	Time	

search techniques include face-to-face interviews, focus groups, telephone interviews, examination of warranty cards and mail questionnaires. One company offers a monthly prize to people who return warranty cards and another puts an 800 telephone number on every product. Both are thus conducting proactive market research continuously.

Industrial and Consumer Markets

Industrial (or business-to-business) and consumer markets differ. The latter marketplace frequently involves very high volume of low cost products with many channel intermediaries (such as wholesalers, distributors, or retailers). In such a marketplace, the ultimate consumer has very little direct influence on what kind of product is available. The industrial marketplace in many cases is based on direct company-to-company dealings, often with intimate working relationships between the product manufacturer and the customer. Of course, there are also areas where the two marketplaces are very similar, such as personal computers and general purpose fasteners. Nevertheless, if your product is for one or the other marketplace, the distinctions color much of what you do. For instance, some market research techniques are more useful in one marketplace than the other.

Market research for consumer and industrial markets differ in the availability of information and how it is distributed. Market knowledge is usually concentrated for industrial markets. Exhibit 3-8 portrays highly concentrated information in industrial markets where a few people (often only a handful) know essentially everything there is to know. The early interviewing is designed to identify these people and learn which questions to ask them. Conversely, for consumer markets,

Exhibit 3-8. Concentration of market information.

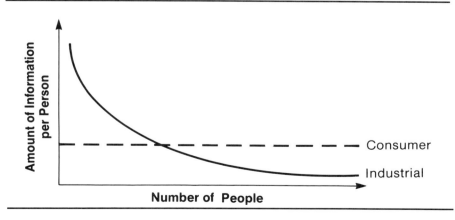

everyone has essentially the same amount of information. That is why consumer market surveys frequently require interviews of 1,500 people (which is a population sample size that provides plus or minus 3 percent accuracy).

Timing

Market research must be done during the optimization phase and the specification must be based on the results, not some wish list or preconceived belief. Consider the unhappy story of Pronto Computers. In mid-1982, Pronto decided to develop a new business microcomputer by stressing and concentrating on three product attributes: computing speed, data storage capability, and ergonomics. In terms of development duration, they were successful, since the first system was shipped one year after the company was founded. Less than two years later, however, the company filed for bankruptcy. In their haste to develop this new 16-bit microcomputer system, the development effort was apparently launched without thoughtful market research. Market research, which should have been done before the product's attributes were specified, was undertaken only when it became apparent that sales were less than necessary for company survival. At that last date, it was no longer possible to focus the company's limited resources on a needed, as opposed to technically feasible, product. Market research, which is a crucial element early in the optimization phase, must precede the design and production (or selling) phases, not follow.

In some cases market research must be performed in conjunction with other feasibility activity. For example, if there is a very broad range of technical options requiring investigatory work, market research may help to narrow the range and thus focus the technical feasibility activity on a few more promising targets. In other situations, the feasibility activity itself may be mostly market research, as, for instance, if a totally new market is being investigated.

Three Pitfalls

One general caveat in conducting market research is to recognize that you must consider both in-kind competition and functional competition, as shown in Exhibit 3-9. Many people conducting market research look only at the direct, in-kind competition. Unfortunately, in many cases it is the functional competition that is the major threat. Your new product success obviously depends on it offering the customer a differential advantage. This requires that you have a full understanding of your present and potential competition.

There is another market research problem. Some naive optimists are misled by the market share fallacy. They see a huge market and believe they can easily capture some small portion of it (such as one percent, 5 percent, or 10 percent). This small fraction (tiny in their eyes) is meant to be reasonable ("a piece of cake," "like falling off a log," or "any idiot can get that small share"), but, in practice, it is not. Never substitute a percent share of a big market for actual market research. Only the unwary or naive count upon capturing a small percentage of a large (or growing) market.

Finally, the timing for the product, and the market research, may be too early or late. Some markets are not ready for a good product. In the late 1950s, a chemical company produced a synthetic felt hat, following Du Pont's introduction of synthetic leather for shoes (which itself was a product that eventually failed). The hat was virtually indestructible (television advertisements showed a garbage truck running over the hat on a rainy night and the owner picking it up and replacing it on his head). It could be washed in a washing machine and it could be folded for storage. However, the entire market for men's hats was declining and consumers did not appreciate the value of non-woven synthetic materials for apparel. Now, however, such materials are used successfully and routinely in apparel.

Secondary Market Research

Secondary market sources include all kinds of published and statistical data. If your company is in a given industry or line of business, then a regular ongoing examination and collection of published data can save time when new products within this industry or business are being considered. When you must conduct new market research, the use of electronic database searching (such as the Dialog Information System, for

Exhibit 3-9. Two kinds of potential competition one must consider.

	In-Kind Competition	Functional Competition
Vacuum tube	GE and RCA	Transistors
Steel	Many companies	Kevlar
Cheese	Many types and brands	Other foods
Laser radar machine vision	Other laser radar	Structured light and stereo

instance) is usually much faster than consulting a library. The goal of secondary market research is to rapidly acquire the vast majority of relevant published literature and data about a product or market.

You can also collect commercial intelligence on an on-going basis. This has to be stored in some systematic way in your company to assure reasonable access. Commercial intelligence sources include field sales force reports; memos by all company personnel reporting on talks with distributors, customers, or users; data available as a result of the Freedom of Information Act; news articles about competitors; competitors' employment advertising; resumes obtained by your employment department of people who have worked for competitors; tear-down or analysis of competitors' products; and similar information. Patent filings, which you can locate in electronic databases, may also be a helpful source of information on what your competitors are doing. If your competitors include public corporations, then the ownership of one share of each competitor's stock assures you of timely access to all public information filed with the Securities and Exchange Commission.

Primary Market Research

Primary market research consists of queries aimed at customers, prospective customers, users, channel intermediaries, or other knowledgeable people. You normally conduct this after you complete the secondary market research. This sequence improves the quality of questions you can ask. However, to save time, it is possible to conduct the initial phases of primary market research before the secondary market research is fully completed.

Market Segments. When you conduct primary market research, it is usually crucial to segment the market and potential market. For instance, segmentation might be as shown in Exhibit 3-10. As an example, the veterinary market can be segmented by customers in accordance with the nature of their practice: small animals (usually household pets);

Exhibit 3-10. Some possible market segments.

- *PRODUCT APPLICATION*
- *CUSTOMER TYPE*
- *CUSTOMER SIZE*
- *GEOGRAPHICAL LOCATION*
- *USAGE RATE*
- *PRODUCT USE CLASSIFICATION*

large animals (usually commercial); or mixed. If you plan to sell veterinary medicine, you would try to determine how many veterinarians are in each category and how many animals there are of each type. In the case of airlines, for example, geographic segments are crucial: People living in hub cities will have different needs from those who do not; and people living on the two coasts of the United States will have more opportunity for transcontinental domestic flights than those living in the middle of the country.

It might be helpful to segment by purchase behavior, as illustrated in Exhibit 3-11. People who will not become customers and those who just bought from a competitor can still provide extremely valuable information, especially if you inquire about their reasons in a non-confrontational manner.

This latter segmentation was very helpful in the case of one company selling standard business microcomputer software as a result of direct responses to their advertisements in popular computer magazines. Formerly, these advertisements stressed low price exclusively. Prior to conducting any market research, the company believed that low price was the essential ingredient for success. Thus, they were lowering their price every month to advertise lower prices than their competitors. Upon interviewing their current and recent customers, it became apparent that people were buying for reasons other than low price. Specifically, recent customers stressed fast delivery from the company's large inventory and their knowledgeable telephone sales help. A mail survey, using names randomly selected from recent bingo card requests, sampled all categories of customers, as well as some non-customers (presumably these were primarily of the may become category). The results confirmed that low price was important, but not decisive; in fact, prospective purchasers would happily pay substantially above the lowest possible price if they could be assured of rapid delivery, knowledgeable

Exhibit 3-11.   A way to segment by purchase behavior.

Customers

- *Current*
- *Recent*
- *Stale*

Noncustomers

- *May become*
- *Will not become*

sales and technical service, and the supplier's dependability. As a result, the company quickly made changes in its strategy and advertisements and raised its prices.

You may also wish to devise segments based on channels of distribution, where different channel intermediaries may have different desires that you will have to reconcile. For example, the car buyer desires a quality car, one that does not require frequent repairs. However, the car dealership desires repair work to keep its shop busy and profitable. Market research must identify this kind of reality and you must resolve how to balance these contradictory desires.

Interviewing Techniques. Detailed techniques that I have found helpful in conducting face-to-face or telephone interviews are in Appendix D. Such interviews are commonly one-to-one.

A useful alternative is to interview several (typically from five to twelve) people in a focus group. This is a well-established market research technique. Recently, however, I read the following.

A New Twist to an Old Technique

An important dimension of effectiveness can be added to the focus group, one of the most widely used qualitative evaluation techniques available to market researchers.

This added dimension involves the follow-up questioning of individuals in focus groups within forty-eight hours of the group session in which they participated. It has proven an invaluable source of additional information. The concept is neither new nor unique, but considering the value of the information that can be drawn from respondents, is vastly under-used, in our opinion.

Anyone in the business can use the technique. We have formalized the follow-up idea by incorporating its use for all our group sessions. This has resulted in a significant increase in the data available to clients. We call it "FOCUS P.S."

Normally, focus group sessions, consisting of eight to ten respondents, last from an hour and a half to two hours, after which the recording equipment is turned off, and the respondents and moderator go their separate ways.

The key consideration in the follow-up technique, however, is that the respondent does not turn off, but continues to consider and mull over the material covered in the session. In our experience, some respondents, who may have been reluctant interviewees during the session, actually formulate their opinions *after* the session is over.

This rather obvious (in retrospect) phenomenon is manifested by continuance of the discussion in the elevator, in the parking lot, or coffee shop, with the net result being a loss, to the client, of valuable additional data.

We find that this post-session information can be gathered from respondents by the use of a self-administered questionnaire, mailed the day after the group session, or by a telephone interview, or both, depending on the nature of the inquiry. These follow-up techniques are still being tested and evaluated. The main thing is that we no longer are losing these vital thoughts and feelings that crop up *after* group discussions. The client winds up with a lot more useful information for his research dollar.[1]

Feature Trade-Off Analysis. If you are evaluating a specific product or service (existing or contemplated), you can ask respondents to rank attributes such as price, delivery, availability of service, and performance features. For a new car, top speed and fuel economy (that is, miles per gallon) are examples of performance features. For a telephone system, performance features include ease of access (that is, how quickly you get a dial tone) and amount of background noise. Initially, it is generally important to allow for "other" when asking about attributes, because the respondents may well identify factors you have not yet recognized as important. After this information has been gathered, you may then wish to perform a quantitative trade-off analysis.

One such method is conjoint analysis, which you can use to measure the importance of each attribute for a new product or service. Carbon composite airliner brake sets reportedly survive more landings and weigh less than the conventional steel brake sets. Therefore, the price of such new sets can be higher. Exhibit 3-12 summarizes the reported attributes. The dollar value of more landings and less weight could have been determined by conjoint analysis (although, in actual fact, it may have been established by other methods.) Similarly, a new kind of cement reportedly has longer life, greater strength, requires less water, and hardens more quickly than conventional cement. These new attributes have high value, especially for road construction and some other applications and where water is scarce, and thus can command a higher price. Again, the acceptable price premium could have been established by conjoint analysis.

As I said before, products and services have attributes such as price, availability, technical support, ease of repair, warranty, as well as performance features (for instance, top speed, frequency response, and operating costs). All potential customers do not value these attributes in the same way. Thus, it is often important to evaluate the relative importance of each attribute for a representative sample of potential customers and users. This permits you to produce the new offering with the combination of attributes that is most likely to satisfy the largest possible

1. Earl I. Wilson, President, Earl Wilson and Associates. Reproduced by permission.

Exhibit 3-12.   Airliner brake set attributes.

	Steel	Carbon Composite
Landings	1,000–1,500	2,500–3,000
Weight (lbs.)	9,000	7,200
Price	$300,000	$750,000

portion of the chosen market. This can be done very effectively by conjoint analysis, which is described more fully in Appendix B.

This powerful and simple technique is a way to translate market requirements into a quantitative design specification, which is the major goal of the optimization phase. I have also used it at the end of focus groups to provide a quantitative check on that otherwise qualitative market research.

The Truly Novel Product. Market research for a breakthrough or revolutionary product is a challenge. People were not expressing any need for 3M Post-its; in fact, the initial (traditional customer test market) market research was not encouraging. Truly novel products require that the manufacturer create a want, which eventually may become a need. In the case of Post-its, these were given to a number of secretaries, who found them to be useful. Polaroid, which brilliantly created a market for instant photography, was for many years unable to develop other products to satisfy different existing, but unfilled, needs.

There is always a management quandary in such situations. At what point do you decide the putative want cannot be created? In fact, an ardent proponent of the new product will rarely quit arguing for its continued development. Thus, since no dropped case can be conclusively proven, such decisions are usually made solely on a judgmental basis and, unfortunately, often provoke personal antagonism.

DO-IT-YOURSELF MARKET RESEARCH

Doing your own market research without professional expertise is not quite as risky as do-it-yourself brain surgery, but it does incur unnecessary risks. Despite this fact, many owners of smaller businesses and managers in larger businesses choose to undertake self-guided market research.

A number of fallacies may promote this choice: fear of loss of confidentiality, which could be ensured by a suitable secrecy agreement with a reputable, ethical management consultant (for instance a Certified Management Consultant); anticipated expense, which may result in a false economy if the do-it-yourself effort is not objective, efficiently conducted, or insightful or if it detracts from running the on-going business; and hoped-for speed, which presumes that the do-it-yourselfer does not require any learning time and can practice the art as efficiently as a specialist.

If you feel you must conduct market research without expert assistance, there are some steps you can take to reduce risks. The first step in any market research project is to define the information desired. Thus, you should prepare a written statement of your goal before doing anything else. This goal statement often can be refined during the secondary market research.

The next step gets to the heart of the matter, conducting some kind of primary market research. Remember, if you want to sell a product or service, you only have two choices: Sell more to existing customers or add new customers. Obviously, a company can only survey its customers if it maintains proper sales records, which, astounding as it may seem, is not always the case. To put this differently, maintenance of good customer records may help you develop your next product faster if market research will be required.

At this point, the do-it-yourselfer encounters the crucial limitation of this approach, namely self-deception. Our personal capacity to fool ourselves seems infinite; we just don't hear negative information, especially subtle nuances. Even worse, when interviewing another person, we unconsciously bias the interviewee. Inevitably, an interviewer who has a personal stake in the market research produces a skewing influence in how the interviewee answers questions. Many interviewees, for instance, are afraid of a confrontation or even its possibility. They will not truthfully respond to many important questions for fear of provoking the interviewer or making the interviewer defensive. (Consultants are thus valuable because they can be completely objective in conducting an interview.)

There is a similar problem if the market research is conducted by a subordinate of the person who believes in the idea being studied. It is very unusual for such a subordinate to candidly report negative market research findings to an enthusiastic superior. In the case of Nimslo's 4-lens camera that produces three-dimensional pictures, it seems likely that management's enthusiasm for its product blinded them to the market research findings or biased the market research it performed. It is hard to explain Nimslo's dismal actual sales, in contrast to original expectations, any other way.

Thus, if a manager is committed to conducting market research personally, it is best done by mail survey. This reduces the contamination or skewing that accompanies direct personal or telephone contact with an interviewee, but it does permit direct response from a potential customer or user (which secondary market research does not provide).

Some practical advice about preparing and sending out mail surveys that you should understand are:

1. Keep the questionnaire short and simple. You can gather only limited information by this method.

2. Pre-test the questionnaire on a small sample of the intended audience. People always read one or more questions in a way that you had not intended them to read.

3. Provide a response inducement if you want to receive a large response. The incentive must be something that is perceived by the audience as attractive enough to justify the trouble to respond. Money included in the survey mailing may be an inducement to open the letter, but it provides only a marginal incentive to complete and return the questionnaire. A gift for responding, for instance a penknife or card case, is an inducement only to a person who wants that kind of gift. Probably the best that can be done is to conduct a random drawing from responses received by a certain cut-off date and award the lucky winner with a check for $100 or $250. However, any award inducement requires respondents to furnish their name and address, which some may not choose to do. Always include a postage-paid return envelope with your questionnaire.

4. If you have appropriate sales records, it is relatively easy to mail questionnaires to customers. Even if your past records are poor, you can still identify present customers; in fact, you can enclose a questionnaire with each purchase. It is more difficult to reach noncustomers. Purchased address lists are often not what you expect and will have some obsolete addresses. Normally your main interest is noncustomers, so perhaps you can solicit names from inquirers (for instance via bingo cards) or store walk-ins.

5. You are never certain who fills in a mail survey. Some people delegate such tasks to children or secretaries. Also, some respondents will not be really knowledgeable about the subject but will complete the questionnaire merely to obtain the response premium. Therefore, it is important to have at least one question that provides a logical consistency check.

6. Respondents are likely to differ from nonrespondents. Therefore, it may be important to try to reach nonrespondents by some other means to get a better understanding of the differences.

Questions can be posed to permit free-form answers (essay type), yes/ no answers, or ranking of several choices. Each has its value, although the yes/no is least likely to provide any profound insights. Essay type answers are best sought only if you are conducting a small sample, because these require reading (often of poor handwriting) and the answers are often ambiguous. If you can phrase a question so that the respondent can rank several choices (for instance, "Put 1 next to your first choice, 2 next to your second choice, . . ."), you can often turn the questionnaires over to a junior person for analysis.

HIGHLIGHTS

Specifications are the critical underpinning of a fast new product development effort.

A good specification must be aimed at a real market problem, and should be measurable, specific, tangible, and verifiable.

It is useful to specify the follow-on members of the same product family, perhaps with less precision, when you prepare the specification for the initial new product.

Every member of the triad shares responsibility to see that the specification is clear, complete, and achievable.

It is helpful to write the specification as text for an advertisement or the product's operating manual.

It is crucial to conduct objective market research.

To save market research time, you can stockpile secondary market research information and overlap primary market research with secondary market research.

If you must conduct your own market research, objective information is more likely to come from mail questionnaires than interviews.

Chapter 4

Design for Low-Cost and Quick Manufacturing

You have to convert the optimized specifications into a producible design. How well you do this ultimately determines your profitability. My preferred phased approach has distinct design and preproduction phases. These may be combined into a single phase in some companies or in special situations. If the manufacturing engineering function is located within the engineering department, you may be more likely to combine the two phases; if it is a wholly separate function or part of the manufacturing function, you are more likely to benefit from separate phases.

LINKING THE OPTIMIZATION PHASE TO THE PRODUCTION PHASE

During the previous optimization phase, you translated the user's requirements into a product specification. You must now derive a low-cost manufacturable design that you can produce in a timely manner. Thus, the goal of the design phase is to prove that you can achieve the specification. And after you are confident of that, you are ready for the preproduction phase in which the goal is to verify that the manufacturing documentation is complete and accurate. Exhibit 4-1 illustrates this linkage, and also enumerates several criteria that, if satisfied, can lower your product's cost. To put this differently, everything that happens in the subsequent production phase is truly determined by what you do in the design and preproduction phases. If the new product is successful—and that is clearly your objective—you will produce it for a long time; therefore, any problems that are not eliminated by careful design and preproduction work will be ones your company must endure through-

Exhibit 4-1. The design and preproduction phases linking the optimization and production phases.

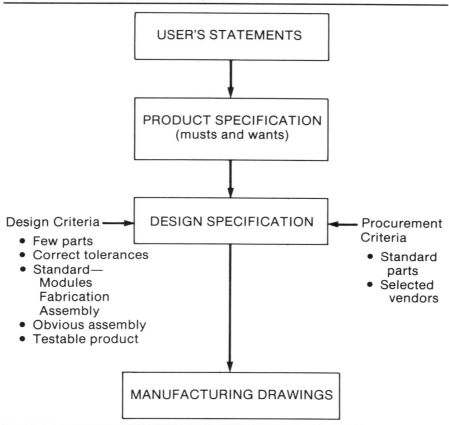

out the product's lifetime. In some cases, you may be able to correct these designed-in problems later, but that is usually very costly compared to avoiding them.

There is a different perspective in which to see this linkage, namely the kinds of issues that are of concern in the optimization and production phases. Some of these are shown in Exhibit 4-2, which illustrates that the concerns change. However, it is the cleverness of the design choices that determines what occurs subsequently in the production phase. For example, if two different companies start with identical product specifications, they will probably have different product designs and costs because their design executions will differ.

Some unfortunate companies try to improve the gross margins of products that are in production. There are only two ways to do this: Raise your price or lower your cost. However, the price you can charge is set by the selection of the product attributes you specified in the

Exhibit 4-2. Changing concerns in the optimization and production phases.

Optimization Phase Concerns	Production Phase Concerns
Product features	Quality
Product performance	Scrap and inventory levels
Product styling	Manufacturing flexibility
First shipment date	Date of routine shipments
Expected factory cost	Real factory cost

optimization phase, so it is likely to be hard to increase this subsequently in a competitive marketplace. Similarly, the design and preproduction work will establish your product's cost, so you will not be able to do very much about that once the product is being shipped. Therefore, if your design and preproduction work is not highly effective, you can be locked into low gross margins. The converse is also true: You can enjoy very high profit margins as a result of effective design and preproduction phase work.

This dependency also underscores why a triad is so critical. In a sense, the manufacturing department member of the triad participates in nonmanufacturing work to ensure that production phase concerns are dealt with when it is practical to do so. Unfortunately, in many companies, there are insufficient manufacturing engineers to do this. These people are scarce because they are a component of manufacturing overhead cost, which manufacturing management wants to minimize. This problem can be overcome by assigning the expense of those manufacturing engineers who are working on early phases of the new product development activity to the new product development budget, which is where this necessary expense truly belongs.

Even the criticality of periodic sales forecasts on subsequent production lot sizes or rates can be reduced by careful early work. The total production time of the product is the time duration from the date when you must order the first raw material, parts, or other component subassemblies until the date when you have finished goods that can be shipped. On the other hand, your customer does not really care about that time interval; its interest is in delivery time. This interval is the time from the date a purchase order is placed with your company's salesperson until the date the product is received by the customer. If your total production time is long compared to the customer's delivery time, your sales forecasts must be superbly accurate. If not, you will either be unable to satisfy some customer delivery needs or you will have an excess of finished goods in inventory, as Exhibit 4-3A suggests. A long total production time puts you at risk. Exhibit 4-3B portrays the happier converse situation of a short total production, where short total production time eliminates that problem. In the real world, this latter situation is one that some contract job shops and aerospace companies enjoy, but it is hard to achieve if customers demand short delivery times.

ACCELERATING TECHNIQUES

The use of quality function deployment (the house of quality) shown in Exhibit 4-4 and simultaneous engineering may help, provided the par-

Exhibit 4-3A. Long total production time.

Start production   Deliver product

Time you are at risk
[——————————————]

Customer's Delivery Time
Order product   Receive product

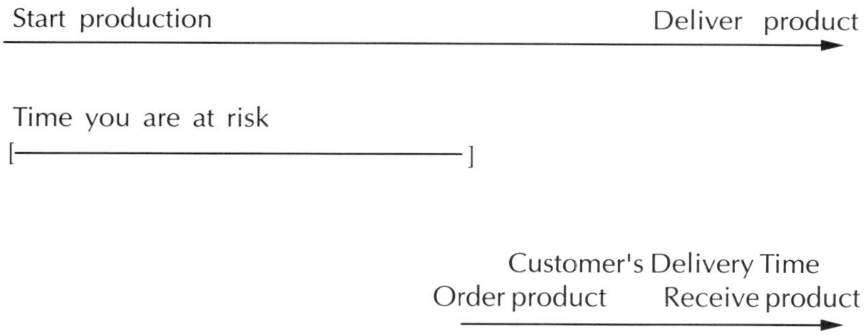

Exhibit 4-3B. Short total production time.

Start production   Deliver product

Customer's delivery time

Order product   Receive product

Time "cushion"
[——————]

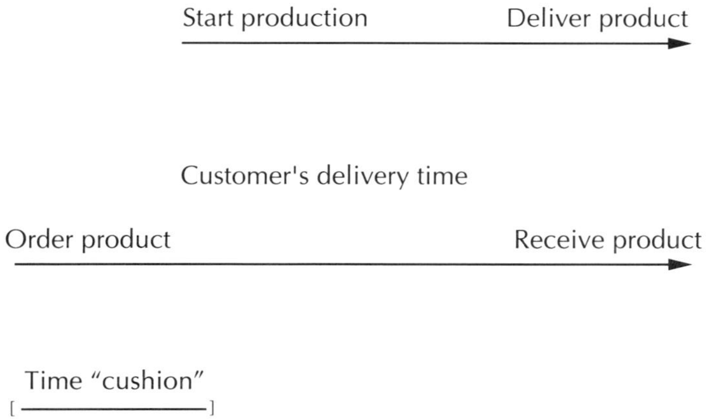

Exhibit 4-4. Using quality function deployment to translate customer requirements into a product.

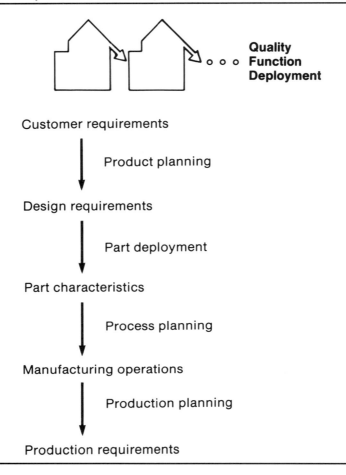

ticipants themselves stress speed and low cost. That is, a triad team that chooses an inherently slow process or material with lengthy procurement time, even if using a fast approach to do so, does not save as much time as possible. Designing a product or manufacturing process so that factory rework is rarely required is much better than making rework easy. Proponents of quality function deployment assert that the process can reduce differences in the interpretation of the specification, cross-functional disharmony, design changes, product warranty costs, and time-to-market.

Similarly, you must choose parts, processes, and operations that are inherently fast. For example, one company arranged for corrosion protection without plating, since a plating operation would have required a production turn-around cycle at a subcontractor facility that was inherently longer than desired. In general, the triad must look at the time for each procurement, production process, and assembly operation to shorten the time-to-market and the routine on-going production duration itself.

Another technique is concurrent product and process development. Sometimes you can do this by making early arbitrary subsystem partitions, which, with more thought, you may conclude are not necessarily the best choices obtainable. Nevertheless, if you make a circuit board or cabinet housing a bit bigger than ultimately required, you can move ahead with the design of other parts and their manufacturing processes.

THE DESIGN PHASE

Assuming the design work is a distinct phase, here are the considerations previously summarized in Exhibit 2-6 (Chapter 2).

1. START POINT. Assuming that there is an attractive combination of achievable product attributes at a realistic production cost, it is then appropriate to undertake the design phase. The design phase can start immediately after the triad completes the firm specification. This phase separation ensures that you will focus the much more expensive and time-consuming design activity on an optimum combination of product features. Although there may indeed be complex and challenging work to undertake during this phase, it is a phase which can and must be tightly scheduled. However, because it typically has substantially greater complexity than the optimization phase, it is appropriate for the critical path network schedule and development budget to have both time and cost contingency. The amount of this contingency is obviously a trade-off with the risk that the leadership triad and its support team will miss the development schedule or budget. How this trade-off should be made depends on the nature of the competitive situation and the extent to which early commitments have to be made to a specific product introduction date.

2. GOAL. The goal of the design phase is to prove that the specifications can be met.

3. TYPICAL TASKS. These are listed in Appendix C.

4. KEY DECISION. The key management decision the triad makes is whether to recommend production (and, ipso facto, its predecessor, namely preproduction). Thus, the end of the design phase can only occur when there is sufficient information to permit a discounted cash flow analysis. The really big expense in most organizations occurs during the

preproduction or production phase and includes such things as tooling or even new production plants. The commitment to dedicate corporate resources to these very expensive undertakings should never be made lightly. While there can never be any complete guarantee of ultimate success, it is crucial to minimize the likelihood of committing major resources to a program that is unlikely to have an attractive, or at least acceptable, financial return.

5. END POINT. Assuming the return appears satisfactory, the design phase will end with complete production documentation, sometimes elaborated with breadboards or other working model embodiments, and the critical path schedule for the preproduction phase. At this point, the triad must be convinced the product can be manufactured cost-effectively with high quality. Also, the triad will have a critical path network schedule for the preproduction phase.

6. SCHEDULE. The schedule for this phase is set by the critical path network that was prepared during the end of the optimization phase.

7. MANAGEMENT AUTHORIZATION. Management should approve the entire phase. If it will be longer than three months, the progress, the current status, and the forecast for the forthcoming quarter should be reviewed quarterly.

8. MARKET INTRODUCTION. The date for the product introduction is set, but only to the expected quarter.

9. BUDGET. The budget for design phase work can vary widely, depending on the specific product. It is set during optimization.

10. SCHEDULE VS. COST RISK TRADE-OFF OPTIONS. You can authorize procurement of long-lead tooling and other items for the preproduction phase without committing to undertake the phase.

11. TRIAD ROLES. Normally, this phase makes more use of technical (usually, engineering and design) personnel than any other phase. However, even with a superbly detailed specification, both marketing and manufacturing personnel remain involved to ensure that the design does not (1) exceed the specification's requirements and (2) lead to unreasonable manufacturing demands. In addition, these two functions will have other nondesign work to do to have their houses in order for a timely product introduction.

THE PREPRODUCTION PHASE

Assuming preproduction is a distinct phase, following are the considerations previously summarized in Exhibit 2-6.

1. START POINT. This phase normally starts with complete design documentation and a working breadboard.

2. GOAL. The goal of this phase is to prove that the documentation is complete and accurate. The principle reason for separating preproduction from production is to minimize any premature expenditures, which lowers your risk. In a sense, the goal of the preproduction phase is to have absolutely everything in order so that the production phase can be carried out in an efficient and cost-effective way. Thus, all of the work, such as detailed designs, test specifications, chemical formulae, and similar items required to permit a manufacturing release must be complete.

3. SOME TYPICAL TASKS. These are detailed in Appendix C.

4. KEY DECISIONS. The key decisions in this phase have to do with production methods, tooling design, and vendor selection. Exhibits 4-1 and 4-2 illustrate some of the impact these decisions will have. The next section covers this topic in more detail.

5. END POINT. Typically, you will complete a satisfactory prototype or pilot lot (or pilot plant run) during this phase. Finally, the preproduction phase ends when the marketing (or sales) department specifies the initial production lot sizes and the manufacturing department accepts this and issues a production schedule.

6. SCHEDULE. The schedule for this phase comes from the critical path network diagram the triad created at the end of the design phase.

7. MANAGEMENT AUTHORIZATION. Management should approve the entire phase. If it will be longer than three months, the progress, the current status, and the forecast for the forthcoming quarter should be reviewed quarterly.

8. MARKET INTRODUCTION. The date for the product introduction is set, but only to the expected month.

9. BUDGET. The budget for the preproduction phase work can vary widely, depending on the specific product. It is set broadly during the optimization phase and more precisely during the design phase.

10. SCHEDULE VS. COST RISK TRADE-OFF OPTIONS. You can authorize procurement of long-lead tooling and other items for the production phase without that being a commitment to undertake the production phase.

11. TRIAD ROLES. Normally, this phase makes more use of manufacturing engineering personnel than any other phase. However, even with a relatively clean design, marketing, engineering, and manufacturing personnel must still be active participants for the same reasons I cited in the design phase discussion.

SOME DESIGN ISSUES

There are several things that must be kept uppermost in mind during these two phases, since the product's manufacturability is critically affected.

1. You want to use the fewest possible number of total parts as well as the fewest number of different parts. This will lower your documentation, procurement, inventory, assembly, and service costs. Ideally, these will all be standard parts used in other products, even if this requires some minor compromises on this specific new product. Similarly, you will use the loosest tolerances that ensure adequate product quality, since these parts will normally be less costly. The mundane choice of unambiguous part numbers can also reduce confusion and lost time.

2. It is important to strive for assembly methods that cannot be botched. Automating these methods, now or in the future, may also save time and money. Again, it is desirable to use existing assembly methods, since learning, and the attendant scrap, may be reduced.

3. You want to use common modules or sub-assemblies wherever practical. This offers similar benefits to standard parts. As I pointed out in Chapter 3, this is also important if you wish to exploit the concept of product families. In one case many years ago, the company for which I worked designed a family of 110-style pocket cameras. The designs of two of our products were completely identical with the exception of one part (and the logo on the front). The lower-priced model had one extra part, which was an aperture stop in the lens so that the f-number would be worse (higher) than the higher-priced model.

4. You want to make use of the fewest number of vendors, ideally ones you have worked with before. There are three benefits of this: (1) Procurement costs can be reduced; (2) these proven suppliers can frequently provide intelligent input to the design process; and (3) the reliability of what they provide is presumably satisfactory.

5. Designing the new product so it can be tested to verify that it meets the specification, hopefully with an existing piece of test equipment, gives your manufacturing department an easy way to ensure consistent product quality. And, if the product fails the test, it is important that the test produce diagnostic information so that you can quickly fix the shortfall.

6. The design and preproduction work must strive for minimum product cost, and each part, component, assembly, and process must be critically examined for its cost implication. The product's factory cost target is clearly dependent upon the planned total volume, production rates, and specific schedule, so these have to be set by the triad; and the cost target must receive just as much design and engineering attention as the product's performance and technical attributes. Some new

software is available to help estimate what a part will cost to produce; commercial versions currently handle only parts made by metal machining operations.

In summary, if you can stick with proven processes, standard parts, existing vendors, common modules, and similar unexciting ingredients, subsequent production will be much less troubled. When you must use something new, minor revisions to what you have done before will be less of a problem than anything totally outside your company's experience.

HIGHLIGHTS

Participants in the design and preproduction work must stress fast new product development to achieve a short time-to-market.

A short total production time during routine manufacturing lowers your risk.

You can only obtain a low-cost product design by very careful engineering, design, and manufacturing engineering work that emphasizes low cost.

Choices for part design or procurement, fabrication processes, and assembly methods provide the opportunity to reduce time-to-market, total production time, and manufacturing cost.

Chapter 5

Manufacturing

Your success in product manufacture is almost entirely determined by the prior development phases. Nevertheless, such techniques as just-in-time (JIT) manufacturing can be helpful. There are also concurrent nonmanufacturing tasks that must be completed prior to market introduction.

DEPENDENCY ON PRECEDING PHASES

Dependency on preceding phases is the payoff which follows a lot of very hard work. Your new product is being made. As I have suggested, what happens now has really been established by what happened in those earlier phases. Sure, there will be strictly manufacturing department challenges and problems, such as a late supplier or a machine that is out of adjustment. But the fundamental constraints are derived from how the specification from the optimization phase was executed during the design and preproduction phases. You cannot overcome the difficulties in a design that is hard to manufacture by expanding your plant, splitting the work between two (or more) plants, or renegotiating labor agreements with your company's unions.

The real-world transition to manufacturing is difficult for practitioners. Exhibit 5-1 contains some quotations from practitioners who were asked to identify their key problems in achieving faster new product development. While not as prevalent as the problems in optimizing specifications (Exhibit 3-1, Chapter 3), this transition clearly has many troubling problems.

The difficulty in manufacturing start-up is normally greater for more expensive products (and complex processes), as illustrated in Exhibit 5-2. As the exhibit indicates, you may build only one or a few of such products, so there may be no earlier prototype or breadboards from which to learn. In such cases, a lot of debugging and learning from mistakes occurs only when the product reaches the factory floor. Manufacturing managers are naturally unhappy in such a situation, since they are often partially measured by scrap rates.

Thus, the key manufacturing department personnel must have been part of the triad, and participated in every trade-off option choice. As I said before, some manufacturing personnel do not want such in-

Exhibit 5-1. Quotations from practitioners: some cited challenges for faster new product development.

"Timely and successful implementation from design into manufacturing."

"Transferring prototypes to production."

"Hand-off from engineering to manufacturing."

"Transition into manufacturing phase in a timely manner."

Exhibit 5-2. Difficulties in manufacturing start-up.

New Product's Sell Price	Example	Some Issues
$100,000,000	New chemical process plant	Typically build only one. No manufacturing replication. Done at installation site.
$1,000,000	Industrial production equipment	Rare to have fully functioning prototype before pilot lot. Features and final test often customer specific.
$10,000	Scientific instrument	Breadboards of key components and some prototypes usually exist. Initial pilot lot of 10–25. May require simultaneous build of final test equipment.
$100	Device	Many units may exist. Final tests probably debugged. Pilot lot of 50–500.

volvement because many new product development efforts are stopped prior to reaching the production phase. However, consider the beneficial effect such involvement can have on inventory levels, which is frequently judged (incorrectly) to be solely a production concern. Raw goods inventory can be reduced if you have insisted on the fewest practical number of parts, and the maximum possible use of standard parts; work-in-process (WIP) inventory can be reduced if standard modules are employed; and finished goods inventory can be reduced by both accurate forecasts of sales requirements and a short production dura64on. While there is nothing that says marketing, engineering, and manufacturing engineering personnel are not aware of these points, the proactive participation of manufacturing personnel in earlier phases can assure these and similar concerns receive appropriate attention. (Manufacturing engineering personnel may be a part of the manufacturing department, in which case they may be the ones to represent these interests; however, in some companies that function is located within the engineering department or in a staff role.) In a nutshell, you want to be certain that the product design is robust enough to assure that production quality is high and factory cost is low.

You also want to consider some other issues early. For example, you do not want to hastily change the extent of your company's vertical integration for one product, even if it will be for many products and for a long time. Such an overhaul requires changes in procurement practices and production tools, processes, and labor training, all of which are likely to be costly in time and money. Capitalizing upon programmable automation is alluring but difficult. In addition, if your manufacturing has traditionally been done by purchasing finished goods from suppliers, the decision to start with purchased subassemblies, parts, or raw materials has vast implications. Similarly, there are problems if you traditionally have started with raw materials. In this instance, the decision to start instead with fabricated parts is likely to leave you with a lot of (usually expensive) machinery and labor that is underutilized.

In addition, there is the issue of where and how many manufacturing sites to use. If there is only one domestic factory, can it also produce goods that are suitable for export? Or, if there are both domestic and foreign plants, will there be enough production volume to assure economic production lot sizes? For bulky or heavy products, shipping costs are a significant consideration demanding early deliberation.

Clearly, there are many other seemingly non-manufacturing decisions in which manufacturing personnel should, in fact, must, participate. As a final example, cognizant manufacturing department personnel must approve design changes, which assures that these can be accomplished in a cost-effective and timely fashion.

THE PRODUCTION PHASE

Whether the production phase should be separate from the preproduction phase depends on the specifics of the product. If there is long-lead tooling, you should certainly initiate its procurement in a timely way, and that might logically occur during the preproduction phase. In exceptional situations, it might even be appropriate to order long-lead tooling during the design phase, but that clearly has a very high risk. In other cases, you may provide a design specification or complete design and obtain the entire product from another company. While this option is sometimes faster, whether or not it is as profitable as self-manufacture depends on many factors. In any event, this is worth considering in certain situations, but it comes under the category of a make vs. buy decision, which is beyond the scope of this book.

Assuming production is a distinct phase that is primarily carried out in your company's factory, I will now cover the considerations previously summarized in Exhibit 2-6.

1. START POINT. This phase starts with prototypes and debugged documentation. There are no longer any unknowns.

2. GOAL. The goal of the production phase is the routine shipment of the new product at rates that satisfy the period's sales forecasts.

3. SOME TYPICAL TASKS. These are listed in Appendix C.

In addition, the regulatory approvals included in the previous phases sometimes require production samples as a precondition for final certification. If so, you must obtain these now. For example, the Food and Drug Administration (FDA) requires that all drugs and much medical equipment be tested for certification. All electrical equipment requires certification by the Underwriter's Laboratory (UL) or a similar organization. Products that can emit electromagnetic radiation have to satisfy requirements imposed by the Federal Communications Commission (FCC) or its European equivalent (VDE). In cases such as these, you normally must submit samples that are typical of production units, and the duration of the tests is outside your company's direct control. It is obviously critical to plan for these tests in the production phase, and do just as much early work with the relevant certifying organizations as possible. If you can get these tests started before the entire production line is stalled waiting for the approval, you can save great expense.

4. KEY DECISIONS. Most of the key decisions that govern this phase are made before it starts, primarily in the design and preproduction phases. Within this phase, you may make a decision about the specific configuration of a production line, or which workers will perform specific assignments, or similar issues. For routine, on-going production

(which follows the production phase in the sense I have described it), you have to pick optimum lot sizes and production rates to best satisfy buyers without unduly high inventory levels.

The most difficult decision is when to publicly announce the schedule for the new product's availability, which I discuss later in this chapter.

5. END POINT. The production phase ends when routine shipping is achieved. At that time, the new product is no longer new, in the sense that you now can manage it with standard manufacturing management techniques. Its production is no longer a one-time (that is, start up of production) project.

6. SCHEDULE. The schedule for the production phase comes from critical path network diagrams that the triad creates during the end of the preproduction phase.

7. MANAGEMENT AUTHORIZATION. Cognizant management must approve the entire phase.

8. MARKET INTRODUCTION. The product's introduction date is set before the phase commences. However, as I discuss later in this chapter, you do not have to announce that date until it is to your advantage to do so.

9. BUDGET. Budget practices vary. In some companies the production phase expense is part of the new product development program's budget, and this can include both period expense items and capital budget items.

In other companies, all the period expense items are considered to be ingredients of standard factory cost, and only the capital budget items are separate. In this latter case, there can be high variances initially, due to start-up difficulties.

10. SCHEDULE VS. COST RISK TRADE-OFF OPTIONS. The main tradeoff is taken earlier, in deciding how much long-lead equipment and supplies to commit prior to the start of this phase.

11. TRIAD ROLES. The marketing personnel are preparing the new product's roll out, which I discuss later in this chapter. They will also inspect and accept the initial production units, which is a signal that this phase is almost complete (subject only to achieving routine production). Engineering and manufacturing personnel are likely to make minor design changes to ease unforeseen production bottlenecks, but they too are largely done.

JUST-IN-TIME (JIT) MANUFACTURING

JIT is clearly and deservedly the current manufacturing craze. By reducing raw, WIP, and finished inventory levels to those required just at the moment, you can gain tremendous advantages. For instance, you gain flexibility and reduce factory floor space requirements.

JIT is a new way of looking at the whole manufacturing process. The goal of JIT is to deliver parts to subassemblies, and subassemblies to final fabrication in very small quantities just as they are needed. Implementing JIT can result in dramatic cuts in waste and overhead, immediate quality improvements, and outstanding gains in productivity. JIT was first developed and implemented in Japan and now increasing numbers of companies in the United States and elsewhere have achieved similar improvements by adapting these techniques.

By decreasing setup times, users of JIT have found a way to make manufacturing in small lots cost effective. Die changes that used to consume an eight-hour shift at General Motors' Grand Blanc, Michigan, plant now can be done in as little as five minutes. This is an example of the so-called quick change concept, which abets JIT.

As the lot sizes come down, the entire process becomes simpler. Instead of being dumped at the beginning of the line and pushed along, parts in smaller numbers are pulled from station to station just in time to be used. Every step you take toward simplification exposes more problems and thus provides opportunities to correct them:

1. Consider the effect on waste. In a push system, a defective machine continues making batches of bad parts, which will not be noticed at the next station until the inventory is used up. With JIT there is not any inventory, so the first defective part is noticed immediately after it is produced. Consequently, there are no bad lots and hardly any waste.

2. Consider the effect on the worker. In a push system, when a worker's machine goes down, everybody upstream keeps working and the material piles up in front of the crashed station. In a JIT system everybody stops working and the machine is fixed immediately. As a result, the worker gets help and the line gets going.

3. Consider the effect on quality. In a push system you accept a certain defect rate and try to enforce it with hordes of inspectors. With JIT quality is built in all along the line and 100 percent inspection becomes possible.

Nevertheless, in common with many of the actions that you can take to improve productivity (which I discuss in Chapter 14), there is a lengthy learning and retraining process that you must not overlook. Just as a totally new product often creates high scrap and quality reject levels when you commence manufacturing, new production processes and equipment will lead to similar initial problems. In the case of JIT, intensive preventative maintenance is crucial, and you will have to negotiate JIT agreements with your suppliers and organize vendor certification programs. You will even have to reorganize your factory floor and product flow.

As you begin to reap benefits from JIT (or other productivity improvements), you may find that you have more labor than you now require. Have you both the freedom and will to get rid of the excess? If you do reduce the production staff, this may create a ripple effect, revealing excess levels of middle and upper management, and maybe excess plant space. Are you prepared to deal with that?

CONCURRENT NONMANUFACTURING TASKS

Assuming that the production phase is fairly long, which is a common situation, there are concurrent nonmanufacturing tasks that you must also complete. (If the production phase is not of long duration, you will have to do these tasks in an earlier phase.) These tasks are all to prepare for sales of the new product.

1. You have to decide when to announce that the new product will be available and on what date you intend to start shipping it. You must balance competing buyer information needs and your own wish to pre-empt the market against the possibility of creating vaporware, that is, a product that is only ephemeral, not real. Thus, if you do announce the product early, you may allow prospective purchasers to plan on using your product and you may induce them to abandon plans to use a competitor's product; if you announce too late, you may not allow your customers enough lead time to make full use of your product. There are other risks in an early announcement: You may tip off your competition about your plans in time for them to react to your disadvantage; you also run the risk of announcing a date that you later find you cannot meet; and, if the new product replaces one of your existing products, customers may stop buying the existing product to await the new one.

2. You have to train many people about the new product. Your own sales and service personnel must understand it and you must educate both customers and users. This means you must prepare advertising, public relations announcements, users' manuals, dealer support, sales support, and service literature.

3. You must produce and distribute spare parts for use by your service personnel. While this is usually a manufacturing department production task, I include it here because it is not part of the new product's production per se.

HIGHLIGHTS

The success of the production phase is largely determined by how the specification was implemented in the design and preproduction phases.

The goal of the development activity is completion of the manufacturing phase, at which point your new product is being shipped routinely.

Adopting just-in-time methodologies can help you shorten your time-to-market as well as your routine manufacturing duration.

Many nonmanufacturing activities to prepare for the sales phase must be carried out concurrently during the production phase.

Chapter 6

Maintenance

A well-understood phased approach will diminish interruptions. Unplanned support for existing products can destroy the schedule for your current new product development efforts. Therefore, if you separate maintenance of existing products from all development activity, you will not interrupt the people working on the new product programs. You can assign this maintenance work as a responsibility of other people. This diminishes fire-fighting interruptions and the attendant delay of new products.

TWO MAINTENANCE OPTIONS

Maintenance activity is frequently called sustaining engineering or continued technical support. It is necessary because, inevitably, there are user, customer, or sales department problems whenever you introduce a new product to the marketplace. Unless your company's policy is "use voids warranty," you are going to have to dedicate talented resources to the maintenance and support of products. Ideally, you do not want to delay other new product development programs to support existing products that are already out on the field.

You have two choices:

1. You can establish a separate department charged with responsibility to support products that have achieved routine shipping status; or
2. You can let the people who develop new products also do the maintenance on prior products.

Various mixed options can be found between these two pure extremes, the advantages and disadvantages of which are summarized in

Exhibit 6-1. For example, some companies move one or a few people from the development team into the sustaining engineering function for a period of time after product introduction; then, after the initial problems are mostly resolved, these people return to their new product development role.

If your company dedicates a separate group of people to perform this important function, you can avoid a situation in which you must pull away marketing, research and development, engineering, manufacturing engineering, or other manufacturing personnel from forthcoming new products. Conversely, if required maintenance will be the responsibility of people who must also develop new products, you must reduce the amount of time they will have available for new product projects by the amount of time you expect they will have to spend on maintenance. This can easily amount to as much as a quarter of their available time, so it is not insignificant. If you maintain time records, you can consult these to determine historical averages for your company; if you do not have such records, you will have to survey people in your company to determine how much allowance to make.

Both the extreme alternatives and various mixed options do not totally eliminate the problem of a resource conflict between new product development and maintenance activities. In the words of one manager, "my most difficult challenge is the resource conflict with sustaining

Exhibit 6-1. Some advantages and disadvantages of two options for dealing with maintenance activities.

Separate Sustaining Engineering Group	Additional Duties of People Who Also Develop New Products
Advantages	
No intrusion on new product development.	"Once burnt, twice scared." That is, this reduces the likelihood of making a similar mistake in future new products.
	The original creators of software are often the only people who can fix "bugs" quickly.
Disadvantages	
Can insulate the triad from real market feedback.	Can delay a new product if the maintenance time exceeds expectation.
Maintenance workload fluctuations may not match staff size or skills.	

activity." Inevitably, there are occasional resource demand peaks to deal with a flurry of maintenance needs. Thus, your realistic goal is to minimize these intrusions into the development activity.

MAINTENANCE ACTIVITY

Assuming maintenance is a distinct activity, I will now cover the considerations previously summarized in Exhibit 2-6.

1. START POINT. Maintenance activity starts when there is some problem with a product that is supposedly in routine shipping status. Each time someone identifies a problem with one of your existing products, you should authorize a maintenance project with a schedule and budget. In some cases, this will lead to a quick fix with the present product, and in other cases it will also lead to the initiation of a subsequent totally different new product development effort.

2. GOAL. The goal is to solve the identified problem. This must not be used as an excuse to start a bootleg product improvement project that goes beyond the immediate problem; if it does, that will delay fixing the immediate problem.

3. TYPICAL TASKS. These tasks are whatever is required to accomplish limited quick fixes. If there is a persistent type of problem, the use of Taguchi methods to quickly isolate a root cause can be fruitful.

4. KEY DECISION. Authorization of a new product development or improvement program may be justified. In fact, a benefit of having an explicit maintenance activity is that you gain exposure to changing market conditions and needs, which can point the way to future new products.

5. END POINT. Output is a minor revision and sometimes a new product or process idea.

6. SCHEDULE. Typically the schedule is one day to a few weeks.

7. MANAGEMENT AUTHORIZATION. Approve the entire project.

8. MARKET INTRODUCTION. Marketing is not applicable to this class of activity.

9. BUDGET. The total for all maintenance activities can consume up to perhaps 25 percent of the entire new product development (or R&D) budget.

10. SCHEDULE VS. COST RISK TRADE-OFF OPTIONS. Fast resolution of customer or user problems is important, so you may have to take some cost risks to be responsive.

11. TRIAD ROLES. In general, the entire triad (rather than a single component function) should decide how to resolve each maintenance

problem. Much of the work may only require one function, however. In some cases the marketing function can solve the entire problem by issuing revised product claims (in advertisements, brochures, or other product literature), to clarify some market confusion that is creating the problem. In other cases, the technologists may have to make a fundamental software or hardware fix. In still other situations, manufacturing personnel may have to adjust the production process, for instance, to achieve more uniform quality.

HIGHLIGHTS

You must recognize that maintenance will be necessary and can delay new product development.

Two ways to avoid such delays are: (1) Prepare your development schedules on the assumption that people will have to spend time doing maintenance tasks; and (2) establish a separate group to do the required work.

Chapter 7

Feasibility Efforts: Required But Separate

You can reduce your new product risk if you establish a mechanism for separate feasibility activities. Although feasibility activities typically precede a new product development activity, the topic is treated last (in Part II) to emphasize that feasibility must be separated from time-critical new product development. The idea is to separate product development from invention or proof of feasibility. With a phased approach, subsequent development phases are not dependent upon making inventions on a pre-set schedule. That is, the feasibility efforts produce a series of proven concepts and demonstrations or clear records of why something does not yet work acceptably. You stockpile the inventions (or other results) from feasibility work, awaiting their use in subsequent development activities that have critical time schedules.

WHY HAVE SEPARATE FEASIBILITY ACTIVITIES?

There is one inescapable fact in developing new products: You cannot invent on schedule. Therefore, you cannot schedule a realistic market introduction date for any new product development program that requires an invention. Similarly, if you must use technology that is new to your company in a new product, you cannot forecast the new product development schedule accurately. Thus, the *raison d'être* of feasibility efforts is to build a stockpile of useful proven technology that you can exploit when the need arises. (Sometimes, for analogous purposes, feasibility efforts are examinations of unknown markets or investigations of new production processes.)

If you want to take advantage of this stockpile, someone has to examine it periodically. Thus, every result, good and bad, must be recorded and systematically indexed. Many years ago, 3M Company abandoned some work on microcapsules when they could not find any problem which their use solved; this solution (that is, microcapsules containing a temperature-sensitive color indicator) that was looking for a problem was recently dusted off and utilized to produce indicators for microwave cooking.

Another reason for feasibility activities is to record what does *not* work, as well as why that is the case and what has to change to permit its use at a later time. In some cases, you may defer the development activity until a clear and convincing feasibility effort is successfully concluded. As disappointing as this may be, it is less costly to postpone a new product development program and its attendant costs until there is proven technology upon which to draw.

Two recent cases illustrate severe undesirable consequences of premature market introduction. Kodak introduced lithium batteries with a claim these would have a shelf life of ten years. After about one year on the market, the claim had to be withdrawn, along with many of a customer's products that depended on this claim. Searle may not have let researchers resolve some testing issues during the early development of the Copper-7 intrauterine contraceptive device; and now, many lawsuits by women claiming injury are pending. Whatever the merits (and results) of the lawsuits, publicly traded stock of Monsanto, which had purchased Searle, fell substantially on the news of this.

I know of one company that undertakes new product programs that involve development of complex new chemistry and associated instruments to measure certain reactions involving these new chemical formulations. Unfortunately, it frequently commits itself to unrealistic product introduction dates when the feasibility of the new chemistry has not yet been proven. This has resulted in the inefficient use of personnel and facilities. Worse, it causes the R&D and engineering departments to lose respect for the marketing department and vice versa. This company could improve its situation significantly if feasibility projects (without market introduction date commitments) were initiated when technology was unproven.

FEASIBILITY MUST BE FOCUSED

Exhibit 7-1 shows that you pursue only those projects that are consistent with the corporation's strategy. Feasibility projects must be chosen to support your company's strategy. This seems obvious, but there are companies in which *any* novel market, technology, or production process seems to be fair game for feasibility work. If you use feasibility efforts to investigate novel technologies (or other things) solely because

Exhibit 7-1. Pursuing only those projects that are consistent with the corporation's strategy.

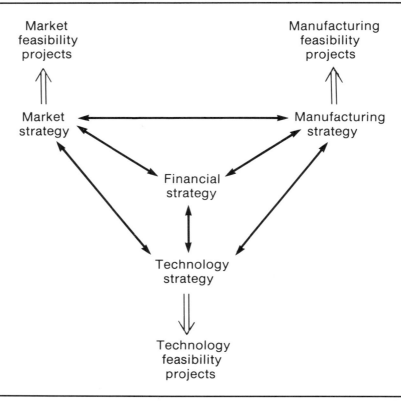

of their novelty, you will divert resources from potentially useful work that supports your business. If your company is totally bereft of prospects in its own business, or closely related businesses, there may be pressure to use resources for work in areas that are obscure to you, but I know of no case in which such random feasibility has been successful. It is unlikely to have a winning payoff.

Focus has value. Pick a worthy objective, define it, and work toward that goal. As an example, Squibb chooses its projects only in areas in which it has both appropriate technologists and a reasonable chance of making a meaningful breakthrough. Since resources are obviously limited, even in very large companies such as Squibb, this means you will have to limit what you work on if you want to ensure that you have enough people (and other resources) for big prospective winners. In Squibb's case, they are concentrating on hypertension and cholesterol reduction, a narrow niche in which there is a reasonable prospect that daily medication will be efficacious, producing large sales.

FEASIBILITY CAUTIONS

There are three cautions about feasibility efforts: (1) These do not ensure useful innovations; (2) if successful, the transfer to development can be difficult; and (3) you must not raid these efforts to staff development activities.

Useful Innovation

Innovation and profitability depend on several factors, which are listed in Exhibit 7-2. Just spending money on R&D (or other feasibility activities) is no assurance that you will obtain a payoff. In fact, as the table suggests, you may do just as well (or better) by investing in capital equipment or staff upgrading. As I show elsewhere, some people mistakenly believe that there is some magic optimum amount to spend on R&D. Rather, what you want to do is spend enough (whether capital or expense) to ensure success with a few big winners.

Transfer to Development

Let's assume that you have a very successful feasibility project. What do you do now? Even if you have a market problem that this feasibility output addresses, getting development people to embrace someone else's breakthrough can be difficult. NIH (not invented here) inhibits such a transfer.

There are two ways to overcome this barrier:

Exhibit 7-2. Successful feasibility efforts: one way to achieve desirable corporate results.

Innovation and profitability depend on:

- R&D effectiveness
- Capital investments
- Quality of all people
- Climate
- Luck

1. Let (or induce) the people who did the innovative feasibility work move on to also participate in the development activity.
2. Routinely have some development people work on feasibility efforts, so that they can transfer the work to subsequent development projects.

Isolate Feasibility Resources

There is a natural proclivity to interrupt feasibility work and transfer resources (either people or equipment) to time-urgent development or maintenance projects. If you allow this to happen, you may never see any results from feasibility projects for two reasons: The interruption itself may become a permanent termination of the project providing resources; and the mere fact that feasibility work is deferrable may become a self-fulfilling prophecy as this action can demotivate people working on other feasibility projects.

What your company should do is dedicate some fraction of the new product development (or R&D) budget to feasibility activity. Then you must authorize feasibility projects within this framework. After you establish a total budget for the year, it should be inviolate (subject only to its proportionate share of budget cutting if corporate expenses must be trimmed during the year). For flexibility and to have a carrot to encourage people to submit new ideas, you should not authorize all projects at the start of the year. You may be able to maintain existing feasibility projects even in times of corporate expense reduction.

The protective isolation of feasibility activity still allows you to end projects that are successfully completed and to terminate those that are no longer sufficiently promising. In the latter situation, a negative result is still the mark of a worthwhile feasibility effort, provided you clearly document what has been done and why you are suspending further work. In some cases, you will later reactivate this suspended work, for instance after a key competitor drops out of some market niche, a costly ingredient becomes economical, new production technology permits a lower factory cost, or new technology permits you to accomplish what was not previously possible.

THE FEASIBILITY ACTIVITY

When stressing fast new product development, it may appear to be counter-productive to propose an extra feasibility activity that is separate from the time-critical development activity. Some companies work on the hope that necessity is the mother of invention, and thus omit any feasibility activity. If this wish were realizable, we would already have cures for all forms of cancer and malaria, cheap food for deprived people, inexpensive and safe housing for the homeless, and other socially desirable products and services. Unfortunately, wanting a breakthrough does not guarantee it, so provision for feasibility activity is a lesser evil than the late introduction of a product for which an invention was required or the fast introduction of a product that has flaws. Assuming feasibility is a distinct activity, I will now cover the considerations previously summarized in Exhibit 2-6.

1. START POINT. Start a feasibility activity project when there is a possibility of something useful. This is not limited to exploration of new technology, although that is the most common reason to initiate a feasibility project. You may start a feasibility project to conduct highly exploratory market research of a totally unknown market or whenever there is some promising new manufacturing technology. In many cases, you may have many short feasibility efforts in which you do a little of both. For instance, there may be several short, iterative market and technical investigations to more sharply define the best initial market niche and required technology. In some situations, these will be sequential, and in others they will be conducted in parallel.

2. GOAL. The goal of any feasibility effort is proof (or denial) of the possibility that you are exploring.

Most commonly, the goal of the feasibility phase is to eliminate technical unknowns. You authorize technological investigations, particularly in the research and development department, consistent with overall corporate strategy and especially the market strategy for the business areas in which the corporation wishes to engage, as illustrated in Exhibit 7-1.

3. SOME TYPICAL TASKS. What's typical depends on why you started the effort. For new technology, the critical tasks are usually laboratory experiments, breadboard demonstrations, and various analyses. In investigations of new chemical processes you usually focus on bench and pilot scale trials. When investigating an unknown market, the key task is exploratory market research.

4. KEY DECISION. The key decision is how long to continue a given line of exploration. A priori it is rarely clear at what point you should drop a particular effort. Thus, the entire triad leadership and sometimes other top management should participate in deciding which projects to authorize and which to discontinue.

5. END POINT. What your company expects to obtain from successful exploratory work is plentiful and varied proofs of concepts. These feasibility demonstrations include such things as development of new bench chemistry formulas or techniques, breadboard models, sample

lots of new materials, a software module using a new programming language, or similar demonstrations. One of my colleagues many years ago made models of novel, complex mechanisms using Mecanno sets (the English version of Erector sets). Each successful (and unsuccessful) result must be documented clearly and completely, ideally in language that is comprehensible to all other triad members, whom we hope will make use of it.

6. SCHEDULE. Feasibility activities are typically less than two years duration.

Because there are substantial technical unknowns during feasibility phase efforts, it is not possible to schedule the dates on which a specific successful breakthrough will occur. Rather, schedule the tasks that will be accomplished during the forthcoming period, which is typically of three months' duration. For instance, you can schedule the performance of three specific experiments, but there can be no assurance that any of these experiments will, in fact, be successful. (In fact, even if the experiments are successful, this does not mean that you will undertake a development activity.)

Critical path network schedules will improve the timely completion of the planned activities during a feasibility effort.

7. MANAGEMENT AUTHORIZATION. Regardless of the duration of the total planned feasibility project, you should normally approve a maximum of only three or six months' work at a time. Obviously, if a fast schedule for some exploratory research would allow it to be completed in four months, you would not work with a three- or six-month time schedule, but rather with a four-month time schedule. Similarly, there will be occasions where procurement lead times to carry out certain experiments require a schedule longer than six months.

8. MARKET INTRODUCTION. Feasibility activities are related to a general product plan, but not to a specific product introduction. Such efforts must support corporate strategy.

9. BUDGET. The total budget for all feasibility activities is some small fraction of the entire new product development budget. While it is impossible to be specific, this might be 5 to 10 percent of the total budget.

10. SCHEDULE VS. COST RISK TRADE-OFF OPTIONS. The hallmark of good feasibility work is thoroughness. You do not want to skimp on either time or expense in such an effort (nor do you want to fritter away resources on needless frills).

11. TRIAD ROLES. As I said above, the entire triad leadership should decide which projects to authorize and how long these should continue. Most commonly, the bulk of the work is carried out by R&D or advanced engineering personnel. In some cases, particularly where

your company is entering an unfamiliar market, exploratory market research will be conducted by the marketing department; or, for new production technology or processes, the bulk of the work may be done by manufacturing engineering or other manufacturing personnel.

OUTSIDE SOURCES

There are various ways to have feasibility work performed externally. The National Science Foundation has a division that helps move new technologies from academic research laboratories to industry rapidly. The various national laboratories (such as Oak Ridge, Los Alamos, and Jet Propulsion) have Offices of Technology Applications (or similar titles) to assist with the transfer of laboratory technology to the private sector and these can sometimes be a source of new technology. Exhibit 7-3 contains a representative list of some technologies that were recently available for licensing from one national laboratory.

In industries such as scientific instruments, your innovative customers may have developed breakthroughs that you can exploit in new

Exhibit 7-3. An illustrative list of technologies that were available for licensing from one national laboratory.

- Quality control program for analytical chemistry laboratories
- Techniques for producing monodispersed biocatalyst beads for use in columnar bioreactors
- High-temperature thermal insulation structures
- Nickel aluminides
- Whisker-reinforced ceramic matrix composites
- A new radionuclide generator system for clinical studies
- Capillary processor and pipettor for processing whole-blood samples into measured aliquots of plasma
- Automatic coordinate measuring system
- Lead-indium phosphate and lead-scandium phosphate glasses for optical components
- Ultrasonic ranging and data system
- Demodulation circuit for ac-circuit spectral analysis
- Triple effect absorption chiller using two refrigeration circuits
- Absorption refrigeration cycle having improved thermal performance
- Motor current signature analysis process
- Radioactive material shipping design
- Fermentation process for sewage treatment

products. Also, there are both for-profit and nonprofit organizations that perform advanced development work under contract, sometimes for a fee that depends upon subsequent market success. Many companies pay for or subsidize research conducted at universities, including foreign universities, in return for licensing rights to any useful technology. Finally, there may be opportunities for joint ventures with another company. Whether the use of such outside sources is advantageous depends on your company's situation.

HIGHLIGHTS

A separate feasibility activity can eliminate development delays caused by attempts to invent on schedule, since these attempts are usually unsuccessful.

Feasibility projects must be chosen to support your strategy and must be carefully managed.

Resources dedicated to feasibility activities must be isolated from intrusive demands to assist with time-critical development and maintenance activities.

Feasibility projects may be carried out separately in the marketing, R&D, engineering, or manufacturing departments or in some combination.

Feasibility projects may also be carried out in external organizations, sometimes under contractual arrangements that give your company exclusive or first refusal rights and sometimes where you merely await information and then bid for licensing rights.

Part III

Structure for Shortening Development Time

Chapters 8–10 cover organizational options. By adopting a phased approach, you have already separated the time-critical new product development activity from unscheduled feasibility and intrusive maintenance activities. Now you want to devise organizational structures to separate the new product development work from the imperatives of the on-going business and to separate high priority new product development efforts from less valuable ones. In a sense, this part of the book is concerned with the people issues you must confront. While there is no right way to organize every company, there are some key principles that are important: Promote multifunctional (also called cross-functional) cooperation; and concentrate your limited resources, both people and things, on a few prospective winners.

Chapter 8
Organizational Form

There is no universal prescription for the best organization. You can succeed, or fail, with any. The three most common organizational forms are functional, matrix, and project manager. There are also some alternate hybrids and recent changes by companies. Another option is the dedicated project team.

ORGANIZATIONAL PITFALLS

A common lament is: "New products take too long; we have to reorganize." Indeed, your organizational form or the details of which individual fills what role is important. The key issue is not so much how your company is organized but, rather, where and how the new product development personnel fit into it. A major new product development problem, as one manager explains, is "interference from other activities in new product development." This manager goes on to pinpoint "competing projects and department versus project allegiance" as difficulties encountered.

Simply put, there has to be a triad or some other mechanism that is both committed and empowered to keep everyone focused on the new product's optimized specification and the concomitant development schedule. You can only achieve the specification's musts if your new product development effort is not diverted by organizational distractions and the various departments' hidden agendas of wants, possibles, or wouldn't it be elegant ifs. This focus, ideally a myopic focus, must also emphasize the importance of maintaining (or beating) the schedule.

New products are brought to market quickly in companies organized in every conceivable fashion because there are many facilitating mechanisms. Conversely, of course, some new products fail in well led and organized efforts. Thus, you must not focus exclusively on the organization's form, since this alone, while important, is not enough to guarantee timely new product introductions.

THREE COMMON ORGANIZATION TYPES

Exhibits 8-1, 8-2, and 8-3 portray the three most common organization forms: (1) functional; (2) matrix, which in this context is normally called the product manager organization; and (3) project or program manager.

In the purely functional organization, the only cross-functional co-

Exhibit 8-1. The functional organization.

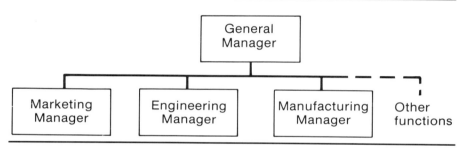

Exhibit 8-2. The product manager organization.

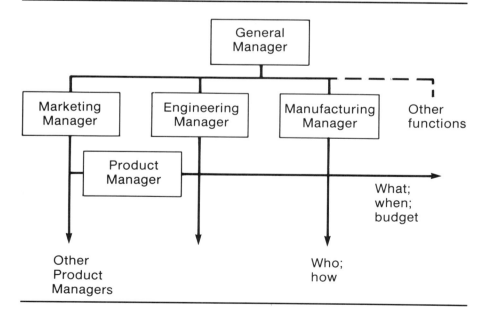

Exhibit 8-3. The program or project manager organization.

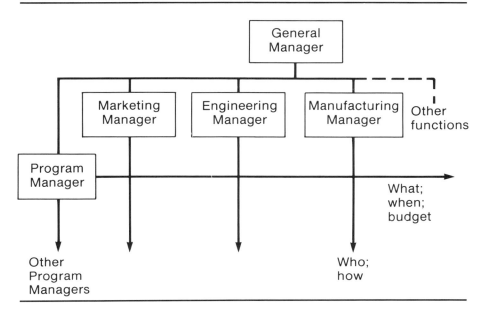

ordination occurs when the president or general manager is involved. A company (or division or strategic business unit) is typically organized functionally to run the on-going business most efficiently; this is rarely best for new product development because cross-functional cooperation is inhibited if not actually discouraged. In fact, I think this pure form is least attractive, because the functional managers in such an organization tend to promote the parochial interests of their own departments, which can be fatal for encouraging cooperative triad teamwork. As one functional manager puts it, "I'm so busy with day-to-day responsibilities that these interfere with information gathering and the development of new products."

The product manager form, which is a matrix organization that is common in consumer product companies, installs a coordination mechanism under the functional managers; however, these product managers typically report to the functional manager of marketing (perhaps through an intermediate manager, such as the director of product management). While there may still be a parochial orientation, this form is often quite successful for new product development if not for fast time-to-market. In some cases, the product manager is responsible for both mature and new products. These call for different skills and divide the product manager's attention. If you adopt the product manager form, your new product development may be quicker and more successful if the product manager is responsible only for new products, perhaps only a single new product.

The project or program management form, most frequently found in high technology industrial product companies, is a matrix form similar to the product manager form. It usually differs from that form in that the focal point person normally reports directly to the president or general manager. (Sometimes the line of direct reporting is through a director or vice president of program management.) This assures that the cross-function coordination role has the power to resolve priority conflicts. In one company with which I am familiar, where this form is employed, some functional managers continue to override the project manager and timely new product introductions are still elusive. This need not be the case, but it does illustrate a pitfall.

In larger organizations, there is some evidence that you will do better in meeting schedules if you build your organization around project teams or a matrix with strong project leadership. Unfortunately, many larger organizations are organized functionally or have a nominal matrix in which the project leader lacks real power. Small companies are sometimes a one-product company, so the entire company is, in effect, a project team.

A common characteristic of these three forms is that all the required personnel are rarely assigned to a single specific new product development project on a full time basis. Some of the required personnel may be assigned full time, but many are working on other new products or other company business. In situations where a person has multiple assignments, the triad leadership will have difficulty getting timely support if the priority of or a contributor's personal interest in another assignment is greater than the triad's new product development effort.

The organizational problems are much more severe if departments are physically separated by a noticeable distance. In one client company, marketing is on the second floor of one wing and engineering is on the first floor of another wing; hostility is high and cooperation is low. In another client company, both are on the same floor, but separated by about the length of two football fields, so face-to-face meetings require a conscious effort. When each department is in a different building or country, divisive tendencies can add overwhelming complexity.

You can make any of these organizations work successfully. Fast new product development can be promoted if the project or program manager form is modified so that the single person project manager is replaced by the triad.

NEW CORPORATE PRACTICES AND ALTERNATE HYBRIDS

Many major American corporations are changing their long-established organizations to improve the effectiveness of new product development.

As one specific example, Kodak has shifted to a ". . . market-focused organization . . . [to obtain] better and quicker results." This organizational revision is also intended to promote improved cross-functional cooperation between marketing, the technology functions, and manufacturing. Kodak has already introduced several new products using the new organization. There is not yet any public data on speed improvements; nevertheless, the changes are both promising and reflect what is occurring elsewhere.

Two alternatives to the classical functional organization are shown in Exhibits 8-4 and 8-5. The first of these, the business manager approach, is rather common. Business managers are responsible for both the marketing and engineering functions for a group of related products, and they feed their product designs to a manufacturing function. This can promote cooperation between the marketing and engineering functions, but it does not improve the interface with manufacturing.

The second, the product-process department has recently been proposed as one mechanism to encourage more manufacturable designs, and as a way to promote simultaneous (or concurrent) engineering. While it may indeed do that, it does not promote cooperation with marketing nor inherently resolve competition for factory resources.

THE PROJECT TEAM OPTION

Some companies want to go further to overcome the problem of a person's divided attention, so they adopt the project team option. In this organizational form, all the people who must work on the new product

Exhibit 8-4. The business manager form of the functional organization.

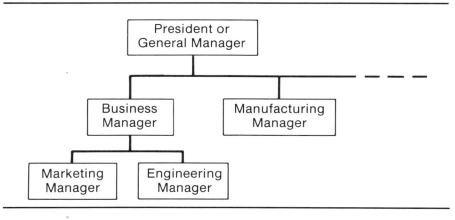

Exhibit 8-5. The product-process department variation of the functional organization.

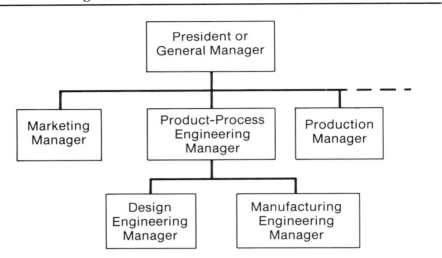

development project are assigned to it on a full time basis. If they are fully dedicated, this ensures that they have no distraction due to other assignments that compete for their time. If you have a very large, long duration effort, you should consider this option, because this choice can be very successful in such a situation.

However, there are some inherent problems. The project team option rarely exists in pure form (except in a small start-up company). That is, the new product development project always has some need for people, such as certain staff experts, who cannot be assigned on a full time basis. In addition, some of the people who are assigned to the new product development team are only marginally useful at certain stages of the work; thus, the corporation would get better value if these people worked on something more suitable at such times. On balance, however, the choice of this organization form is probably the lesser evil for major new product development efforts.

HIGHLIGHTS

Companies are typically organized functionally to manage the on-going business, which provides the income.

The functional organization is rarely best for new product development and can be especially difficult for achieving quick time-to-market.

Two common alternatives to the functional form are the matrix and project manager, both of which can improve the focus on new product development.

Other variants, such as the business manager and product-process department, also may deserve your consideration.

For major new development efforts, you should probably form a project team that clearly empowers the triad (or, at least, an individual) to be the focus of a dedicated new product development activity.

Chapter 9

Improved Resource Effectiveness

Obviously, all levels of management can facilitate or hinder faster new product development by the way human resources are organized and managed. This chapter covers some of the actions to take and avoid, starting with the crucial, but sometimes overlooked, need for priority choices. After you make these choices, you want to ensure that the highest priority efforts have all the resources they require when they are needed, which may be best accomplished by sequential emphasis. Finally, the role of the venture team and a champion is described.

SETTING PRIORITIES

Consider the problems cited by managers of new product development efforts that are shown in Exhibit 9-1. In all these situations, senior executives in their desire (or perhaps greed) to introduce new products have avoided the tough decisions on where to concentrate the corporation's limited resources.

A key responsibility of senior executives, perhaps the key responsibility, is to establish priorities for new product development efforts. You cannot tolerate a situation in which every)program has very high priority. Hedging your bets over the many possible new product development efforts will impede the few most critical ones. You must also be certain that all people have the same understanding about which programs have what priority. Such priority decisions can only be made by senior executives. As an example, the head of a major pharmaceutical company's laboratory has said, "We have to be sure we understand our priorities and allocate our resources accordingly."

Unfortunately, this is sometimes not done. The failure to set priorities frequently turns into a decision to starve new product development programs to the point where they lack required resources. Some new product development efforts have to be terminated not because they do not have promise or have failed to make progress, but rather because those resources can be better applied to some other opportunity. The same is true of feasibility and maintenance efforts, which must sometimes be canceled or deferred to free up resources for a few best opportunities.

Recently, Bausch and Lomb reportedly did exactly that, dropping many research projects and concentrating the bulk of its development budget on just a very few. At another corporation's research center, there are now only a dozen active new product development projects where there were three times as many a few years previously when the staff and facility was much smaller! In summary, senior executives, and all other responsible managers, must not let promising efforts struggle along without adequate resources. Bringing a few products to market quickly, so that they are successful, is far more useful than working energetically on many but not being able to bring them to completion.

Sequential Emphasis

Exhibit 9-2 portrays a conceptual model illustrating the benefit of sequential emphasis or resource concentration on one new product effort, then another, and so on. The situation for three new product efforts is

Exhibit 9-1. Resource concentration problems cited by new product development managers.

"We have many more profitable efforts possible than our resources allow."

"Making the priority judgment—do we have ten projects going or do we focus all energies and people on one or two?"

"Contention for limited design resources."

"We have too much to do, too few to do it, and it is needed too soon."

"The number of current projects exceeds the number of people. Then we add more projects. And then we divert people to unscheduled tasks."

"Balancing priorities when developing several products at the same time."

"Carrying out development of new products or features concurrently with production of existing products."

"We are organized functionally with teams for new products, but the functional managers frequently pull a critical person when the new product team needs that person."

Exhibit 9-2. Conventional vs. sequentially concentrated resource allocation.

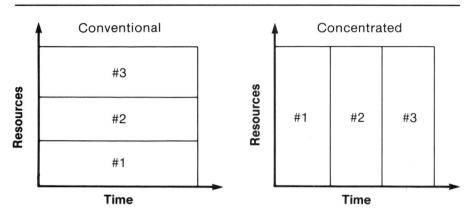

illustrated. In the conventional approach, all three projects run simultaneously. However, in some situations, you will be able to apply all or many of your resources to first one project, then another, and finally another. When you can do this, the first and second new products will reach the market sooner than conventional resource allocation permits and the last will still reach the market at the same time. While you cannot build the Egyptian pyramids in one day with ten million laborers, the concept of sequential emphasis is a valuable objective. What you are striving for is a situation in which the highest priority new product development effort has all the required resources it needs when it needs them.

Obviously, there is no point putting ineffectual or unneeded resources on the highest priority new product development effort (or any other one). This extra burden will in fact hurt by diverting management attention. The goal is to assist the leadership triad so that they never have to wait in a queue for their resources.

INTRAPRENEUR AND INTERNAL VENTURES

Many large corporations are ponderous, and both decision making and execution are often sluggish. This reality can frustrate new product initiatives. Consequently, such large corporations and others often allow (or encourage) both new product venture teams and champions. The goal is to harness and capitalize upon, not stifle, in-house entrepreneurial talent. In so doing, you can satisfy psychological needs of many employees and perhaps obtain novel new products.

Many companies practice intrapreneuring, which has existed for many years as a form of internal venturing. The notion is to allow employees of a very large corporation to form and manage a business venture that is designed to bring a new product to market. Intrapreneuring and internal venturing is primarily an antidote to large organizations' bureaucracy and is not required in small organizations where the entire company may itself be a venture. The distinction between a venture team and a project team is one of subtle degree: Membership in a venture team is normally voluntary. That is, venture team members have signed on in return for some kind of financial (or psychic) reward, which depends on the outcome of the venture.

The new products on which the venture team works are normally ones that are not directly related to the existing product lines or markets of the parent corporation. There are no data to prove that this organizational form promotes faster new product development per se, but it does get new products to market that might not otherwise be introduced. Despite this caveat, you may wish to consider this form as a relief valve to let innovative steam escape from the plugged up new product development system often found in large corporations or in any size organization when other techniques to encourage speed are also installed.

The 3M Corporation is frequently cited as the best example of success in this practice and many other companies also adopt it. While 3M has produced a steady stream of innovative new products for many years, it has been criticized by some observers for mostly producing variegated small new product successes such as microcapsules. Notably, however, 3M has also developed and introduced Post-it Notes, a new product that is a stunning success.

Du Pont is also a practitioner of internal venturing. In the 1970s, this company looked primarily for very large opportunities, generally those with reasonable prospects for more than $100 million in sales volume. Now, the company is investing in internal ventures from which the sales volume may be substantially smaller.

IBM has established many internal ventures, which they call independent or special business units. The underlying rationale in this company is that the requirements for developing and introducing a new mainframe computer would strangle any less complex undertaking. One of these ventures successfully spawned and quickly introduced the IBM PC.

Starting in the mid-1980s, Kodak has also sponsored numerous startup ventures, some of which (Edicon, for example) have been successful. Similarly, starting in the early 1980s, Dow has funded hundreds of projects, a few of which (Citrucel and Starburst, for example) have been successful.

There are significant management issues about where to house these ventures within the corporation and when (or if) to fold them back into the existing more formal structure. Also, as I suggested above, these ventures should be staffed by volunteers. The absence of volunteers to join such a venture may be a danger signal to management that people do not see how to succeed and that the venture should not be authorized or continued.

THE CHAMPION

A champion may exist in any form of organization. A champion is a single individual with an idea and what I call the 3Es: enthusiasm; energy; and enterprise. The new product champion is the person who works nights and weekends to overcome each obstacle as it is encountered—and that typically means most nights and weekends. The champion's drive keeps everyone moving quickly. He or she can see the role the new product will play and believes in its importance. Such a champion can generate excitement and can be a big help in developing your new product quickly. Ideally he or she is a member of the leadership triad.

The absence of anyone on the development team who is committed to the new product is usually fatal. You should terminate new product efforts if there is no one who has some measure of passion for the result. Similarly, you cannot appoint a champion to be the spark plug for your own pet new product idea.

There can also be a problem with a truly dedicated champion. They are often naive or mavericks, sometimes both. Their myopic devotion to their project's goal can blind them to other corporate issues and needs. Similarly, they are frequently a problem if their pet project must be stopped. If their project is not your company's highest priority, they can be a nuisance, if not actually destructive.

HIGHLIGHTS

Establish clear priorities for new product development activities.

Give the highest priority new product development effort *all* the resources it requires when the leadership triad needs them.

If your corporation is very large, consider establishing internal ventures and encouraging intrapreneurship.

Encourage and support champions when they are working on important new product development efforts.

Chapter 10
Teamwork

New product failures are more likely to occur when different departments are not cooperative, so harmony has value. These are various techniques to promote interdepartmental harmony.

HARMONY HAS VALUE

There is no point to developing your new product quickly only to see it fail. Energy invested in fighting between different departments inside your company diminishes your ability to fight the competition outside. It is therefore important to promote harmony between the several departments involved in the development work.

The Marketing-Technology Interface

The absence of teamwork between the marketing department and the technology departments (R&D and engineering) is correlated with new product failure. Harmonious teamwork between these two groups is one link in the chain leading to success. Exhibit 10-1 summarizes data which reveal that a harmonious interface is much more likely to produce a successful new product than the converse. That chain leading to a successful new product includes other links, such as a good product idea and a real market need. Harmonious and effective teamwork cannot make a silk purse out of a sow's ear, or, to put it differently, teamwork will not overcome the absence of a good product idea. So, assuming there is a good idea, a real market need, a believable plan to make a profit, and you have developed a plan for fast development, you want to assure harmonious interdepartmental relations.

Many factors promote disharmony between different departments

Exhibit 10-1. Effect of R&D marketing interface's harmony on 289 projects.

States	Project Outcomes in Percentages		
	Success	*Partial Success*	*Failure*
Harmony	52	35	13
Mild disharmony	32	45	23
Severe disharmony	11	21	68

The following definitions are used:

Success: High plus medium degrees of commercial success (blockbuster plus above expectations)

Partial success: Low degree of commercial success plus low degree of commercial failure (met expectations plus below expectations)

Failure: Medium plus high degrees of failure (protected our position but lost money plus took a bath we won't forget)

Reprinted by permission of the publisher from, MANAGING NEW PRODUCT IN-NOVATIONS by William E. Souder (Lexington, Mass.: Lexington Books, D.C. Heath and Company, Copyright 1987; D.C. Heath and Company).

and a few of these are illustrated in Exhibit 10-2. One of the underlying factors causing disharmony between the marketing and technology departments, perhaps the most fundamental, is the very different time orientation that good technologists and good marketing people have. The technologists usually have a very long time orientation, whereas marketing people usually have a very short time orientation. This inherent cultural difference can be exacerbated by the barriers which are present in any functionally organized company.

Interestingly, in high-tech companies, where many marketing personnel also have a technical degree or training, there are fewer cultural differences, even though disharmony may still be prevalent. This is illustrated by the comment of a marketing manager:

> In a technology driven company, new product conception often begins in the engineering department as an outgrowth of existing technology. While engineers are excellent product designers from a technical standpoint, their understanding of product features required to market a product is quite minimal. I currently have a new product which the engineers want to take in one direction, but the market requires something much simpler. Whenever I attempt to set direction for this product, I am told by engineering that it is not feasible to develop the product the market really wants. Much effort is being expended to develop this high-tech product for which, in its current form, little or no market exists.

Exhibit 10-2. Some typical departmental attitudes.

	Marketing	*Engineering*	*Manufacturing*
New products	Lifeblood of business	Opportunity to create	Start-up problem
Quality	No complaints from field	Infinite life, brick outhouse	No scrap
Time	Ship tomorrow	Enough to do it thoroughly	Quick production cycle
Features	Any that are asked for	Any that can be conceived of	One model, one style, one size

Even worse, physical separation of different functions can dramatically increase the alienation. Unfortunately, because the technologists frequently need specialized facilities such as laboratories and model shops, it is not uncommon for the technology departments to be physically separated from the marketing department's offices. At one time in my career, I managed the technologists and domestic manufacturing functions for a corporation; the marketing function reported to my immediate superior, but both he and the marketing department were located in another building that was three miles distant. Even that short distance greatly exacerbated the inherent problems.

As another example, one of my clients situates the technology and marketing functions in different wings of the building, and even that separation creates significant cross-functional problems. These are illustrated by the following comments:

> [*Marketing vice-president*]: There is no development schedule credibility . . . we are a market driven company, so we can't let the R&D department pursue random technology . . . a market change causes R&D consternation.

> [*R&D vice-president*]: Marketing changes goals too frequently. . . . [T]hey can't make up their minds. . . . [T]here are no technical visionaries in marketing . . . marketing aims at yesterday's market . . . marketing does not provide sufficient lead-time . . . they want to run *my* projects.

There are data that show that the R&D function is more reluctant to cooperate than the marketing function, and both functions are sometimes unclear about how to share in new product development. If this is your situation, you must confront it. A different study shows that new product R&D projects are much more likely to be successful when they are first suggested by a team from the R&D and marketing departments (and/or customer) than when suggested by the R&D department working in isolation. To put this differently, when R&D is the sole source of first suggestion for new products, the projects are likely to have relatively low probabilities of success. The unhappy outcome when the technologists work alone or initiate projects in isolation is caused in part by their fascination with technology. Good technologists are most interested in exploring new technology, which induces them to practice the Columbus method of selecting and guiding projects: They start off not knowing where they are going; arrive not knowing where they are; and report to senior management not knowing where they have been.

The technologists can be much more effective, as the data reveal, when their efforts are cooperatively guided by market reality. For instance, the technologists can be very effective if they develop clever solutions to real market needs that have been validated by market research, perhaps with their own participation in this market research. Or they can scan new technology to lower the cost of existing products (since these are already filling a market need) or improve the features of existing products.

Other Departments

Harmony is not exclusively an issue between the marketing and the technologist departments, as was illustrated in Exhibit 10–2. The manufacturing department, which may very often be located in a third facility because of its specialized equipment, is crucially involved. For instance, your company has to be able to produce the new product in a way that does not create burdensome inventory problems. As I have said previously, the early involvement of the manufacturing (and manufacturing engineering and purchasing departments, if these are not directly part of the manufacturing department), and their cooperation, is also very important. Similarly, you should involve functions such as industrial design early in the development activity. This can preclude having their creative input cause delaying or costly styling changes later.

One manager has said to me:

> I can't agree more that marketing and engineering must work in a harmonious relationship and also that manufacturing must be an integral part of the development team. I also think that the quality organization is a vital part of a successful product development team. . . . In our company the quality organization brings specification compliance to the table as well as monitoring how to perform the test in production. In many cases we must develop special testers in parallel with the product being developed.

Other functions also have varied points of view, a few of which are summarized in Exhibit 10-3. Even within a single function, there are often very different orientations. For instance, within research and development, the fundamental researcher, the applied researcher, and the departmental manager will see many things very differently.

Triad or more extensive multifunctional teams are used commonly by many Japanese companies. This is almost certainly a significant contributor to that nation's success with new products.

Outside Organizations

The timely development and success of your new product may also depend upon the work of people in one or more other organizations. For instance, prompt work by suppliers is clearly going to save you time. You may need cooperation from customers and users to obtain realistic tests of your initial prototypes or early production units. The marketing function frequently conducts field trials, but you can get better products when other triad members, especially the technologists, also participate.

TECHNIQUES FOR PROMOTING HARMONY

While there are many techniques for promoting harmony, I wish to discuss four: (1) reduction of disharmony; (2) sharing; (3) transfers; and (4) network diagrams.

Reducing Disharmony

Disharmony is an inherent risk and it is therefore necessary to be proactive in trying to reduce it. Pretending the disharmony does not exist is

Exhibit 10-3. Some aspects of the different points of view in different corporate functions.

Function	Orientation Regarding Money
Corporate management	Quarterly earnings statement and lines of credit
Marketing	Product line profit and sales volume
Sales	Order quota and low price
Research and development	Enough to purchase newest research equipment, fund forefront work, and permit travel to technical conferences
Engineering	Adequate project funding
Manufacturing	High gross margins
Purchasing	Lowest cost suppliers

not productive. It is most important not to let minor interdepartmental problems fester; rather confront and resolve them as soon as they are noticed.

The use of a project start-up workshop may be very helpful. Such sessions, which may require a few days at the start of a project, build consensus and promote harmony. They can also provide a mechanism to develop project management (or other) skills the team can use.

In addition, equitable top management treatment of all groups can promote harmony by reducing power and status differences. Similarly, a common location, to the extent it is practical, is helpful. If the departments are not proximate to one another, then many mechanisms that assure frequent cross-fertilization visits should be installed. These mechanisms may include periodic review and planning meetings. In a sense, the trick is to get your various departments to focus on fighting the competition rather than each other.

Sharing

It is almost impossible to have too much shared activity between the departments. Challenging and thorough discussions, while sometimes difficult, assure that each department understands the other, so these generally lead to increased mutual respect. Such multifunctional meetings will be more harmonious and productive when the participants have roughly equal ability to express themselves, assert their (or their function's) point of view, and persuade others.

Having multifunctional teams responsible for every phase, rather than a single department responsible for each, as illustrated in Exhibit 10-4, is crucial. These teams may obviously include more than the minimum triad constituency. In fact, the specific composition of the triad is itself dependent upon the nature of the new product. As an example, Exhibit 10-5 contrasts the minimum triad composition for hardware and software new product development projects.

Triad teams, the value of which I have stressed already, are clearly helpful in developing harmonious interdepartmental relationships. People who overcome difficulty together, or share meals and travel, frequently build personal friendship bridges. Where one department has a prima donna role or takes solitary action, resentment and disharmony can build. Xerox has used small product teams, and credits these with reducing both the labor and time to introduce its recent new products. The Warner Division of Dana reports similar dramatic improvements in new product development duration and, even more impressive, also the substantial reduction of production cycle time.

While it is too early to predict how new group-shared software, so-called groupware, will help, this may be useful to you. The idea is that

Exhibit 10-4.   The use of multifunctional teams.

A.   One department per phase can destroy teamwork and delay a new
     product.

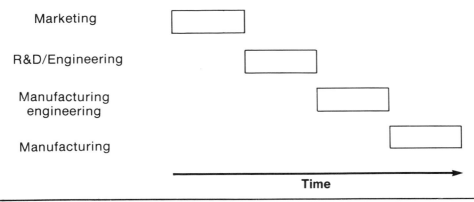

B.   A cooperative multifunctional team can shorten new product
     development time.

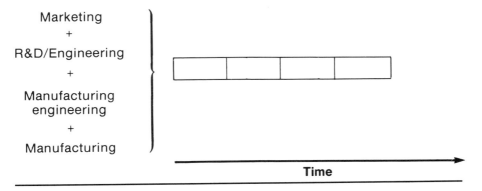

various people can contribute to the development and revision of a document from individual terminals. Thus, you may be able to improve and
accelerate instruction manuals or other required documents.

Finally, joint rewards will foster collaboration. These rewards may
be tangible or not. For instance, shared presentations at trade shows or
to top management are primarily a psychological reward and can be very
effective.

Transfers

Moving people from one department to another for short periods (three
months, for instance) or even permanently is a very effective mechanism
for building better understanding and cooperation. Applied Materials

Exhibit 10-5. Minimum triad composition for two different kinds of new product development projects.

Hardware	Software
Marketing	Marketing
Technology (R&D and Engineering)	System analysis
Manufacturing (manufacturing engineering and production)	Programming and documentation

relocated some personnel (and their families) from California to England to facilitate the development of a new ion implant product. One of my clients has also used similar temporary international transfers. Such personnel transfers can also reduce the NIH (not invented here) obstacle, a significant barrier to rapid new product development which is so prevalent, especially between geographically remote business units.

Even if departments are close to one another, transfers can help promote teamwork, usually with beneficial reductions in new product development time. An engineer may never be a superb marketing person, but there is work he can perform in the marketing department for a short period of time. Similarly, a marketing person may be able to perform administrative or product testing work during a temporary assignment into the engineering department. Transfers between the engineering and manufacturing departments can do wonders to avoid design complexity and to reduce manufacturing costs.

Philips, the Dutch electronics company, enjoys a worldwide reputation for the superb quality of its various research laboratories. Unfortunately, there has been much less success in the follow-through, that is, in profitable product output. Now, the company is beginning to transfer people from the research laboratories into operating units after about a half-dozen years. Since some of these people who are transferred out will eventually return to the research laboratories, the process provides cross-fertilization. Many other companies have similar problems with the conversion of work from central research facilities to operating divisions, and these companies can also use personnel transfers to reduce their own development obstacles.

Network Diagrams

Network diagrams, which are discussed extensively in Chapter 12, are one of the most effective tools to assure that your new product is introduced as quickly as possible. If you can't draw the network diagram, you don't know enough about your product to announce the introduction schedule for it. Fortunately, the network diagram provides an ideal vehicle to help promote teamwork.

Marketing naturally will exert pressure for an early product introduction, which is inherently in conflict with the technologists' commitment for perfection and their longer time horizon. Having the triad development team of the marketing, technology, and production people jointly set the initial specifications and schedule is thus both prudent and a promoter of teamwork and harmony. Because there are more things that will cause a development schedule to be overrun rather than completed early, the triad should insert a reasonable time contingency in the critical path schedule.

The joint network diagram can be constructed in many ways. Perhaps one of the easiest ways to make the first cut at it is for representatives of each of the involved departments to use self-adhesive notes for each task that must be accomplished and to arrange these on a large sheet of paper or a dry marker board. After the initial list of tasks has been arrived at and their dependency established, the information can be entered into an appropriate microcomputer project management software program for subsequent calculation, manipulation, and printed output.

HIGHLIGHTS

Interdepartmental harmony and teamwork is important in promoting successful new products.

The marketing-technology interface is especially prone to disharmony, which leads to new product failure.

You can promote harmony by proactive reduction of disharmony. A project start-up workshop may be especially helpful.

Other techniques to promote harmony and cooperation include shared activities and personnel transfers.

The use of critical path network diagrams can promote harmony and should also encourage more rapid new product development.

PART IV

Tools and Techniques for Shortening Development Time

Part IV describes several tools and techniques that you can use to shorten any new product development activity. In a sense, this part of the book deals with mechanical devices you should consider. Not every technique can be used in every company or for every development activity, but some will prove useful to you in your own situation. Also, your own managerial style will affect how, or whether, you adopt some of these tools and techniques. This is appropriate, since you must be capable of using any tool or technique.

Chapter 11
Efficient Time Use

Efficient time use involves both avoiding delays and achieving clever savings. Dead time between phases, or anywhere else, will delay the new product introduction date, and you want to avoid such losses. There are several shortcuts to the normal new product development duration that you may be able to use. Some approaches are to do things differently, that is, in ways that depart from the company's *modus operandi* or by taking unusual advantage of external resources. Other mechanisms are pure time-savers, which include temporary expedients, omitting or compressing tasks, or doing required tasks in parallel. There are shortcuts that are sometimes superficially appealing, but which do not really shorten the development duration and may have unattractive or unanticipated consequences.

ELIMINATING DEAD TIME BETWEEN PHASES

The phased program, as opposed to an unphased program, has greater potential for delay between phases. Although delays caused by failure to obtain approvals from senior executives are still fairly common, they are not inherent in the phased approach I favor. But you must recognize the potential pitfall, adopt an effective alternative, and accomplish the phase-to-phase transition with minimum effort.

THE PHASE REVIEW PITFALL

Gaps between phases, as illustrated in Exhibits 2-2(a), 2-2(b), 2-7, and 2-10(a), are lost time. Such periods delay the introduction of your new product. While those figures portray relatively long time intervals, even short time intervals create unnecessary delay. A new product introduction can be one month late if there is a single one month delay (due, for instance, to a specification change, design error, or manufacturing inefficiency) or equally tardy if there are myriad one-hour and one-day slippages. The most insidious of small delays is the time lost for phase or major milestone reviews. Every hour (or day or week, or whatever) that is spent awaiting a top management or board of directors approval is a total loss.

Why does this happen? All too often, the answer is, "The chairman (or president, or general manager, or someone) is traveling this week, and we will have to delay that meeting." Another aspect of this as expressed by one manager was, "There is a long lead-time to convince upper management." This is a common situation, but it can be avoided if your senior management *wants* to shorten the time-to-market. To achieve fast new product development, you must avoid such self-imposed delays.

Timely and Effective Phase Reviews

You must have a twin goal at your phase (or major milestone) reviews. In some cases, as one group of new product managers reported, "our reviews are ritualistic status symbols." This is maladaptive and you must rearrange the corporate culture and practice so that no time is lost and in such a way as to ensure their effectiveness. To ensure that no time is lost, the triad should propose a meeting date one or two months prior to the review meeting. If one or more senior executives cannot attend on the selected day, there are three options available:

1. The triad should try to devise a way to advance the review date to a time when there is no conflict;
2. The people who are unable to attend on the chosen date may choose to send an empowered substitute; or
3. The review date, and the new product, must be delayed.

The last of these three options is least attractive, whereas the first is most attractive, if it can be done. In the real world, where it may be difficult to accelerate already tightly scheduled work, the first may be impractical. In this case, since we wish to avoid the third option, triad members must strive for the middle option.

For the middle option to work, senior executives must be willing to accept the necessity for this option, in the interest of fast new product development, and must be willing to delegate their decision authority to others. To make this more palatable, the senior executives should recognize that they always have the right to subsequently re-examine the new product development program. However, if the senior executives exercise this inherent prerogative, it must not become an extra or onerous burden to the triad or the new product development team. Most, but certainly not all, of the time spent preparing for and participating in program reviews comes at the expense of time spent working more productively on the development effort itself. Senior executives and the triad leadership must strive to find the most productive balance between stepping aside to ask critical questions and uninterrupted work.

What the Phase Review Must Accomplish

The end of a phase or a major milestone is a point requiring a decision to continue or discontinue the new product development program. Such reviews must result in either go or stop. One way to assure promptness in this decision is to adopt the following ground rule: THE FAILURE TO STOP A PROGRAM IS EQUIVALENT TO A GO. That is, the only way to stop or redirect a new product development program is to formally declare that it has ended. This rule has the attractive virtue of assuming that a program will be successful and will move from phase to phase quickly.

Such a rule helps speed new products to the market and does not force executives to cede any real authority. They can always sleep on the go decision, return from a trip and consider what their empowered substitute at the review has heard, or reflect on other changed events that affect the corporation's available resources and then stop (or kill) a new product development program.

In general, the most difficult new product development decision is the decision to kill a program. It is not only difficult for top management, it is also difficult for the triad. There is both an emotional and financial investment in the effort to date. There is also always the possibility that a little more investment will overcome the present difficulty (whatever it is). The decision to stop a program is also psychologically difficult because we appear to be put in the position of saying that we were wrong to have authorized it. It is thus easier for newly appointed executives or objective outsiders to review programs and recommend their discontinuance.

You must learn to separate the decision to stop a program from the notion that stopping is a failure or that the people who have worked on it have done a bad job or were ineffective in some way. (Obviously, it is indeed possible that the triad or new product development team is inept, but you will have to stop many new product development efforts for various other reasons.) The decision to stop a program is merely a statement that it is no longer promising enough *at this time* to justify the continuing use of scarce corporate resources. To put this differently, as a result of the work to date, we now know enough to believe that there is a better use for our corporation's limited resources.

There is a caution, of course, which is that the difficulties of a program that has been under way for some time are likely to be more apparent than the difficulties of a program not yet started. Lack of present in-depth knowledge makes the far-off hills look green, and the pitfalls may not be apparent. Feasibility activities and short development activity phases reduce the likelihood that you will discard a merely difficult new product development effort in favor of a beguiling illusion.

The phased approach provides limits to open-ended commitments. Thus, it helps everybody make the toughest new product development decision of all, namely the decision to kill, or suspend, less promising new product development efforts. As I said before, killing a new product development effort is tough because the people who do so are in essence saying they were wrong, since typically they are the same people who previously authorized it. However, if all that has previously been approved is a particular phase of the new product development effort, rather than the entire effort, it is sometimes much easier to not approve a subsequent phase. Resources then can be reallocated and applied to those efforts that are judged more promising.

SAVING TIME WITH NOVEL APPROACHES

There are some potential shortcuts in the use of unusual procedures, alternatives to conventional new product development, and, specifically, quality function deployment and simultaneous engineering.

All corporations have a variety of standard operating procedures (SOPs). Some of these govern employment practices and are designed to ensure that the corporation does not violate any nondiscrimination legislation. Other have to do with procurement and purchasing, some of which are intended to ensure that minority businesses receive fair consideration. You must comply with these and similar legally mandated SOPs.

Conversely, there are many other SOPs that are based on outdated requirements or preferences of some corporate executive. For example, there are instances where you are supposed to complete a long, complicated form before doing something. Normally, you can violate the requirements of this kind of SOP when it will save you development time. If you do so, it is obviously prudent to explain the timesaving justification in advance. This advance (or concurrent) notification is especially important where the SOP is based on the emotional needs of a senior executive. As you may still be criticized, it is smart to be reasonably sure the eventual timesaving will be both significant and apparent. One way to accomplish this is to calculate the cost per day of the new product development effort (burn rate) and show how your deviation from the norm will actually save money.

In addition to formal procedures, every company has a culture—a way in which things are done or not done. In common with SOPs, you can deviate from the normal cultural pattern to save time. However, again be sure this deviation will save time, and invest some of that time saving in giving advance notice to the relevant people.

Some companies establish small groups that are exempt from the normal cultural and operational pattern to save time. This is more useful in larger corporations, where the bureaucratic obstacles are more prevalent.

You can also encourage your corporation to change its procedures so compliance is less time-consuming and burdensome. Obviously fewer forms and fewer required signatures will help.

Alternatives to Conventional New Product Development

There are two kinds of new product development alternatives that may permit an earlier than normal market introduction. There may be a simple or expedient version of the product that can be introduced quickly to establish a limited market position. While this limited version is not your *raison d'etre* to undertake the development effort, it can still be profitable, especially if it and the ultimate product (and any versions in between) share common parts, processes, and tooling. Further, its introduction may provide important feedback from the marketplace. This feedback can be applied to the ultimate product intended by the development process and thus reduce the risk involved in the major product.

In one case, while touring a division facility, a corporate executive saw a working model of a new instrument and commanded that it be introduced at an important industry trade show. The product development team did not see how they could do this, but they did believe they could introduce a simpler version to serve a limited segment of the entire intended market. This can shorten the time to get to market with a new product. Exhibit 3-2 illustrates this situation. In fact, they still missed that date by a bit, but there is agreement that the approach was worth trying and that they performed the development work faster than they would have otherwise. The ultimate product that the executive wanted was an integral part of the development plan, but it was scheduled for a later introduction date, one that the development team felt was achievable.

Some Japanese companies are using incremental product feature innovation to introduce new products quickly. This approach to new product development is worth considering, since it provides you with a continuing stream of new products.

In some cases, you cannot gainfully use a staged family of new products; that is, you cannot benefit by introducing the first product in a family quickly. Nevertheless, you may still be able to shorten your development time by using parts, processes, or tooling from existing products. Unfortunately, it is often difficult to persuade creative people to not invent, to merely make do, but it often saves time. Assuming the previous part, process, or tooling works satisfactorily, you can save additional test and quality assurance time. However, you must be alert to the possibility of subtle differences or obscure interactions, which can render the previously satisfactory solution unsatisfactory in the new application.

If your own people do not know how to accomplish the development by the desired introduction date, perhaps some other company does. For instance, there are some design companies that claim a record of very fast new product development. Sometimes there is a completed product you can buy for resale as your product. Or, there may be a company with which a joint venture will save time. Two potential problems with this second alternative are (1) sharing may not be as profitable as doing the development or production entirely within your own company and (2) giving exciting or interesting work to others may demotivate your personnel if they believe they are capable of doing it too. In any event, you do not want to be trapped into a lengthy development duration by your own people's NIH (not invented here) syndrome, so you should always consider purchasing any existing solutions to your development needs.

Quality Function Deployment and Simultaneous Engineering

Both quality function deployment (house of quality) and simultaneous engineering have shortened the time-to-market in reported cases. The value of these two techniques for engineered products almost mandates that you adopt one or the other. The largest time savings come from the improved communication between the design engineers, manufacturing engineers, and the people who will have to manufacture the product, since this reduces design changes.

TIME SAVING TECHNIQUES

More conventional shortcuts are pure timesavers. These fall into four categories: (1) using temporary expedients; (2) omitting tasks; (3) compressing the normal time for a task; or (4) performing tasks in parallel.

Temporary Expedients

There are many temporary expedients that you might use to get your new product to market quickly. These are situation specific, so no general rules can be offered other than to be constantly alert for such opportunities.

As an illustrative example, Blue Cross of California saved five months merely by stapling two reports together. The company was developing a new (service) product, an insurance package for companies of from 50 to 250 employees. The goal was to offer these companies what market research indicated they desired, a combination of both a PPO (preferred provider option) and an HMO (health maintenance organization). At the time the new product development effort started, Blue Cross of California had both of these offerings available, but they were maintained by entirely separate software systems. Integrating the software to provide a single report required time-consuming programing, so to get on the market quickly the separate reports were initially stapled together.

Omitting Tasks

Sometimes there are tasks that you normally perform that are nice to do but are not required. These will vary from one company to another, and you can only eliminate them by critically asking "is this task truly *required* for this product? A full battery of standard tests often includes some that are not really appropriate for your current new product.

Similarly, there is often a formal series of market research tasks that the company carries out habitually. Once again, you may eliminate some work and time by a critical examination of the need. You may be able to omit portions of the market research which you normally conduct. For example, some companies are choosing to omit a portion of consumer food and grocery product test marketing. This saves a great deal of time and reduces the risk that your competitors will learn about your product prior to national introduction. In some cases, you can substitute concept testing for more elaborate and time-consuming market research.

The most obvious market research shortcut, and the most dangerous, is to conduct no market research at all. In some cases this occurs because some articulate and persuasive employees assert that they know the market situation. This need not be risky, if they, or you, truly know everything there is to know about the market you are proposing to serve. For example, the three founders of Zygo Corporation knew essentially everything there was to know about precision optical measurement techniques and the market to be served. They had already spent many years making these extremely difficult measurements while employed by a major corporation producing precision optical instruments.

They realized that the advent of the laser permitted these extremely difficult measurements to be made more simply and they formed Zygo Corporation to commercialize laser-based interferometry. This new measurement technique greatly simplified the prevailing, difficult, time-consuming measurement tasks. The new corporation was the successful pioneer with this class of interferometric measuring equipment.

Appendix C contains a list of typical tasks required for developing a new product. Obviously, no such list can ever be fully complete for all possible situations and companies. In all likelihood, you will have to add additional tasks for your next new product. You can also delete many of the tasks as you construct your triad's development plan and those omissions will save you time.

Compressing Tasks

There are many situations where it is practical to add resources (either personnel or facilities and equipment) to shorten the normal time for a given task. This can have a big payoff for long duration tasks on the critical path. In general, you can easily justify even a development cost premium or increase to shorten critical path tasks. (Unfortunately, this doesn't work everywhere, especially where you are developing new software. In this situation, adding more software personnel can delay tasks by requiring more communication and integration time than you otherwise save.)

In other cases, there may be new ways to carry out a given task that is quicker than your normal way. For example, suppose you have a group (either in your company or external) that is developing advertising for the new product. Imagine that everyone is unhappy with the creativity of the present theme. Sometimes the use of inexpensive facilitation software will quickly produce a creative breakthrough. (I discuss productivity improvements, which can also compress task durations, in Chapter 13.)

Performing Tasks in Parallel

Rearranging the project schedule plan to perform some tasks in parallel can usually save a great amount of time. Cincinnati Milacron reportedly built a prototype of a high-performance machining center (HPMC) in 257 days instead of the normal two to three years by dividing the HPMC into separate modules which were designed separately and then fit together. Another common example of parallel work is the early purchase of long-lead items. There is an obvious risk in doing this and such a purchase must never become the justification for subsequently authorizing the next phase of development where progress is otherwise insufficient or if there are better alternatives.

NONSENSICAL SHORTCUTS

There are some no-noes. You obviously cannot eliminate, and frequently cannot shorten, legally mandated regulatory reviews or tests, such as those by the Food and Drug Administration (FDA), Underwriters' Laboratories (UL), or similar organizations. Thus, you have to plan for these, and do the best you can to facilitate them (for instance, by being sure to have all required data and documentation ready, in the specified or expected form, before they are needed).

There is a common, but asinine, shortcut. Some development teams prepare an unrealistically short new product development schedule, to sell the program to upper management. Proposing task or development schedule durations that cannot be achieved is not going to make these happen sooner. This is just fiction and reduces the likelihood the company will allocate its scarce resources in an optimum fashion.

SHORTCUT CONSEQUENCES

Most shortcuts carry some degree of inherent risk, either of a performance compromise or a development cost penalty. You must be alert to these and try to estimate the payoff reward versus the downside. This is so specific to each development and company situation that there are no obvious rules of thumb.

Also, it is difficult to deviate from the corporate SOPs in a company that has an established culture, which is probably any company that has been in business for more than ten years. Those able to deviate are usually persons who know the system or are recognized as established experts or influential politicians. There is probably no way to learn how or whether to take such a personal risk except by gaining experience in your own company.

HIGHLIGHTS

You must avoid dead time, which is common between phases, during your new product development program.

The most effective technique to avoid dead time at reviews is to assure that executives or empowered substitutes are available to make the go or stop decision at the correct time.

You should always consider novel approaches and similar devices to try to save new product development time.

Timesavers include using temporary expedients, omitting tasks, compressing the normal time for a task, and performing tasks in parallel.

Shortcuts are rarely risk-free, so think through the possible consequences.

If the benefits of the shortcut's timesaving appears to be greater than the risks you incur, alert cognizant personnel and adopt the shortcut.

Chapter 12

Project Management Tools

The development of a new product is a project, and, therefore, you can save time by using some of the many project management tools and techniques that already exist. These vary from simple to elaborate, since project scopes vary tremendously. However, your new product development project will normally require only the simpler tools.

The tool with the greatest potential value is microcomputer project management software, the use of which I strongly urge you to adopt. Two features of this tool that are especially useful are schedule and resource forecasts. This software is not a panacea, but its use can help you introduce your new product close (or closer) to when you want.

THE VALUE OF PROJECT MANAGEMENT TOOLS

Project management is the process, partially management science and partially art, of defining an objective for a one-time undertaking, planning the work to accomplish that goal, organizing resources and leading required personnel, monitoring progress, and completing *all* the work to achieve the performance goal on time and within budget! Since this description also applies to the development and introduction of a new product, you can make effective use of some project management methodologies.

Unfortunately, project management has a bad image, since many people associate the term with massive schedule and cost overruns on large aerospace and construction projects. Some other people believe that project management means getting an account number to which labor and other expenses can be allocated. Less well known is that such badly managed projects would undoubtedly have had worse outcomes if project management tools and techniques had not been employed. To put it differently, you can use those simple tools, which have proven to be effective, that fit your managerial style and new product development needs. There is no reason to throw out the baby with the bathwater.

As an example, several years ago I was retained by a small company developing a new product after they realized that their scheduled product introduction date was slipping one month every time another month rolled by. The scheduled shipment date always remained several months in the future. The delays were not from any suddenly discovered problems, but rather because the various team members kept discovering tasks which they had not previously identified that had to be done. I interviewed the half-dozen key managers and asked them to specify everything they knew they had to do. Then I determined all the predecessor and successor tasks for each of these tasks. After that, I assembled all the information on a single critical path network schedule and showed the entire team what they had to do before they could actually start to ship. In a short meeting, we made a couple of minor adjustments and they finally had a realistic schedule, which they did accomplish. While I have forgotten the details, I recall that everyone was surprised to learn that the sales samples had to be prepared immediately. This was typical of the tasks they knew they had to do, but had assumed could be deferred until later; if it had been, they would have suffered another product introduction delay later.

There is a variety of tools and techniques that experienced project managers use to help overcome the stumbling blocks normally encountered during any project, including new product development projects. Project management software is one such tool, and many software packages have become available for use on microcomputers. While many of the project management tools will undoubtedly prove useful to you, the one that is most useful to help you develop your new product quickly is this new (and still rapidly improving) software.

Exhibit 12-1 shows the three dimensional goal—what I call the triple constraint—of your new product development project. It shows a nominal plan for new product development along with tradeoffs to consider. No project, especially a new product development project, goes in accordance with the original plan. What you do not know when you start is where and when you will encounter something unexpected. One of the values of project management software, microcomputer or other, is your ability to allocate some schedule and budget contingency to areas you identify as having higher risk and to then quickly see what a realistic schedule and budget for the complete new product development effort look like. This use of software for contingency planning is very useful in avoiding a commitment to a foolishly unrealistic product introduction date.

SCHEDULING PROBLEMS

As I said above, one of the greatest values in using project management methodologies in developing a new product is for scheduling. Even when you use the best project management scheduling software, you will have some schedule problems. I have discussed this with dozens of executives and managers and there is a broad consensus. To help you realize what scheduling software can and cannot do, and to help you distinguish software problems from schedule problems, I want to mention some of these schedule problems now. These fall into four categories: specification changes; faulty estimates; resources; and technical problems.

Specification Changes

There are three main reasons why there is pressure to make changes to the specifications after the optimization phase is complete:

1. You may have new people, who were not part of the group that set the specifications, join the product development team. These newcomers may see a better way, real or imagined, to carry out the development effort, so they will want to change the specifications.

2. You may obtain new information, which may be based on fact or rumor. This is the problem of the stationary target, which is illustrated in Exhibit 1-9.

Exhibit 12-1. The three dimensional goal (the "triple constraint") of your new product development project.

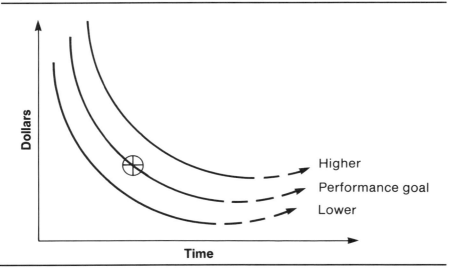

3. Various people may begin to second guess the original specifications. The likelihood of second guessing will be greater the longer the development schedule.

Unfortunately, nothing you do with scheduling software will prevent specification changes nor eliminate the pressures to make such changes. However, a good schedule, that is, one that is credible and has the support of the leadership triad, is easily explained. You can use it to help counteract the tendency to change specifications, which invariably leads to a delay in product introduction.

Faulty Estimates

Software does not determine the development schedule. Rather, the software will calculate the schedule for the assumptions that you enter about task durations and interdependencies. If the estimates are faulty, the resulting schedule will also be unrealistic. Faulty estimates come about for at least three reasons:

1. There is optimism, which leads to omitting contingency. If you have no contingency in the schedule, you will almost surely miss the target introduction date. Conversely, if you have too much contingency, you may not be able to justify the product development effort to top management. Software does not make the judgment about what is a reasonable balance between prudent conservatism and foolish optimism; this has to be done by the triad leadership, based on experience with similar product development efforts.

2. There may be unscheduled demands that intrude upon the resources you plan to use. A proper allowance for maintenance activity will reduce some of this, but, there can be other such intrusions. Once again, only experience can allow you to forecast a realistic allowance for these intrusions.

3. There can be external delays, such as those for material or component procurement. You can reduce the likelihood of making poor assumptions by involving your company's procurement specialists when schedule estimates are made, but this will not eliminate the problem.

Resource Demands

Not only may there be unscheduled demands upon your resources, there may be priority changes. If your development becomes the highest priority, this can help you get resources. Unfortunately, the converse also occurs.

In common with other corporate work in which you engage, you will find that your new product development project is dependent upon many resources that you do not manage. While a good prediction of which resources you will require at a given time, clearly presented, can help you obtain the resources you require when you require them, your success results primarily from superb interpersonal skills.

Technical Problems

No scheduling tool will preclude technical problems. While a provision for feasibility activity will reduce these, you may still encounter them. Once again, contingency based on experience is the best insurance.

PROJECT MANAGEMENT SOFTWARE

You can use a microcomputer project management software package to help complete your new product development project on a fast schedule. In 1988, Philips Lighting Division (in The Netherlands) found that they could save 20–25 percent of the normal new product development time by using microcompter-based project management scheduling software. If your company already has project management software that runs on a mainframe or minicomputer, you can use it rather than microcomputer software to help manage your new product development projects. Schedule slippage can be reduced, if not eliminated, by having a time-based critical path schedule for the development effort. This schedule need not be complex, unless the development effort is complex, but it should include all the tasks that have to be completed. At this point, you may wish to consult Appendix C, which lists typical new product development tasks, to decide which tasks you should normally include in your own schedules. The use of this list can help prevent required tasks from falling through the cracks.

Microcomputer project management packages do three main things for you:

1. They provide a relatively fast way to draw network diagrams and bar chart schedules. The network diagrams may be either PERT (Program Evaluation and Review Technique), CPM (Critical Path Method), or some hybrid format. (Caution: Some packages claim to provide PERT or CPM, but instead provide some variant of uncertain utility, and a few software packages provide only a bar chart schedule.)

Network diagrams are graphic representations of what has to be done during a new product development project. CPM normally portrays the tasks that must be accomplished to complete the project; PERT normally depicts the various events that must occur before the project is completed. These may be drawn with a time base and may also contain information about resources and personnel dedicated to each task. This can be the triad's key tool for coordinating work of many people in all the various functional groups, which is reason enough to use this software.

As I said before, you must expect plan changes when developing a new product. Or you may have decision points where subsequent actions depend on the results to date. The capability to quickly revise a network diagram or bar chart is useful and current microcomputer project management software does provide that capability.

The general situation you are dealing with is shown in Exhibit 12-1, where the nominal plan for your new product development project is the circled cross in the middle. You can easily and quickly explore what if scenarios, such as:

- Putting more resources on the critical path to save time (which usually costs more);
- Trying for a higher performance (typically a changed specification, that takes both more time and money); or
- Exploring other variations of performance and schedule.

2. Software can be used to determine resource requirements. This may reveal that a person with some critical skill (for example, a senior design engineer) or facility (for instance, a focus group facility) is over-committed; such an overcommitment (or resource deficit) is a danger signal indicating that the new product will not be completed as planned. This kind of danger signal can alert the development project manager to replan the project, which can be done quickly with most of the microcomputer software by varying resources in a what-if mode allowing you to see the resultant impact.

3. Most microcomputer project management software packages will also record and display planned new product development project capital and expense cost charges. This capability can be helpful in determining payback. (A few microcomputer packages also allow entry of actual costs, providing a comparison of actual and planned development cost. This feature obviously presumes you have a means to determine the actual development costs. Since this is normally the least important of the three triple constraint issues in new product development, I would not spend much time nor effort exploring it.)

There is another benefit that is more important than these three mechanical functions. If the triad cannot construct a network diagram for the development effort, they probably do not know enough about the new product development project to manage it. To put it differently, if you are unable to construct a time-based critical path schedule for the planned development effort, you will not introduce the new product when intended. The use of project management software forces you to confront the logic of your development effort, which is both important and helpful.

The following two sections provide more detail on project management software's use for scheduling and resource management. I use two specific products (of more than a dozen I have operated) to provide some of the illustrations.

Scheduling

In some software, the graphic output is displayed in a awkward format. Unfortunately, microcomputer software packages have few fixed formats, so the output display is not necessarily as graphically obvious as a form selected for your own visual needs. Exhibit 12-2 contrasts three general types of network diagrams, which are also illustrated in the other cited figures:

1. Task-on-arrow (Exhibit 12-3)
2. Task-in-node (Exhibit 12-4)
3. Event-in-node (Exhibit 12-5)

While a new product development project can indeed be portrayed by any of the three types of network diagrams, the distinction among these is not trivial in practice. As an example, one of the few things a new product development project manager can constructively do is change the allocation of resources dedicated to a specific task. That is, your new product will get to the market quickly because people complete the required work on all the tasks quickly. Therefore, if the display type

Exhibit 12-2. Three types of network diagrams.

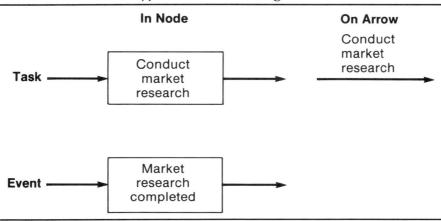

Exhibit 12-3.   Task-on-arrow network diagram.

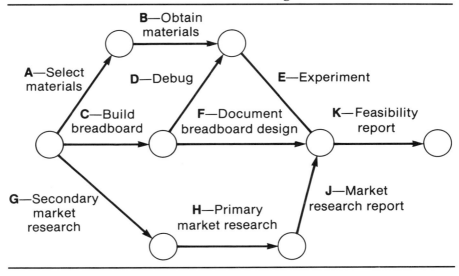

Exhibit 12-4.   Task-in-node network diagram.

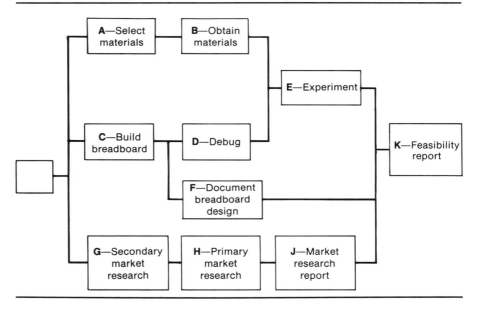

Exhibit 12-5. Event-in-node network diagram.

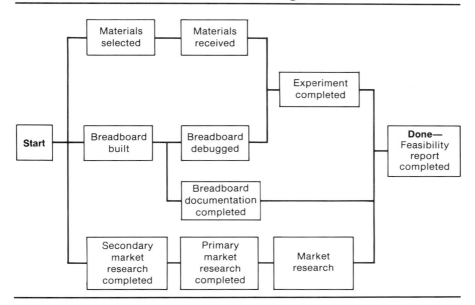

that you have chosen does not depict each task (as opposed to event), it is, in general, less useful. Events are the goal, but you reach them by successfully completing tasks.

I am convinced that a time-based task-on-arrow critical path method diagram is the clearest way to improve coordination and communication of the multifunctional triad team; manual approaches were proposed (correctly in my view) over twenty years ago! Exhibit 12-6 illustrates two versions of time-based task-on-arrow critical path network diagrams. Some popular software packages provide only the task-in-node format, and you can't make the length of each task proportional to the time planned for it. Exhibit 12-7 illustrates this kind of display with TimeLine 3.0. Fortunately, however, TimeLine has an add-on package (TimeLine Graphics), which allows the output to be portrayed in a time-based critical path format, as shown in Exhibits 12-8 and 12-9. Unfortunately, the current version of this particular software does not give you control over where the activities are displayed (vertically), so
(text continued on page 149)

Exhibit 12-6. Time-based task-on-arrow critical path diagram.

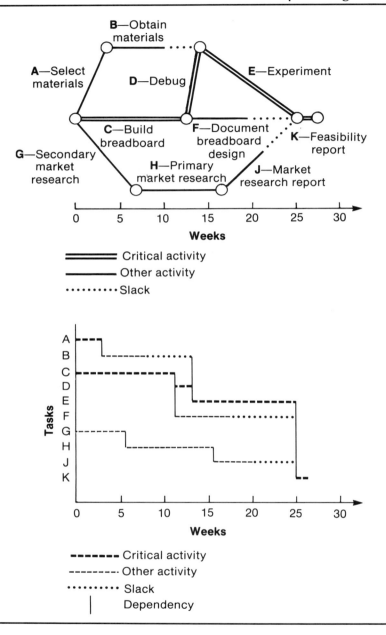

Exhibit 12-7. A microcomputer project management software task- or event-in-node network diagram.

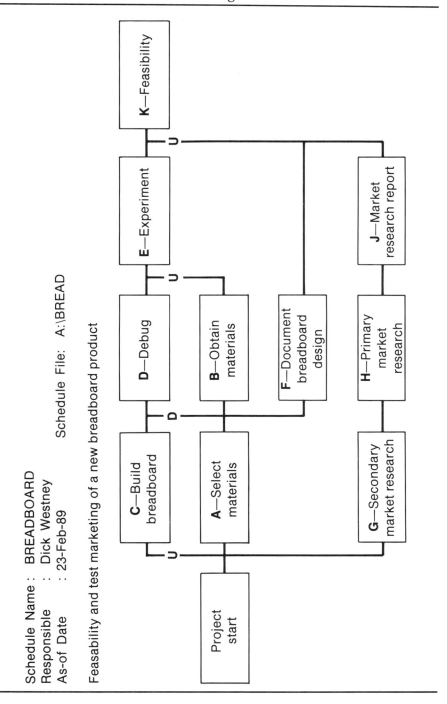

Exhibit 12-8. Time-based task-on-arrow critical path diagram for network illustrated in Exhibit 12-7, prepared with a microcomputer software package.

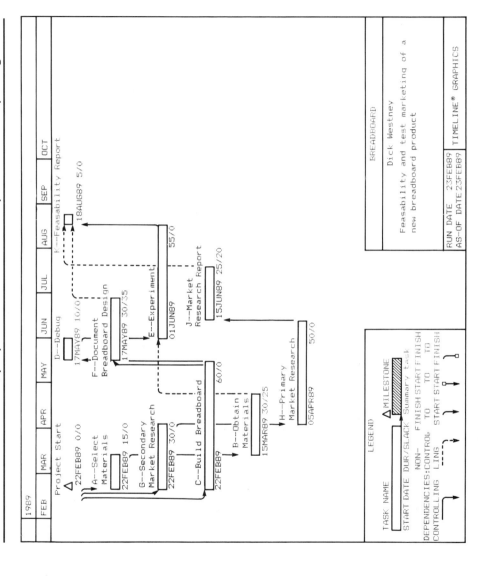

Exhibit 12-9. Time-based task-on-arrow critical path diagram prepared with a microcomputer software package, emphasizing the critical path.

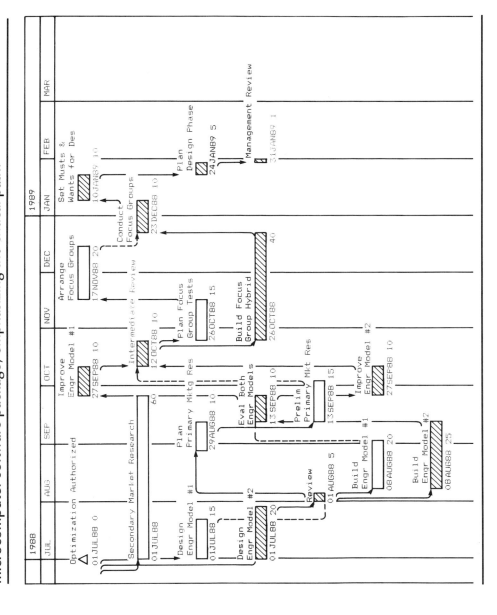

Exhibit 12-10. Task-on-arrow network diagram schedule in which vertical location of each bar can be selected by user. (Original color not reproduced here to distinguish critical activity, noncritical activity, summary, and hammock.)

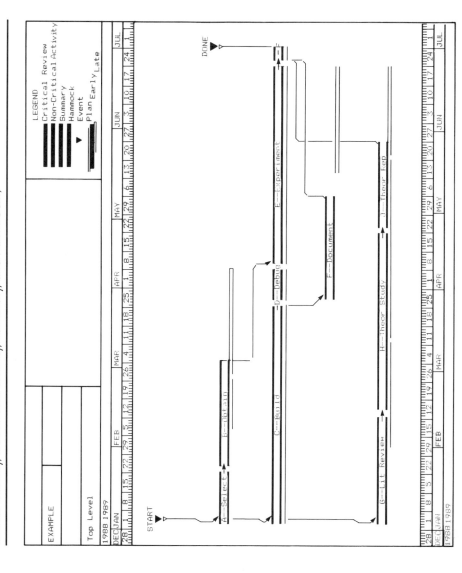

it (in common with any software display) may portray activities with illogical proximities and layouts. Another currently available software package, ViewPoint 3.1, provides a time-based activity-on-arrow where you can vertically position the arrows (or bars) accordance with your preference, as illustrated in Exhibit 12-10.

Resource Management

In many cases the dominant factor that determines what project schedule really can be achieved is resource availability. As you plan your project with project management software, you can enter resources required for each task, which might be as illustrated in Exhibit 12-11. Exhibit 12-12 summarizes the forecast schedule for engineering resources derived from the plan in Exhibit 12-11. Visual inspection reveals that you require six engineers for many weeks; if these are available, you have no problem. Many project management software packages will provide a resource histogram for the entire project, such as shown in Exhibit 12-13. These histograms provide a clear picture of requirements.

Some microcomputer project management software packages offer you the option of determining the fastest schedule that can be realized given the resources (people and equipment) that are available. For example, ViewPoint provides several different ways to manage your resources. Once you have developed your plan and assigned resources,

Exhibit 12-11. Resource allocation plan for project illustrated in Exhibit 12-6. (Task durations in weeks.)

Task	Planned Duration	Mrktg	Engr	Mfgr engr	Mfgr
A	3		1	1	
B	6			1	
C	12*		3	2	
D	2*		3	2	
E	11*	1	2	1	
F	6		1	1	1
G	6	2			
H	10	3	3	3	3
J	5	2	1	1	1
K	1*	2	2	2	2

*Task is on the critical path.

Exhibit 12-12.   One resource requirement for plan illustrated in Exhibit 12-11.

Task	Engineering Requirement Each Week (assuming earliest start on each task)
A	1 1 1
B	
C*	3 3 3 3 3 3 3 3 3 3 3
D*	3 3
E*	2 2 2 2 2 2 2 2 2 2
F	1 1 1 1 1 1
G	
H	3 3 3 3 3 3 3 3 3 3
J	1 1 1 1 1
K*	2

*Task is on the critical path.

you can start looking for possible resource overloads. Its "Resource Profile," Exhibit 12-14, shows total work hours over time for all resources or just one resource. If there is a resource conflict or overload, ViewPoint offers you several ways to resolve resource conflicts:

1. "Level" will attempt to smooth the work-load by rescheduling activities with available float;
2. "Constrained Scheduling" allows you to interactively draw a line at the rate the resource is available to be used, which may reveal that this plan causes you to miss your schedule; or
3. ViewPoint offers "Resource Load Tracing" in which you can discover all the activities that contribute to the resource overload, and perhaps find a few for which rescheduling is possible to resolve the problem.

To put it differently, these (and similar) software packages can force the schedule to conform to resource availability. If you do not like the schedule that you can achieve with the available resources, you can try to replan the new product development effort. For example, you can see the schedule problem caused by limited resources before you are very far into the development effort; then, you can try to arrange for additional resources, perhaps by external sourcing, or reconsider the wisdom of going ahead with a development effort that you will complete later than the triad desires.

Exhibit 12-13. Resource histogram prepared by microcomputer software (TimeLine 3.0).

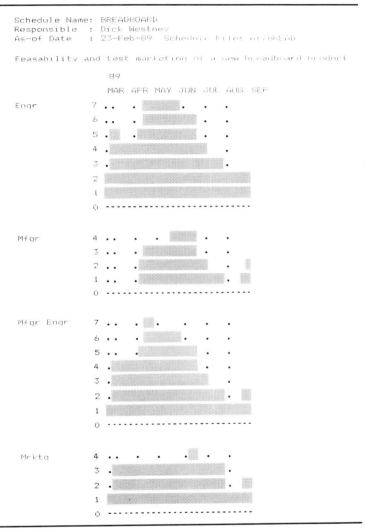

The Role of Project Management Software in Each Activity

Since the objective of the work in each of the activities and phases I have previously outlined is different, the role you expect project management software to play is also somewhat different. My view of how to employ software in each activity follows.

Feasibility Activity. The feasibility activity normally consists of three-month work segments, during which specific tasks, but not suc-

Exhibit 12-14.   Another resource histogram: ViewPoint's "Resource Profile."

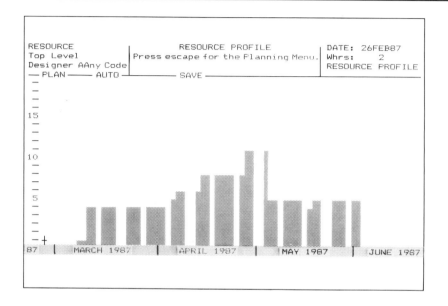

cessful results, have been agreed to. The most useful role for microcomputer project management software is to help provide a critical path network schedule of all of the planned tasks during that three month period. This schedule diagram will help the cognizant manager assure timely accomplishment of all the tasks that may involve many people.

Obviously, if the nature of the new product development effort requires feasibility activity work periods longer than three months, for instance six months or a year, then the critical path network schedule should cover that period of time. But three month efforts are a good rule-of-thumb for the feasibility activity.

One task that is required during each work increment period is to construct the critical path network schedule plan for the proposed subsequent feasibility activity work increment. At the management review which concludes a work increment, the proposed plan for the subsequent work interval must be discussed and either approved or revised. If the feasibility work is successful, the activity might end with a plan for the optimization phase of the subsequent development phase activity, assuming you wish to initiate that effort.

Development Activity. There should no longer be significant fundamental unknowns during the development activity. Thus, you can schedule each phase of this entire activity with critical path network schedules. Normally, this should make it possible to predict the date when first product shipment will occur with reasonable assurance. However, there will be other cases in which there are no significant technical unknowns, but in which the total development schedule duration has significant uncertainty for other reasons.

In any event, the development activity work should start with a critical path network diagram for the optimization phase, and you can schedule the dates for each of the tasks in that phase with no (or very little) uncertainty. The work during the optimization phase should proceed on that schedule without any deviation. If you adopt the illustrative phase structure previously described, the optimization phase work should end with the preparation of a critical path network for the design phase, and the design phase work should also proceed without any deviation from that. In a similar way, you can schedule both the preproduction and production phase with critical path network diagrams. If your phase structure differs from the illustrative one, the same principle still applies.

Although it is relatively less important, project management software has another virtue during the development activity. This software permits project cost estimating, in this instance the cost estimate would be for the development activity work. Because these cost estimates are made for each of the resources assigned to work on the tasks which you include in the critical path schedule, then both the schedule and cost estimate are consistent. Obviously, then, if a change is made to either the resources or the schedule, this will immediately show up in the cost plan for the remaining work. In addition, it is obvious that the cost elements which you enter in the project management software can become cost entries into the discounted cash flow analysis, which you should complete prior to authorizing or incurring major tooling or rollout expenses.

Maintenance Activity. You initiate maintenance activity projects when there is a problem with an existing product that is in routine production. Thus, you can start each of these maintenance efforts with a critical path network schedule describing the entire maintenance activity. This might also forecast the budget you will require to complete it. Thereafter, work should proceed in accordance with that plan. There will be occasions when you must change the initial maintenance activity schedules and budgets because of things you discover while performing the maintenance work.

Using Project Management Software

There are two practical points which I believe should guide your use of microcomputer-based project management software:

1. Use a time-based critical path method diagram which portrays the tasks to be performed, if at all possible.
2. Be sure that the input schedule and budget information represents the consensus of the key people on the new product development team.

Time-based Critical Path Diagram. As explained earlier in this chapter, a time-based task-on-arrow critical path network schedule is unrivaled in terms of clarity for illustrating who is to do what and by when. This format is my personal preference, but many of the microcomputer-based project management packages do not provide it. Many of these software packages will, however, display task-in-node format.

Team Input. One of the most important bits of advice I can offer is that the key members of the new product development team should jointly establish the schedule and budget for each phase of the planned work. This is important for three reasons:

1. These people presumably have better knowledge than anyone else of how much work is required and, thus, how long it will take;
2. If these people establish the schedules and budgets, they are likely to be highly motivated to conform to them; and,
3. This maximizes the likelihood that the new product development program's impact on all the other departments will be given due consideration. If top management or marketing establishes a development schedule for engineering, for example, the engineers are quite likely to be able to prove that the schedule was unrealistic.

CAVEATS

There are several problems with microcomputer-based project management software that I hear of when I talk with managers who are responsible for or participants in new product development projects. (I believe users of software running on more powerful computers would cite these same problems.)

1. You must keep your schedule current. The plan may change for any number of reasons. Or, the plan (that is the interdependency between each task) may remain the same but task durations may change or different resources may be employed. Updating is a nuisance and some people do not keep their plans current. However, an out-of-date schedule is clearly not merely counterproductive but truly harmful.

Once your schedule is not credible, the entire development rationale is suspect; and, if you can overcome doubts about that, you will have great (and unnecessary) difficulty obtaining resources in a timely way. However awkward it is to update software, it is still easier to do that than to update a manually prepared schedule.

2. It is hard to obtain credible time estimates for each task. You can reduce this problem by invoking my golden rule for planning: Get the people who will perform a task to plan it. To begin with, they know more about it than anyone else. More importantly, if they plan it, they are more likely to be motivated to comply with the plan. You can also help yourself by breaking the entire new product development effort into small tasks, since these can be estimated more accurately than large tasks.

3. The software output formats are highly restricted. In most cases, you have no freedom to arrange the display in a way that is best for your own purposes. Also, the printed output frequently requires that many pieces of paper must be carefully taped together. Since a key role for software is to improve your communication and team coordination, these two output limitations can be particularly frustrating.

4. While some of the software is very user friendly that only helps you at the computer terminal. Other people on the development team must understand it and you may have to provide training to a number of people. In any event, you must not make the mistake of assuming that other people will understand the output just because you have mastered the software.

5. Microcomputer software sometimes is awkward or inadequate to sum the resource requirements of all of the company's projects. Therefore, you can only uncover the resource deficits, which are often the main cause for schedule erosion, when each department examines the forecasted workload for every project.

6. Some people use the software (or other scheduling tools) to satisfy their bosses because they are gun shy. The resulting schedule is not their plan, it merely satisfies a procedural requirement, which is clearly a waste of time. In fact, in one company new product development schedules are preprinted onto twenty-four-month calendars requiring only the addition of current dates, which obviously becomes self-fulfilling.

7. No software keeps your project on schedule. While it helps you see and concentrate on critical path (and the nearly critical path(s), which all too easily can become the critical path), it doesn't tell you what to do if there is a slip. You must watch for such problems and react promptly when slips occur. You should be able to recover by using the time saving techniques discussed in the previous chapter.

8. By far the most serious reservation I have about microcomputer

project management software is the trap it opens for a new product development manager's time. This software is a mechanical solution to what is largely a people problem. Ultimately, the development manager must work with people, many of whom are not of his or her own choosing. In some cases, the user is fascinated with the software's technology and elegance, rather than thinking through what is required from it. Using software can become a cop-out for required managerial activity, unless the computer input represents the consensus of the involved personnel. Normally, the time you spend at the computer terminal is time that is not spent working with people or doing your own technical work (which you may have to do if you are also a contributor to the effort you are managing).

You can avoid or minimize this trap by doing all the computer work with the key people on your triad team in a room where there is a computer projection device. Then, everyone can see the computer's graphic display and comment or otherwise interact. Alternatively, you might use software that runs on a local area (or other) network, and arrange for all the key people to also have computer terminal displays on their own desks. This mechanization will have less interpersonal and interfunctional interaction than getting all the key people together in one room. In fact, team peer pressure may help maintain a difficult schedule.

Dozens of microcomputer software packages are already available, more are coming, and some are already disappearing. A few of the more successful suppliers will be introducing software modifications to overcome existing shortfalls. The entire field is changing rapidly. Frequently, articles discuss specific software packages, providing detailed reviews of features, and you can learn about the current software status by reading these. Do not wait for the perfect software; use the most suitable (or least unsatisfactory) now, and benefit from it while you await improvements.

9. The last caveat is that you should not use project management software on very small development efforts. To put this differently, one of the reasons to use this tool is to help maintain a development schedule or live within a development budget. If the worst disaster that could occur during this small effort is a very short schedule slip or a very small budget overrun, then there is no point taking more than that amount of time and spending more than that amount of money to create a development schedule using a computer.

HIGHLIGHTS

Microcomputer project management software packages can help you introduce your new product quickly.

Such software can provide you with a critical path schedule, which might best be shown in a time-based task-on-arrow format.

This software can also help you forecast resource requirements and identify ways to resolve potential availability problems.

You have to find a specific software package that does what you want it to do.

Each software package has virtues and weaknesses. When used where the strengths are capitalized upon, they can help solve some of your new product development problems.

Chapter 13

Productivity Tools

There is a variety of productivity tools that can shorten the new product development process. As a practical matter, productivity tools are themselves rapidly developing new capabilities and utility, so you must spend time investigating the current state-of-the-art when you consider their usefulness for your situation. The chapter provides a brief overview of some possibilities in factory automation, simulation, and electronic publishing to illustrate the kind of emerging capability you might use to shorten your time in developing a new product. Since it is sometimes difficult to justify the capital expenditure for this kind of equipment, there is also a review of justification considerations.

FACTORY AUTOMATION

There are many possible tools that can improve productivity and some of these can shorten your new product development time. In the case of products (as distinct from services), computer-aided engineering (CAE), computer-aided design (CAD), computer-aided manufacturing (CAM), and many other specialized tools are increasingly being used. In fact, virtually all participants who attend my executive seminars on faster new product development have adopted these tools to shorten time-to-market. These tools are especially useful when you are working to develop an entire family of new products because you can automatically record at what point given model changes are introduced.

Even less sophisticated numerically controlled tools can save time, since so-called hard tooling can be omitted. Correct software is all that is required, and it can be rapidly revised if necessary. As an example, computer-controlled laser cutting is reportedly shortening product development time for one company.

Flexible automation may also offer speed advantages, but the re-

quired systems and processes are not yet very mature. Flexible automation exploits programmable equipment rather than hard automation.
This emerging field involves various combinations of robotics, machine-
vision systems, computer integration techniques and artificial intelligence. Because each company has different facilities, systems, product
mixes, and cultures, there is no single universal approach. Unfortunately, a barrier exists because there is no universal communication language. The high cost of required equipment often delays introduction,
but recently some piecemeal steps are becoming possible.

An automated factory can have a shorter production start-up cycle
than a conventional factory. General Electric's R&D center has a computer system on which mechanical engineering design work is completed and manufacturing directions are then delivered directly to
mold-making machinery. The paperless factory is not yet here, but
eventually you will be able to save increasing amounts of time as design
stations are tied directly to production tools. Similarly, the peopleless
(fully automated) factory is not yet here. Perhaps it never will be here,
but many companies are moving in this direction to try to save time.

Production time can also be reduced. For example, in 1985, the
General Electric dishwasher plant in Kentucky required only eighteen
hours to produce a dishwasher that required five or six days two years
previously. Similarly, IBM has a quick turn-around time facility at its
semiconductor manufacturing plant. This facility can produce new circuits in less than a month, and has produced a new circuit in as little as
three days. In distinction, conventional production start-up of new semiconductor circuits may require a few months.

At least one company offers a service to provide prototype chips in
as little as one day, and another is striving to develop a machine that can
produce prototype printed circuit boards in that time. Also, many companies offer equipment that your own company can use to speed up
electronic design and production. Although the full promise is still to
emerge, expert systems are now coming into use to accelerate the design of integrated circuits for specific applications. IBM also has a
method to design chips combining both analog and digital capability in
days, replacing conventional methods that require weeks. Another useful approach to saving time in developing new electronic chip circuits is
to make use of silicon compilers, which allow relatively inexperienced
design engineers to quickly complete designs that would take much
longer by conventional methods. In addition, some vendors sell specialized products to shorten the design time for add-ons to other specific
products.

To take full advantage of factory automation you must integrate the
factory floor, the management information system for the corporation,
and the design and engineering department. Today, there are still sig-

nificant obstacles to achieving this easily. Many of the design modeling systems do not provide appropriate data for sophisticated engineering analysis and production work; many current engineering work stations lack adequate data processing capability; the data transfer rates between work stations, the factory, and the management information system are frequently incompatible; and there is not yet a fully accepted industry standard for exchanging graphics and control signals between dissimilar systems. Nevertheless, this approach can save development time for certain kinds of new products.

Computer-aided software engineering (CASE) is another technology that offers design speed advantages. The notion is to help automate the act of writing software. Software today is often a cause of late product development. In common with other automation tools, the present lack of standards limits the proliferation and general use of this tool.

If your new product development project involves a geographically dispersed team, you can save time by using electronic mail or facsimile. As a management consultant, I have been an adviser to a new product development project manager who is based in Europe. The project involves work in Europe, the northeast U.S., and two sites in California. Regular air mail proved hopeless, express mail helped, and electronic mail really proved to be very time-saving. In working with other clients in Europe, I routinely send a telex or facsimile message at the end of my business day and have their reply on my desk the next morning, and they do likewise. Groupware may also prove helpful when this technology matures.

SIMULATION

You can also accelerate new product development if you can communicate complex concepts quickly to many people with varied backgrounds. Simple models are a very effective means of doing this. One of the most effective simulation practitioners with whom I ever worked was also a brilliant mechanical design engineer. He conceived incredibly clever and elegant mechanisms. After inventing these and working out the principle design considerations, he then made a working model using a Mecanno set. (Mecanno is the English version of an Erector set.) Nontechnical people could then look at this simple model and understand its applicability to the effort at hand. Similarly, I once made a cardboard model of a complex three-axis flexure mechanism to explain what I wanted built.

Today there are early versions of computer-aided model making systems that tie to CAD systems to make models automatically. The manufacturer of one of these systems claims the resulting output can be used directly as the pattern for a mold. However, you may also display realistic three-dimensional models directly on a computer's screen and this may be adequate and faster.

In addition to models, there are exciting innovations in software that can fully analyze multiple performance aspects of unbuilt designs under varied conditions. This can save you time because you may be able to omit some tests or avoid actually building something that will prove unsatisfactory. Other software to analyze assembly is now emerging.

Finally, there are also many other simulation tools, some of which may be used for either products or services. For instance, Apple Computer spent $15 million for a Cray supercomputer to help speed up product development. Apple CEO John Sculley reportedly believed that the supercomputer could simulate new Apple computer hardware and cut six months off the development cycle, which would easily repay the investment.

ELECTRONIC PUBLISHING

The Zilog Z8000 16-bit microprocessor was completed in 1979, but it was a full year later before documentation of adequate quality was available to support the product. Some observers blame this initial lack of documentation for the chip's relatively poor market showing. Electronic publishing systems can, however, dramatically reduce the time for document production and potentially can save a great deal of money as well. One estimate indicates that 30 percent of a product's design cycle is devoted to documentation and that this might be cut in half by use of computer-aided publishing. Less sophisticated word processing software can be used advantageously in other situations.

CAPITAL JUSTIFICATION

Much of the equipment required to enhance productivity requires a capital budget expense justification. In many cases, conventional cost accounting analysis will not justify an investment in useful advanced production technology. A major part of the problem is that conventional capital expense justifications concentrate on direct labor-hour savings, normally measuring overhead expense in units of dollars per labor-hour. Unfortunately, improved productivity frequently reduces direct labor time dramatically, which thus spreads the same total overhead dollars over still fewer direct labor dollars, thus resulting in an attendant apparent increase in overhead.

In addition, there are many other potential benefits of these pieces of equipment that are frequently overlooked in the evaluation and justification. For instance, there may be quality improvements. As an example, Westinghouse has reportedly improved first-pass yields of functional printed circuit modules from 12 percent to more than 80 percent. Faster, automated production can also lead to smaller inventories with reduced warehousing costs. Reduced time in a flexible manufacturing system to change over to the production of a new product is another benefit that may be difficult to quantify.

Clearly, a thoughtless rush to install productivity enhancing equipment is unwise, even though there are obvious problems with the conventional cost justification methodologies. However, the new equipment may well be worthwhile even though the cost justification is apparently unfavorable. As an illustration, I was never able to justify the cost of purchasing the first computer for my own company, but I authorized it; and the unexpected turn-around time saving and quality improvements were, after the fact, more than adequate paybacks.

While cost justification may be difficult (or even impossible) *before* the fact, you should be able to demonstrate successful productivity improvement *after* the fact. Therefore, it is important to have relevant measures of productivity before and after. As an example, you might collect data for both the time and total person-months (for instance, from the start of the optimization phase until the end of the production

Exhibit 13-1.   A possible measure of new product development productivity improvement.

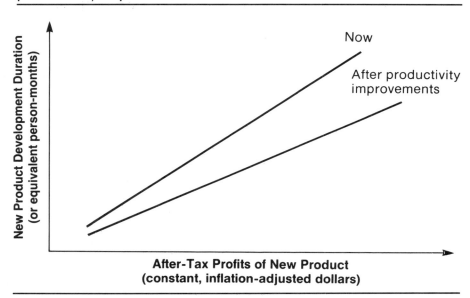

phase) for new products and plot this against the amount of profits (adjusted for inflation) produced by the new products. Exhibit 13-1 illustrates this idea.

HIGHLIGHTS

The entire field of automation and productivity improvement is evolving rapidly and offers many opportunities to shorten your time-to-market for new products.

Factory automation, simulation, and electronic publishing (to cite three specifics) can help you reduce the time for your new product development effort.

These three techniques (and others now emerging) may require the purchase of expensive capital equipment, which is sometimes hard to justify with conventional cost accounting analysis.

Chapter 14

Concentration on the Schedule

Dedicated concentration on the schedule can help speed your new product development. There are at least five techniques you can employ:

1. Measure each individual's schedule emphasis and provide feedback on how they depart (if they do) from what's desired.
2. Continually emphasize the schedule.
3. Conduct constructive project reviews to reinforce schedule emphasis.
4. Isolate the development team.
5. Be certain your time-critical new product development activities exclude work that more properly belongs in either feasibility or maintenance activities.

While you can never obtain myopic devotion to schedule to the total exclusion of everything else (even if you wanted to), you can greatly increase your development team's concentration.

MEASURING SCHEDULE EMPHASIS

I have performed a conjoint analysis (see Appendix B, if you are not familiar with this technique) to assess the importance people engaged in new product development place on the four project outcome factors:

1. Specified performance features (e.g., capacity, sensitivity, accuracy, speed, or throughput rate)
2. A specified standard (factory) cost target

3. A demanding but achievable development schedule
4. A mutually agreed project budget

This was done with several dozen people who are engaged in new product development, all of whom came from four high technology industrial product manufacturing firms which are identified in Exhibit 14-1. The conjoint analysis used an eighteen-card design that included two hold-out cards to help validate the data. The individuals who participated were asked to imagine that they had key responsibility for a new product development effort to achieve the four outcome factors cited above. They were also told to assume the product was typical of their business and would be produced in volume.

The conjoint analysis required them to rank the eighteen cards describing possible project outcomes in order of preference. Each person was assured that their answers would be anonymous. However, they were asked to record their function and background on their reply form.

The possible outcome results they were asked to choose among are shown by the factors and levels in Exhibit 14-2. The detailed results for one group of personnel from one of these four companies is shown in Exhibit 14-3, which reveals that individuals have very different emphasis patterns. The general sort of results I originally anticipated for different functions is shown in Exhibit 14-4. The actual results, shown in Exhibit 14-5, are noticeably different from what I anticipated, and show rather similar patterns for the three functions into which people were categorized. Curiously, the technical personnel were the ones who placed greatest emphasis on schedule, perhaps because they received the criticism when the development effort was late.

The results for each of the four companies are noticeably different, as shown in Exhibit 14-6. Company C personnel stress performance more than the other three companies, all of which are much larger. Company B personnel give more emphasis to schedule than the other

(*text continued on page 169*)

Exhibit 14-1. Industrial product manufacturers in which conjoint analysis was performed to determine new product development emphasis of individuals.

Company	Business	Annual Sales ($ millions)
A	Scientific instruments	100–300
B	Electronic systems and components	1,000–3,000
C	Electro-optical systems, instruments, and components	10–30
D	Laboratory systems, instruments, and supplies	100–300

Exhibit 14-2.   Factors and levels used to assess emphasis that individuals place on new product development project outcomes.

Factor	Level
Performance specifications	Exceed by 20% Exceed by 5% Fall short by 5% Fall short by 20%
Standard (factory) cost target	20% better than plan 5% better than plan 5% worse than plan 20% worse than plan
Development schedule	Introduce product 20% ahead of plan Introduce product 5% ahead of plan Introduce product 5% later than plan Introduce product 20% later than plan
Development budget	Underrun by 20% Underrun by 5% Overrun by 5% Overrun by 20%

Exhibit 14-3.   Emphasis judgments from conjoint analysis performed by thirteen personnel.

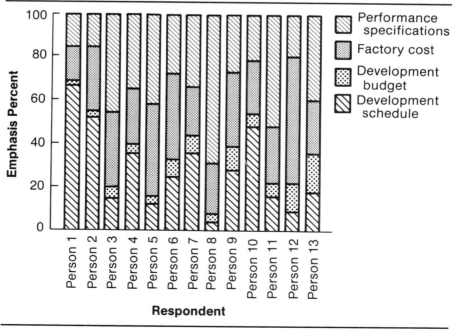

Exhibit 14-4. Anticipated emphasis percentages for different functions from conjoint analyses of new product development personnel.

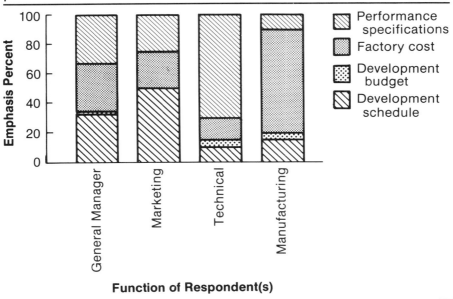

Exhibit 14-5. Actual emphasis percentages for different functions from conjoint analyses of new product development personnel.

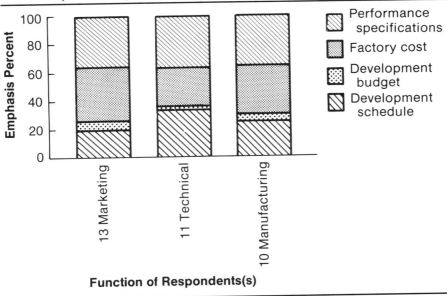

Exhibit 14-6. Actual emphasis for four different companies from conjoint analyses of new product development personnel.

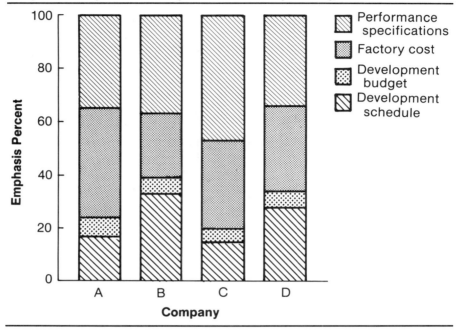

Exhibit 14-7. Ogive showing that only seven of thirty-seven personnel give development schedule more than 40 percent emphasis.

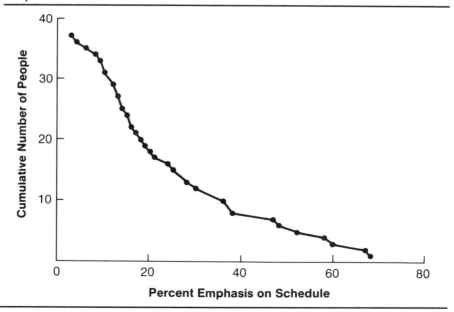

three companies. The most pronounced result of all is the paucity of people who stress schedule. Only seven of the thirty-seven people in this sample gave the development schedule more than a 40 percent emphasis, as shown in Exhibit 14-7.

In short, people working on new products place more value on exceeding the performance specifications than beating the schedule. A better balance in today's competitive world is to meet the minimum performance specification (and target factory cost) while beating the schedule.

These conjoint analysis results demonstrate that you can measure the emphasis judgments of your development team members. This might be done at the beginning of a start-up workshop conducted to initiate the development effort. The leadership triad can show the team what they believe to be the most desirable emphasis distribution. Such feedback can produce individual change. For instance, I have evaluated the judgments of one person at two times: In mid-1987, his development schedule emphasis was 9 percent; at the end of 1988, it was 20 percent, which is clearly a meaningful change.

EMPHASIZING SCHEDULE

Another way to improve dedication to a rapid schedule is to focus on the schedule to the exclusion of other aspects of the development. There are three systematic ways to emphasize the schedule: Use milestones; constantly seek time savers; and employ only relevant measurements. In addition there are other varied miscellaneous actions, which may sometimes help.

Milestones

The use of short phases, which was previously discussed, is an important underpinning for your efforts to emphasize schedule. This new product development program structure assures you that there is a significant endpoint that is not far in the future and this increases everyone's sense of urgency.

You can carry this notion further by having several significant milestones within each phase. These might be spaced every two weeks or so, although other intervals may be more appropriate in your specific situation. While a single milestone need not affect everyone who is working during that interval, each milestone will involve several people. Normally, these visible targets will heighten everyone's schedule consciousness.

Time Savers

If you and the entire leadership constantly seek varied time savers, such as those mentioned previously in Chapter 11, someone may well bring some practical ones to your attention. For example, as time passes and progress is made, it may be possible to reconfigure the entire critical path schedule network. A task that was originally part of the plan, which has not yet been done, can sometimes be omitted, because changes have made it unnecessary. This kind of opportunity may be more obvious to a worker in the trenches, and you are more likely to hear of it if everyone knows that such time savers are always desired. In other instances, the early purchase of some long lead items, which obviously has some risk, may be attractive and appropriate.

Measurements

What management is perceived to measure is what the workers pay attention to. Thus, if management frequently reviews development progress against the network diagram schedule, that act provides a clear schedule emphasis. Posting schedules in prominent locations can help. Conversely, if management pays attention to how neat and orderly the workplace is, then that, rather than the schedule, will receive attention.

Other Varied Actions

You can employ internal advertising. For example, humorous or amusing posters throughout the workplace that emphasize schedule (WHAT DID YOU DO TO HELP THE SCHEDULE TODAY?) can provide a powerful message. Similarly, managers should frequently ask what they can do to accelerate the development schedule. Both of these actions can also increase peer pressure to maintain, or even better, beat the schedule.

PROJECT REVIEWS

Project reviews provide a unique opportunity to emphasize schedule. Based on data I have collected from new product development executives and managers, as shown in Exhibit 14-8, this is not, unfortunately, how project review time is actually spent. Since the amount of time devoted to a subject conveys a message about its importance, this existing practice pattern therefore emphasizes nonschedule aspects.

Exhibit 14-9 shows data for three companies where the lack of time devoted to the new product development schedule seems extreme. The infrequency or irregular frequency of the reviews also deemphasizes

Exhibit 14-8. Percentage of time devoted to different topics at new product development project reviews.

Aspect	Average Percentage
Features	41%
Factory cost	19
Development schedule	29
Development budget	6

Exhibit 14-9. Percentage of time devoted to selected topics at infrequent or irregularly scheduled new product development project reviews in three companies.

	COMPANY E (4 times per year)	COMPANY F (Variable, every 1–6 months)	COMPANY G (Variable, weekly to quarterly)
Features	40%	69%	70%
Factory cost	40	10	15
Development schedule	10	20	10
Development budget	10	1	5

new product development importance. One company uses review frequency to provide a converse signal: Reviews are routinely held at the ends of phases and at major milestones within phases; they are otherwise held monthly if there is no schedule problem or weekly or even daily if there is a schedule problem.

In some companies, senior managers will dwell endlessly on the comparison of actual development expense versus the development budget plan and this is usually the least important issue of all. Exhibit 14-10 shows data for three companies where more or equal time is devoted to the development budget than the development schedule during the monthly reviews. While the optimum amount of time to devote to any topic is obviously judgmental and situation dependent, *a priori* it seems that about 33 percent should be devoted to each of the topics of performance features, factory cost, and development schedule, and only 1 percent to development budget.

Other topics have also been cited to me as occurring in such re-

Exhibit 14-10. Percentage of time devoted to selected topics at new product development project reviews in three companies.

	COMPANY H	COMPANY I	COMPANY J
Features	25%	20%	80%
Factory cost	25	30	5
Development schedule	25	15	5
Development budget	25	30	10
Other		5	

views: witch hunting; parts procurement; quality assurance; launch activities; resource shuffles; and priority changes. The first of these is clearly maladaptive, whereas the others may be important and even highly significant to the schedule.

Sometimes the project review discussion will uncover problems, for which some trade-off between performance features, factory cost, development schedule, and development cost may be required. This provides an opportunity to emphasize schedule. For instance, it is possible that the new product has evolved to a point where it is not yet able to meet the desired specification. The triad leadership can insist that a limited (but functional) product be introduced on time and that a subsequent free upgrade be provided to the initial customers to bring their product's performance up to the original specification. Obviously, this is not as desirable as meeting the original specification on time, but it does have the virtue of getting an adequate, if not ideal, product into the market in a timely way.

Finally, the usual project review ground rules apply: There must be an agenda; only the right people (or their empowered substitute) should attend; and the chairperson must clearly assign action items for follow-up.

ISOLATING THE PROJECT TEAM

There is no doubt that a skunk works can isolate a group of workers from distraction and thus improve their dedication to the effort at hand. If the workers at the skunk works have no other company assignments, no delay will occur because of the inevitable interruptions that routinely occur. Such isolation can eliminate the myriad of one hour and half day interruptions that quickly add up to a week, or more, of unnecessary product development delay.

A separate facility can build an esprit de corps and also improve teamwork. The team that moves to a separate skunk work site often feels they are the chosen few, which is often a motivator.

Unfortunately, some companies make the mistake of believing that a skunk works will, of itself, assure a rapid development schedule. However, this is no more certain than giving a person a baseball bat and expecting a home run. Other things must also be right. In one case with which I am familiar, a group was moved to a separate facility, but it was not given sufficient resources to accomplish the new product development they were attempting. In addition, this group was heavily dependent on the main corporate facility for many of the services that they required and they thus lost a great deal of time driving back and forth between two sites.

ALLOWING ONLY DEVELOPMENT ACTIVITY

You must avoid the leading (sometimes bleeding) edge of technology. You want to insist on using only proven technology. That is, try to deemphasize new technology for the sake of its newness and thus help everyone emphasize schedule rather than technology. The reason you have a separate feasibility activity is to explore important new technology in an environment apart from the time-critical new product development. When the new technology has been practiced sufficiently in prior feasibility efforts, you can more assuredly exploit it in your new product development effort.

Similarly, maintenance activity, if allowed to intrude on development, will distract your team from the new product effort. To put these two points differently, all triad actions should exhibit a sense of schedule urgency.

KEEPING SPECIFICATIONS INVIOLATE

One product marketing manager for a well-regarded high technology corporation has told me, based on data from their post mortems of new product development projects, "changing of design goals in midstream is a major source of schedule slip." Similarly, avoiding specification alterations is reportedly the practice at two Japanese companies, Matsushita and Casio, which try to ensure fast new product development by prohibiting major changes after deciding what their customers desire.

Engineers and scientists have a proclivity to change specifications during the development activity, which can produce a major schedule erosion. The reason such changes occur so frequently is that good technical people can always see new technological possibilities and want to take advantage of these immediately. That is one personal characteristic of the technologist that makes good technical people good. Focusing on the schedule, however, requires maintaining the original specifications and completing the development on time. Some companies even descope, that is, downgrade the original optimized specification, to get a minimally acceptable product to market early. After that, you can initiate a new project to develop an enhanced follow-on product. You can offer this further effort to the development team as the carrot to induce the technologists to concentrate solely on the original specifications during the current project.

The desire to improve the specifications is not confined to the technologists. The other function that frequently advocates a change is marketing. Typically, they want to respond to some real or imagined competitive situation. To put this somewhat differently, better is the enemy of good enough.

HIGHLIGHTS

You can measure each individual's schedule emphasis and provide feedback on how they depart from the desired emphasis pattern.

You can emphasize schedule by using milestones, constantly seeking time savers, and employing only relevant measurements.

Project reviews provide a forum to emphasize schedule.

You can improve the dedication to fast new product development by using a skunk works to reduce extraneous distractions.

Do not allow feasibility or maintenance activities to intrude on the development effort.

Focus on the minimum specification and achieve it before attempting improvements.

Chapter 15

Incentives

Incentives are a means by which managers can encourage desired behavior, and providing incentives for meeting a difficult new product development schedule is one way to clearly emphasize the importance of that schedule.

Possible incentive awards are widely varied, so there are numerous options available and two are described.

THE ROLE OF INCENTIVES

The purpose of incentives is to encourage and promote behavior that produces results you desire. Useful incentive systems require two elements: (1) There must be a clearly understood measure of some aspect of group or individual performance. Arbitrary or variable standards cause confusion. (2) When the performance goal is met or exceeded, there has to be some form of recognition, some reward, which may be tangible or psychological.

When recognition is awarded in the absence of a clearly measured accomplishment, there are always some unrewarded people who feel they were equally deserving and are thus demotivated. Conversely, whatever performance is obviously being measured is usually that to which people pay attention and emphasize. Consequently, insufficient incentives for successful risk-taking and negative sanctions for failure can inhibit faster new product development.

VARIETY OF INCENTIVES

Recognition can be awarded instantly or deferred. It can apply to anyone in the corporation or be specific to a single class of professionals.

The rewards can be given to either an entire group or to one or a few individuals. The form of recognition may or may not be monetary.

Typical incentive plans are directed at individuals and do not necessarily promote either fast new product development or interfunctional teamwork. For example, many companies measure key marketing personnel on a product line's profit or salespersons on the level of orders compared to their sales quotas. Similarly, conformance to the development schedule or budget is a frequent measure for key engineering personnel, and variances, scrap rates, or inventory levels are measures for key manufacturing personnel.

Cash incentive systems are very common in U.S. businesses. Recognition or rewards include bonuses, salary increases, promotions, and stock options.

There is a variety of non-monetary recognitions that you may wish to use, some of which are listed in Exhibit 15-1. As a further example, positive reinforcement is one such mechanism. You can choose to praise a person who has violated a standard operating procedure if that violation shortened a new product's development duration.

Organizational incentives can apply to anyone in the corporation. These include salary increases, promotions, or a better or larger office. Gainsharing, in which bonuses are tied to increased productivity, is another organizational incentive. The attraction of gainsharing is that only the saving is shared; the problem is trying to calculate what that saving is. Professional incentives vary depending on the recipient's specific profession or function. For example, scientists or engineers might have their dues reimbursed in a technical society or receive better laboratory equipment.

INCENTIVES FOR FAST NEW PRODUCT DEVELOPMENT

If incentives are deemed useful in any area of a corporation, they can also be used in other areas, and senior managers can install formal in-

---

Exhibit 15-1. Some illustrative nonmonetary recognitions.

- Demonstrating the new product to the chairman and the board of directors
- Presenting the new product at a press conference or giving a paper about it at a technical conference or trade show
- Team picture in the company magazine or newspaper
- Pat on the back in the presence of co-workers
- Plaque for office wall
- A victory party

---

centive plans to encourage fast development of high quality, profitable products. You can obtain better new product development outcomes when the entire team has a common incentive.

The possibilities for fast new product development incentive plans are virtually infinite, limited only by your cleverness and ingenuity. Two illustrative examples that may be adapted to your situation follow. The first is most appropriate for a large corporation and awards cash. The second is most appropriate for a start-up venture and awards stock.

Large Corporation Cash Incentives

Consider the following concept, which you can adjust to best satisfy your own situation. Exhibit 15-2(*a*) illustrates a new product's time line. The triad first establishes the specification with a reasonable target date for the introduction of the new product. In this case, a reasonable date is one that they, the people who must do the work, believe they can achieve and which is satisfactory to market realities. This target date may be anywhere from a few weeks to many years after the date on which the leadership sets the specification. For modestly complex industrial products, this duration from the specification to target date of introduction is frequently between one and three years; new consumer product introductions are frequently quicker. In addition, this figure shows another time mark two to five years after the target date of introduction. You choose this later time period depending on the expected life cycle of the new product. While a product may indeed sell for five or ten years, you may still choose three years for this later interval, since that is the period of time during which the product will penetrate the market and establish its success (or lack thereof). Again, for a modestly complex industrial product you might choose three or four years for this period.

The actual date of product introduction will be earlier or later than the target date, as illustrated in Exhibit 15-2(*b*). You want the incentive scheme to encourage the people working on the development to get the product to market earlier than the target date. When they can introduce the product earlier than the target date, that reduces the development period and increases the period for product sales to occur. This, in turn, increases the gross profit on those sales, as illustrated in Exhibit 15-2(*c*). The converse is also true. If the development drags on and is later than the target date, then there is a shorter period in which sales occur (between the target and the after target dates). The reason warranty costs are noted in Exhibit 15-2(*c*) is that you do not want to encourage a team to rush a defective product to market. Obviously, such haste can increase your warranty costs.

Now you can establish the incentive pool for the team by building

Exhibit 15-2. A team incentive concept.

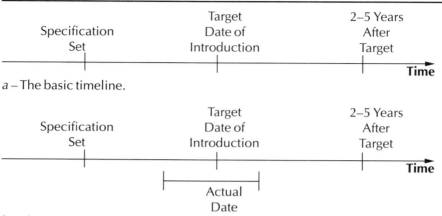

a – The basic timeline.

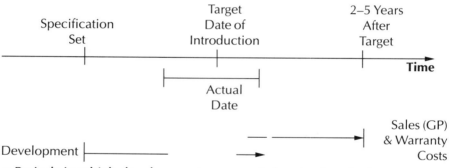

b – The time range in which the product is actually introduced.

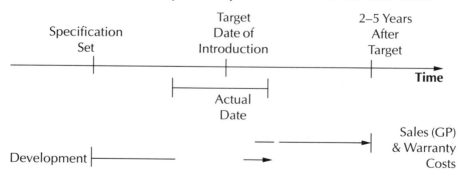

c–Periods in which development expense is incurred and sales occur.

INCENTIVE POOL = (a)(GP–bW–c[D_A–D_B])

PORTION OF POOL TO TRIAD

TRIAD DISTRIBUTES REST OF POOL TO TEAM

d – A possible incentive formula.

on this situation, as illustrated in Exhibit 15-2(*d*). The incentive pool is some percentage (fraction A) of the gross profit minus a different percentage (fraction B) of the warranty expense minus a further percentage (fraction C) of the overrun of actual development expense compared to the original budget for development expense. (There is no credit in this formula for underrunning actual development expense, since a credit could lead to sandbagging in establishing development budgets.)

This type of incentive formula encourages the people who will share it to do the right things: It encourages early introduction because they will obtain more sales and hence more gross profit; it encourages setting the right kind of specifications so that the product can earn a high gross profit; it encourages creating a high quality product to minimize warranty expense; and it encourages not overrunning the development budget. It is the sum total of efforts such as these for which senior executives are themselves commonly compensated with incentive plans. This incentive mechanism transfers a portion of what senior management is judged on to the development triads.

Finally, as suggested by Exhibit 15-2(*d*), you allocate a portion of the incentive pool, perhaps one-third, to the triad itself, to be split upon their recommendation but with senior executives' approval. The triad decides how to distribute the rest of the pool to other people. This permits the triad to allocate a significant share to some individual who made a really significant contribution, for instance a designer with a clever idea, or a worker in a model shop who made an important suggestion while working briefly on the program.

There are clearly practical problems with this concept and I do not wish to minimize them. A colleague of mine has worked out the detailed mechanics of this scheme for one corporation. Because the new product development time durations can be lengthy in the industry where this incentive plan has been installed, he has arranged for partial payments during the course of the development work. These partial incentive payments are judgmental and based on results to date. You must also deal with the fact that the triad, rather than a worker's line supervisor, may make an award to an individual under this concept.

Small Start-Up Stock Incentives

Other plans exist, some of which involve stock or stock options, and you can devise still others. For instance, Pictel Corporation rewarded a dozen key people with two shares of common stock for producing a workable prototype of a picture telephone in fifteen months; they would have received only one common share had it taken longer. To assure that the award was provided for results rather than merely an intense effort, an outside telecommunications expert was hired by the nonemployee members of the board of directors to satisfy other company shareholders. The expert was responsible for approving (or not) the prototype and certifying that it was indeed workable and met minimum requirements. The existence of this kind of clear incentive at the outset of the development effort is obviously a way to emphasize the importance of a fast development schedule.

IMPLEMENTATION CONSIDERATIONS

A key point to recall whenever you contemplate incentives is that they must reinforce what you wish to accomplish. Unfortunately, incentives are sometimes maladapted to schedule emphasis, since counterproductive nonschedule factors may also be included. Devising a measure which isolates only your objective is difficult and may require some trial and error.

In common with the concept I have devised and described above, you also have to deal with the problem of the timeliness of payments. If all the prospective rewards are too far in the future, you may not gain much advantage from the incentive plan. In general, because carelessly designed incentives can be counter-productive, you should design these with the assistance of an expert compensation specialist.

HIGHLIGHTS

The purpose of incentives is to encourage and promote behavior that products results you desire.

Incentives can be used to emphasize the importance of a demanding new product development schedule.

Incentive awards may be instant or deferred, organizational or professional, group or individual, and monetary or other.

Many incentive programs, such as the Pictel example, require the approval of top management or the board of directors.

An incentive plan must be carefully designed.

Chapter 16
Continuing Adaptation

The senior management of a company is largely responsible for establishing the tone of the organization and facilitating (or obstructing) the process by which new products are rapidly developed and introduced. This chapter discusses what senior management can do about procedures, their options when a new product problem arises, how to use post mortems to identify helpful changes, and the organization's climate.

KEEPING PROCEDURES FLEXIBLE

Faster new product procedures cannot be static, because new and better tools are constantly being devised, technology is changing, and people are learning how to execute more quickly. Thus, whatever procedures your company adopts today must continue to evolve. You can make changes as a result of this book (and any other advice) but you must remain flexible. Nevertheless, there are some guiding principles to maintain.

Senior executives are responsible for arranging shorter decision chains, regardless of how the company is organized and the specific new product development procedure. While I believe forms and written procedures can be helpful in bringing the successful prior practices of the corporation to bear and in avoiding well known pitfalls, your goal should be to have only the necessary people involved in any new product development decision.

There is always a risk when you simplify the procedural requirements. For example, in one case, a new product team was designing a spectrophotometer, an instrument which requires a lamp. The technical service group reviewed this design and was satisfied. Nevertheless, the lamp, which inherently requires periodic replacement by the user, was located where service would be difficult (at best). This design flaw was only corrected when a senior executive with several decades of industry experience noticed the lamp's location during a walk through the development laboratory.

Since no procedure can guarantee that you will not commit errors, you want the fewest forms and signatures that are practical. You require mechanisms that assure decisions (and occasional mistakes) are made quickly and that any necessary signatures are easy to obtain. As I said previously, when you lose a day or a week in conducting a major review, you delay the new product's introduction. The same is true for time lost in obtaining a required signature. You simply must have mechanisms in place which preclude this kind of sticky wicket. Some companies assign signature authority to the development team leader(s) so long as they are operating within the development schedule and budget.

OPTIONS FOR SOLVING PROCEDURE PROBLEMS

A salutary adjunct of the phased approach is that cognizant management must review each new product development effort at critical phases. These reviews must not go by the book and produce knee-jerk reactions to problems. Each situation is specific, calling for creative cleverness rather than a general prescription. For example, senior managers should have a clear understanding of, and assurance that, resources are being applied appropriately. Or, when there are insufficient resources available for timely completion of the next phase, the new product development triad and its management can mutually confront the options enumerated in Exhibit 16-1.

In many cases, the three options in Exhibit 16-1 are not explicitly considered and the involved managers implicitly just hope for a miracle. Since miracles do not routinely, if ever, occur, the absence of an explicit option choice produces disappointment, or worse. Conversely, a candid, open discussion of these options helps to establish a healthy climate for

Exhibit 16-1. Three options when there is a problem during a new product development effort.

1. Obtain other (typically external) resources to maintain the development schedule.
2. Continue the new product development effort without sufficient resources, that is, work to a later schedule.
3. Stop the development effort.

faster new product development, even if the specific project must be somewhat later than its best schedule.

A well-understood phased approach is especially helpful in the very large corporation. Very large corporations have the financial and other resources necessary to undertake major new product development efforts, the duration of which may thus span many years. Separating technology development from product development seems to be very important in such organizations. Panasonic reportedly separates these into development of a technology platform (what I have called the feasibility activity) and the product (what I have called the development activity).

To put it differently, it is important that the technology be functionally sound before commercialization efforts are initiated. In addition, there is often a different group, typically a division, with responsibility for commercialization, whereas the technology is often first proven in a corporate or other research and development laboratory. In this situation, it is very important that the customer (for example, a divisional business unit) be identified very early so it can become a voluntary participant in picking up the technology to move it forward. When the management of the commercialization division is thus involved in reviews, the technology developers can get feedback and react to negative information and skeptical criticism very early.

USING POST MORTEMS

Senior executives, with the leadership triad, should arrange for a post mortem at the conclusion of a new product development effort, whether it is successful or otherwise. The act of recording lessons learned forces you to think about what went well and what did not go well.

The post mortem provides the basis for modifying standard operating procedures so that future new product development efforts can be pursued more easily and quickly. It is obviously difficult to conduct such post mortems objectively, so you may wish to have this done by an outsider, for instance, a staff person from another part of the corporation or a management consultant. Once I was retained by a new product development manager to conduct a benchmark post mortem at a major program milestone; the objective was to record the impressions of a dozen key participants at this midstream point while memories were fresh.

The key to a useful post mortem is objectivity; it is not intended to furnish praise for the sponsor of the post mortem, nor should it use outsiders to relieve supervisors of assigning blame to individuals who made disastrous mistakes. The result has to be constructive change and improvement for the future. For example, in one company, a retrospective examination of several new product development efforts revealed a consistent pattern that the triad leadership lacked enough control of team members. This led to a stronger project leadership organization for selected critical efforts.

ESTABLISHING A CREATIVE CLIMATE

The senior management of a corporation is responsible for establishing a climate in which new product development can be accomplished quickly. Senior executives can create a climate that encourages new product risk taking or promote the status quo, as illustrated in Exhibit 16-2. For instance, it is important for these leaders to frequently emphasize that a decision to discontinue an existing product or stop a new

Exhibit 16-2.   Two extreme options for corporate climate.

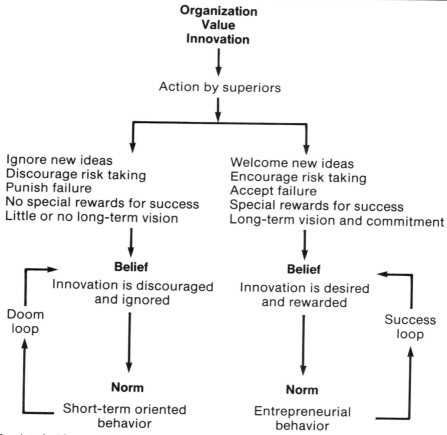

product development program is not opposition to innovation or risk-taking.

Instead, senior management and the new product development leadership triad must provide a climate of positive reinforcement. If any of these executives (or other managers) discover a schedule problem, they can ask what they can do to help overcome the problem rather than blaming someone. They can help by trying to provide schedule acceleration tools, such as responsive model shops, fast reaction purchasing (for example to quickly acquire items required for a breadboard), and other support to speed the new product development effort. Senior executives can praise teams that perform close to, or ideally, on schedule.

The leadership triad and the team members are naturally going to be concerned about their career paths as well as the immediate new product development effort. What impact will success (or failure) of the new product have on them, both collectively and individually? Does their authority correspond to their responsibility? Senior executives must address these concerns, and provide specific assurances. Further, if senior executives are not going to provide support and commitment, they should openly clarify why.

In one case a corporate vice president was given responsibility for the leadership of a new product development effort that had been running for a few years. He decided that the team members, most of whom had been working on this effort for several years, would get a portion of the profits if the effort succeeded, but would be terminated if it failed. This change was a severe personal threat to one key team member (whose wife was very ill), so he quickly resigned to accept a more secure situation.

While it is important that the climate for new product development—especially fast new product development—be positive, that does not mean that senior executives must accept efforts which are defective. For example, one person said to me, "We have projects under way which do not have a plan." Clearly, no responsible manager should allow this, even though they are doing as much as they otherwise can to encourage innovative efforts. Similarly, senior executives must ultimately accept all the attendant risks of introducing a new product to the marketplace, including, for instance, potential liability.

The role of senior executives is to encourage and support new product development efforts. Visible enthusiasm can help. This is not the same thing as imposing their own pet new product development idea onto a reluctant group of subordinates. Unless there is a real champion who is a volunteer among the working level personnel, such an imposed effort is unlikely to be successful.

Clearly, management's institution of the mechanisms I have reviewed in this book will affect many people in the corporation. Senior executives and other managers cannot change the organization's climate overnight. All must recognize that dramatic changes will take time and patience.

HIGHLIGHTS

Faster new product procedures cannot be static.

The actions of all levels of management can facilitate—or delay—faster new product development.

Conduct objective post mortems to record lessons learned and then revise procedures based on these lessons.

The senior management of a company is primarily responsible for establishing the climate of the organization.

Part V
Other Issues

Part V covers some residual topics of importance that do not logically fit into the four previous parts. There are chapters covering the implementation of a new and faster approach to development, developing new services (in distinction from products), and how to continue to seek further improvement in the speed with which you and your company develop new products.

Chapter 17

Implementing a Fast Approach

The general guideline for procedures you adopt to implement a fast approach, phased or otherwise, is to keep these simple and flexible. In addition, each activity and phase requires certain specific elements. You should install a phased approach or modify the approach you now use in your company as you select new feasibility and development activity projects.

GENERAL GROUND RULES

Consider the following statement of philosophy from a good new product development procedure one of my clients has adopted:

> [A] product procedure only acts as a framework around which people can be productive. It helps us to focus our activities and to understand what needs to be done, when it needs to be done, and who needs to do it. A procedure won't give us good ideas and it won't make good products.

There is obviously much more in their brief procedure than this opening statement, which establishes such a helpful focus and underpinning. The procedure itself uses phases similar to those I have proposed and the company is beginning to achieve shorter time-to-market for new products.

Conversely, a company may have a phased approach that is ineffectual because it deals more with form than substance. There are three main problems: (1) voluminous detail; (2) attempting to deal with every imaginable possibility; and (3) assignment of lead departments or compartmentalization.

Developing a Workable Procedure Manual

A written procedure must be both understandable and helpful to the people who will be doing the new product development. Unfortunately, some companies have thick, voluminous manuals to describe their new product development procedure. When this is the case, the sheer bulk normally inhibits voluntary use of the procedure. I know of one company where the bulky procedure manual is approximately three inches thick and is the point of many barbed jokes. The overhead cost, especially time of key people, to keep each copy current is also very high. Another company computerized its procedures so every person has access to the current version on his or her own terminal. You may wish to emulate this approach, since it potentially reduces the overhead cost of maintaining a current procedure manual.

I suggest the following four guidelines to avoid voluminous detail:

1. Keep the procedures or company rules brief, probably less than fifteen pages.
2. Provide a pictorial road map to indicate which procedures are used at what time during the new product development process.
3. Keep required paperwork, such as forms, authorization, and reports to an absolute minimum consistent with adequate control.
4. Provide examples of completed forms so that employees can refer to these when necessary.

Appendix F contains abstracts from the procedures used by two companies for new product development. Some of the elements in these procedures follow those delineated in Exhibit 2-6. While neither of these procedures is contemporary nor has led to remarkably fast new product development, they are illustrative of what you want to include and ways to format your own procedures.

The first of these two procedures has the virtue that it requires only a dozen pages of text for the complete version, although there are appendices containing additional detail. This procedure would be clearer to development personnel if it included an illustration comparable to Exhibit 17-1 to serve as a road map to help understand the procedure. (Exhibit 17-1 is a conceptual illustration. Other activities, phases, and forms might be more appropriate for your company.)

The road map concept can be implemented with examples. The second procedure in Appendix F, which is an edited version of another company's procedure, required only three and one-half typed pages. It

Exhibit 17-1. Illustrative "road map" to guide personnel through new product development procedure.

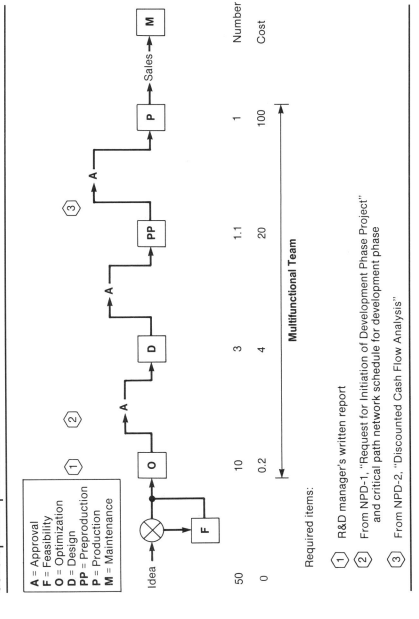

A = Approval
F = Feasibility
O = Optimization
D = Design
PP = Preproduction
P = Production
M = Maintenance

Required items:

① R&D manager's written report

② From NPD-1, "Request for Initiation of Development Phase Project" and critical path network schedule for development phase

③ From NPD-2, "Discounted Cash Flow Analysis"

was followed by seventeen pages of completed examples, which is obviously helpful.

As previously stated, no procedure should ever be allowed to become a straight-jacket. Some companies choose to make options explicit in their new product development procedure and process. The resulting new product development flow sequence diagram thus has frequent optional loops to allow additional work in a preceding phase or to signify discontinuation options, as illustrated in Exhibit 17-2.

While there is nothing inherently wrong in this, it seems to be needlessly complex. It is always understood that additional work may be required or that the development can be stopped. Your company's new product development procedure, whatever the details, will be simpler if it presumes success and is not all-encompassing.

Whatever procedures are adopted should be flexible. This requires permission to deviate from the specific details of the procedure, provided it is undertaken for some very important reason (such as to save time) and has the concurrence of appropriate levels of management.

For example, it may be appropriate in some situations to authorize the procurement of certain long-lead materials required for a subsequent phase during a present phase if this offers a substantial time or cost saving. In other situations, it may be desirable to combine or omit some phases.

Exhibit 17-2. A portion of the new product development flow sequence with an explicit option to do additional development or discontinue work.

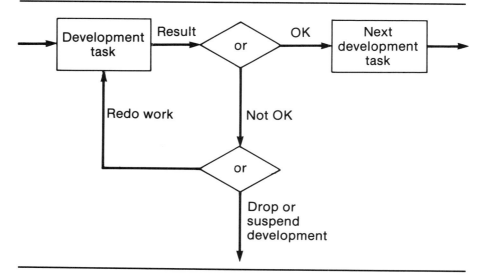

Determining Lead Departments

Exhibit 17-3 illustrates a distressingly common pitfall, namely the situation in which one department is expected to perform all the work in an activity or phase and then pass the result or output on to another department, which then performs the next work. This system of monodepartmentalism for a phase has been likened to passing the baton in a relay race. Unfortunately, the analogy is poor because this method of new product development is slow and rarely exhibits cooperative multifunctional teamwork. In fact, it tends to exacerbate interdepartmental disharmony, as I discuss in Chapter 10. In the words of a new product development manager, "It is a difficult challenge to hand responsibility from one organization to another." The first department blames the next for destroying its good work, whereas the second department says that the output from the first group was unworkable.

GUIDELINES FOR EACH PHASE

There are some additional specific guidelines and elements to consider for inclusion in the procedures you adopt for use during each of the major activities (and phases): feasibility; development (optimization, design, preproduction, and production); and maintenance.

Exhibit 17-3. Monodepartmentalism per phase.

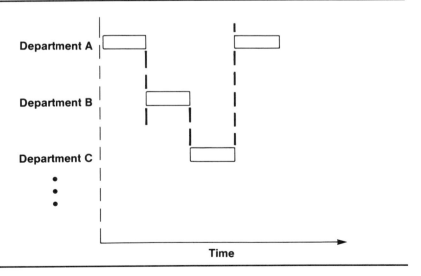

Feasibility Activity

Normally, the manager of the research and development (or comparable) function initiates feasibility activity projects. These projects are chosen to be consistent with corporate strategy, as was previously illustrated in Exhibit 7-1. Cognizant management should review the projects that have been undertaken at least annually, with all senior management, including the functional heads of engineering or development, marketing, and manufacturing. Ideally, all of these people will concur on the projects to be undertaken.

From time to time the research and development (or advanced engineering) department will undertake investigations of a new technology that is sufficiently advanced so that its practical value may not yet be clear to other people, at least during the initial investigatory work. Whenever any feasibility project is authorized, however, there should be at least a hypothetical scenario of how successful work will apply to the business of the corporation.

Some level of management must also review each feasibility activity project every three months for progress against what was scheduled to be accomplished during that interval. At these reviews the members of the work team should provide a schedule for what they propose to accomplish during the subsequent three-month period. It is not necessary for them to guarantee that an experiment will succeed or that they will make a technological breakthrough within every three-month period. However, if investigators commit to carrying out specific experiments or other work, they should indeed be held accountable for actually doing the proposed work.

If it is successful, the feasibility activity for a particular project ends with a demonstration, a model, and a report. From time to time, it will become apparent that a particular project is not yielding a successful outcome and that further feasibility work is no longer justified. In this case, end the feasibility project, and prepare a clear report documenting the work that was accomplished and the rationales for stopping.

The reason that a documenting report is important is that sometime later a market or technology change may justify restarting either further feasibility or development activity work. Unless a clear report is available from the previous feasibility activity, it may be necessary to redo a lot of the previous feasibility work. The reports that conclude a feasibility activity project, whether you recommend subsequent development or not, need not be lengthy; what is crucial is that they be complete and comprehensible to people who will make use of the outcome, namely practical-minded people such as marketing, engineering, and manufacturing personnel.

Two other issues deserve consideration when deciding whether to initiate the development activity:

1. It is important to avoid producing a product or service that may be needed but which is inconsistent with your basic business strategy. In the long run, an effort that is diversionary to the basic business will be starved for the required resources.

2. Be leery of any technologically advanced product. The research or engineering staff will often be overly enthusiastic because it is technically challenging and thus exciting. Unless there is a clear market opportunity, it probably will be more profitable to leave your development money in a bank account.

Development Activity

In the conduct of the development activity (however it is subdivided into phases), each project has a triple constraint composed of a performance goal, a schedule goal, and a budget goal. The performance goal is typically the complete design and prototyping of the product that has specified user attributes and a correspondingly suitable selling price (or factory cost). The development effort, which is a project, also has a project time schedule and a project expense budget. These latter two are the time and expense of carrying out the development phase work. Be careful not to confuse compliance with the development project's expense budget, which is stated in dollars, with attainment of one of the performance goals of the product development effort, namely the selling price (or a specified factory cost), which is also expressed in dollars. The selling price (or factory cost) is a performance attribute, in common with various other technical or utility features of the product. The development expense budget is one of the three dimensions of a development activity project's triple constraint.

Other guidelines for development activity projects include:

1. Be sure there are clear product or service attributes such that appropriate effort is devoted to features that are important to the majority of the ultimate market. Identify the critical attributes for success (musts) and concentrate the development effort on these; devote effort to secondary attributes (wants) only after it is clear that the critical ones have been or can be attained.

2. Try to persuade your best development people that the biggest market opportunity is the most challenging undertaking to which they can devote their skills. Do not let your best people work on relatively unimportant development efforts, even if in-

tellectually exciting, while major development efforts are supported by the second team.

3. Avoid investment in new versions or models of obsolete products. A touch-tone keyboard and a digital display is not going to create a successful 78-rpm record player. You must be certain your market target is sensible.

Exhibit 17-4 illustrates a form that you might use to initiate the development activity. If the must and want attributes are not clear at the start of the development activity itself, then the start of the development activity must be broken into separate optimization and design phases. Then you would have another form, comparable to that in Exhibit 17-4, to complete at the end of the optimization phase to authorize the start of the design phase. It is rare that you can thoughtfully construct these musts and wants without conducting market research.

You can schedule and manage the work in the development activity as an engineering (or similar) project. As stated in Chapter 12, you can apply the proven tools and techniques of project management here. In particular, a fast development schedule will be more likely if you plan the work with a critical path network schedule and then monitor it with weekly or monthly project reviews.

In terms of financial commitment, the most critical management review of the entire phased approach is usually the one to start the production phase. To save time, as stated in Chapter 14, this review should be the same review that confirms the successful completion of the preproduction phase. This normally is the time at which you must authorize the major expenditures (for example, for tooling, inventory, and promotion). Thus, there should no longer be significant unknowns about the market, the competition, or the product. At this point, the development activity usually includes a discounted cash flow analysis to forecast your financial return for the new product. This can't be done until the specifications (musts and wants) are complete, the design is fairly advanced, and the market research is complete. (Earlier justifications for feasibility and development activity work can only include educated financial estimates, since critical data are not yet available.) However, remember: Use financial analysis to determine the consequences of the actions you will take in carrying out your development project, and do not let financial analysis determine what your development will be.

Last, but by no means least important, is the challenge to avoid changes during the development phase work. Good engineers will see many possibilities to improve upon specifications, just as excited marketing people will see opportunities to change the target specifications

(*text continued on page 199*)

Exhibit 17-4. A Development Project Authorization Form.

REQUEST FOR INITIATION OF DEVELOPMENT PROJECT

Product Description _____

Date _____

Submitted by:

_____ Product Manager

_____ Project Engineer

_____ Manufacturing Manager

Approved by:

_____ Product Planning Manager

_____ Controller

_____ Vice President, Marketing

_____ Vice President, Engineering

_____ Vice President, Manufacturing

Costs greater than $250,000 or exceeding approved budgets:

_____ Vice President, Finance

_____ President

Costs greater than $500,000:

_____ Chairman of the Board

Exhibit 17-4. (continued)

Program objectives: _____
_____
_____
_____

Justification: _____
_____
_____
_____

Technical specifications:
  Musts: _____
_____
_____

  Wants: _____
_____
_____
_____

Estimated sensitivity of volume to costs & schedule:

	Musts	Musts + Wants
Target Product Cost / Sales impact of:		
− 10%		
+ 10%		
+ 20%		
Scheduled Introduction / Sales impact of:		
− 6 months		
+ 6 months		
+ 12 months		

Critical considerations (if any): _____

_____

_____

_____

Expected impact on personnel or space needs: _____

_____

_____

_____

Schedule:
  Completion of development project: _____

_____

_____

  Estimated market introduction: _____

_____

_____

_____

SUMMARY

Group	Advantages	Risks
Engineering		
Manufacturing		
Marketing		

in many ways. These enhancements, desirable as they may be, should be deferred. BETTER IS THE ENEMY OF GOOD ENOUGH, and the product whose specifications (the musts and wants) are constantly changing is the product that will never be produced at all. The enhanced product should be the next product, subsequently justified and authorized as an additional development effort.

There will be occasions when you should or must terminate a development activity project because the specifications at which it is aimed are demonstrably no longer sufficient. When this is the case, suspend work and re-examine the opportunity for the product concept if, for instance, the market conditions have changed. The Edsel was developed after thorough market research, but that research was obsolete before the car was produced. You can always terminate a development project, even if it is in the middle of the production phase, and consider whether to authorize a new development activity project to replace it. In some cases, the entire activity should be abandoned.

Maintenance Activity

Maintenance activity projects are usually short. They tend to be quick fixes. Perhaps a customer has a problem with an early version of the product, or the sales force encounters some difficulty with the product. These kinds of problems may lead to the initiation of a maintenance activity project, the goal of which is to fix that particular problem. You should start these maintenance activity projects just as quickly as possible after the problem is identified; it is unwise to wait until monthly or quarterly progress reviews are held. In some cases, the resolution for these problems will suggest the opportunity for an entirely different new product development activity. When that is the case, the people charged with the maintenance activities should provide the marketing, engineering, and manufacturing departments with adequate guidance as to what is required in a new effort. After you have installed and adjusted your own phased approach, you can then initiate all subsequent maintenance activity projects using your new procedure, regardless of whether or not the product's development was done with the phased approach.

INSTALLING A PHASED APPROACH

It is not easy to install an improved new product development procedure. As ancient as it is, Machiavelli provides important cautionary advice:

> It must be remembered that there is nothing more difficult to plan, more uncertain of success, nor more dangerous to manage than the creation of a new order of things. For the initiator has the enmity of all who would profit by the preservation of the old institutions, and merely lukewarm defenders in those who would gain by the new ones.

To put this counsel differently, in the words of a new product development manager, "trying to change methods while product development is moving along at a frantic pace" is a difficult challenge. There are two methods by which you might logically install a phased approach in your company:

1. Impose the new method immediately on all existing and additional new product development programs; or
2. Introduce the new method as you start additional new product development programs.

Exhibit 17-5 shows four projects. The first two are in progress at the time you decide to initiate your company's new phased approach, the third will start after that date, and the fourth is quiescent (paused between two phases or activities) then. Clearly the first should be exempted from the new procedure and the third should comply. In the case of the second, you have to make a trade-off between time lost to restart it and letting it proceed for a long time as a hangover or grandfather clause exemption. In the case of the fourth, you have a comparable decision for the activity or phase that will soon start. Now, let's consider the two courses in more detail.

Immediate Installation

The obvious virtue of this method is that you might improve your company's entire process immediately. Unfortunately, there are three problems with this method that argue against doing this:

Exhibit 17-5. Starting to apply your company's phased new product development procedure.

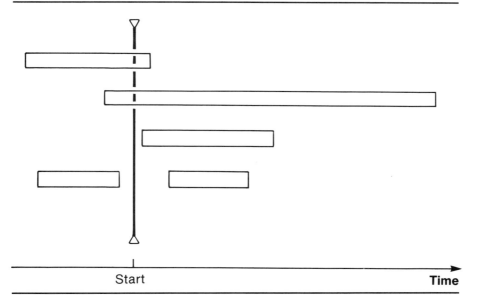

Start   Time

1. You have to put a new set of untested procedures into practice without the chance to learn how they can be adjusted and improved for your own company's style.
2. You must educate your entire staff immediately.
3. Some existing new product development programs (for example, the first, second, and fourth illustrated in Exhibit 17-5) will lack the proper base of orderly background information that an effective phased approach requires.

New Program Initiation Installation

The advantages of installing at the initiation of a new program are the exact converse of the disadvantages of immediate installation. By starting small, you can see where your new procedures have rough edges that can be smoothed off. And, since the obvious goal is to simplify the total procedure and minimize paperwork, this gives you a chance to modify your new procedure quickly and easily. Also, you have to train only the people who have key roles on a few new product development programs, with the concomitant benefit that you do not have to educate the entire staff if you subsequently make modifications to your procedures. And there is no necessity to back up to improve the information background in programs that have been initiated in your previous (perhaps unsystematic) way.

The disadvantage is that it may take two or three years to impose the phased approach on all new product development programs. However, this seems to be a comparatively small penalty given the advantages of this installation method. Realistically, you must allow sufficient time to dramatically improve the way your company develops new products quickly; a simple quick fix is unlikely to yield substantial gains.

Exhibit 17-6 illustrates the concept of installing a phased approach as you initiate additional new product development projects. The hypothetical situation covers ten new product development projects (labeled A through J) over a period of several months. Your own company might initiate either more or fewer projects, but that changes the details, not the principles. Also, your company's new product development projects may be shorter or longer than those illustrated, which, again, only alters the details. This procedural initiation should be done at the start of the new product development program's feasibility activity or optimization phase (or, rarely, if the optimization phase can be omitted, at the start of the design phase).

Situation at the start of the first month. Your company initiates five new product development programs (projects A through E). Project A is a feasibility activity project, forecast to require three months, all of

(*text continued on page 215*)

Exhibit 17-6A. Start of first month.

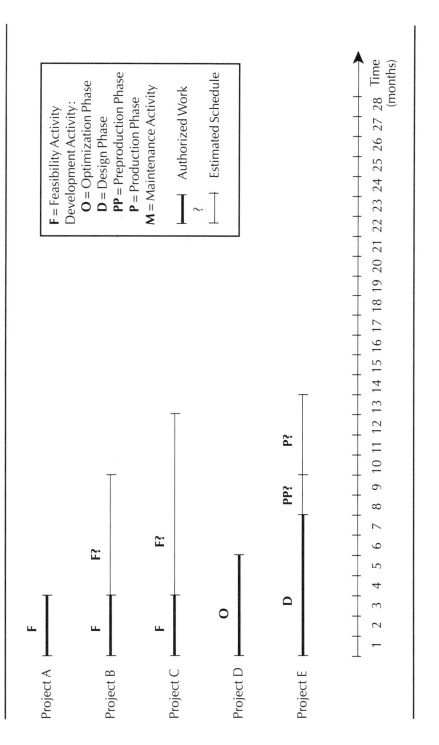

Exhibit 17-6B. Start of fourth month.

Project A   **F**

Project C   **F**

Project D   **O**

Project E   **D**

1 2 3 4 5 6 7 8 9 10 11 12 13 14 15 16 17 18 19 20 21 22 23 24 25 26 27 28   Time (months)

Exhibit 17-6C. Start of sixth month.

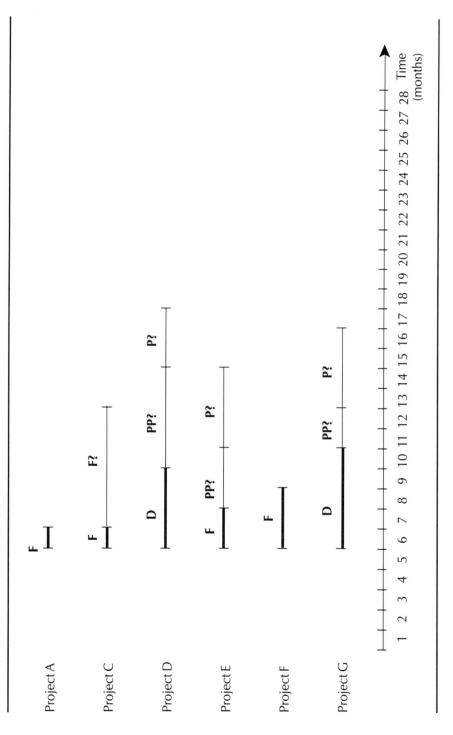

Exhibit 17-6D. Start of seventh month.

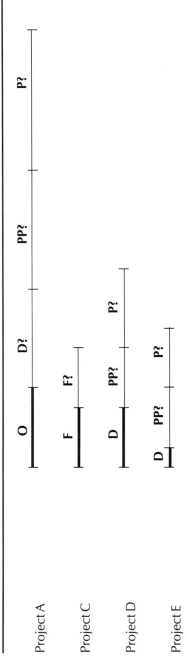

Project A

Project C

Project D

Project E

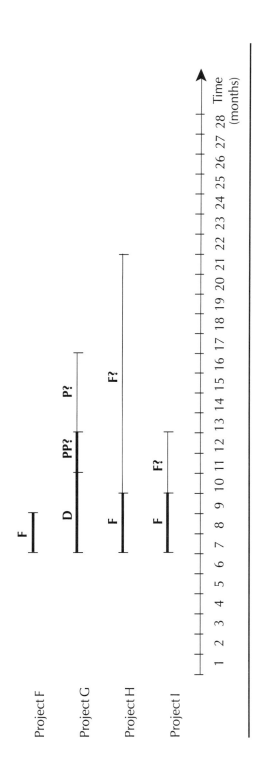

Exhibit 17-6E. Start of eighth month.

Project A

Project C

Project D

Project E

Project F

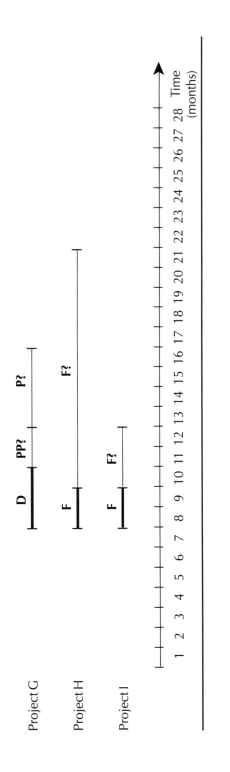

Exhibit 17-6F. Start of ninth month.

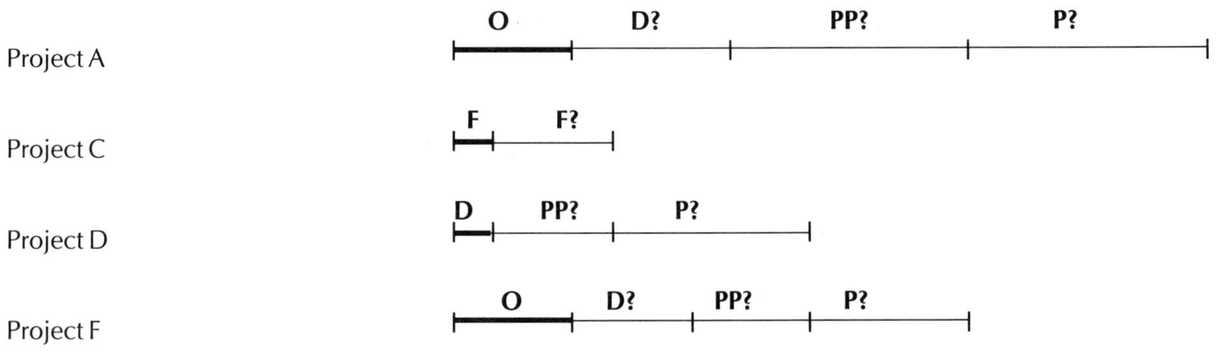

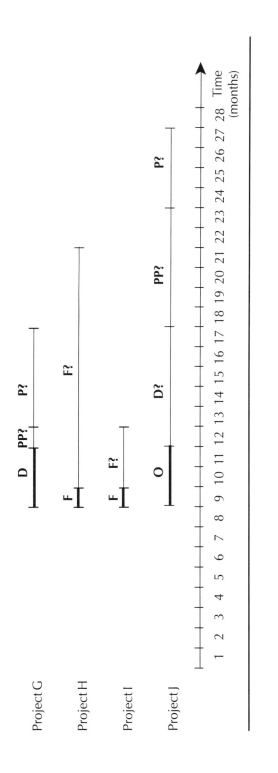

Exhibit 17-6G. Start of tenth month.

Project A   O   D?   PP?   P?

Project C   F

Project D   PP   P?

Project F   D   PP?   P?

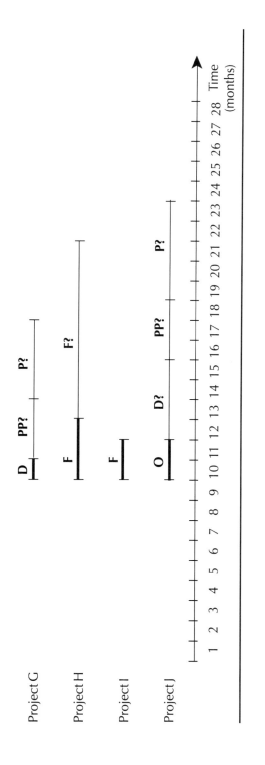

Exhibit 17-6H. Start of twentieth month.

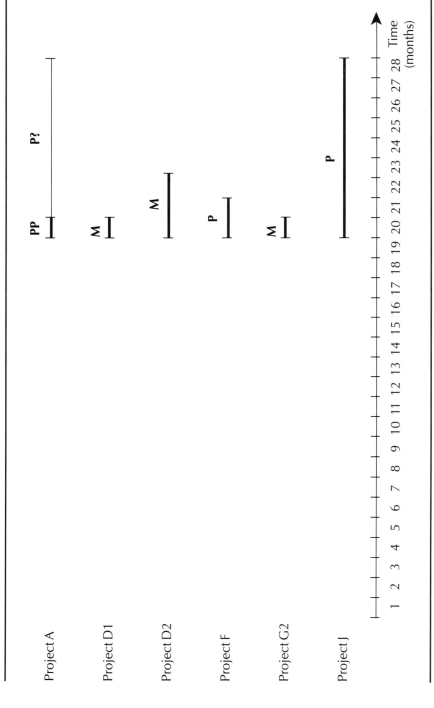

which are authorized. Project B is also a feasibility activity project, forecast to require nine months, of which only three are authorized. Project C is also a feasibility activity project, forecast to require a year, of which only the first three months are authorized. Project D starts with the development activity because there is no unproven technology; however, there are so many options for what should be developed (with attendant total development activity time uncertain) that only a five-month optimization phase (and no design phase) is authorized. Project E does not require any optimization, since the specific embodiment that the market requires is clear. It thus starts in the design phase, scheduled for seven months. In addition, the triad estimates the subsequent phases (if subsequently authorized) will require six more months.

Situation at the start of the fourth month. The team working on project A has produced promising results and an additional three months of feasibility work is authorized. Project B is discontinued. Project C is progressing as expected and an additional three months of feasibility activity work is authorized. Projects D and E continue, although it now appears that Project E's remaining phases will require seven months.

Situation at the start of the sixth month. There is no change in the situation for projects A, C, and E. The team responsible for project D delivers a satisfactory optimization phase result, so your company authorizes a four-month design phase and the triad team estimates that the subsequent phases (if authorized) will require eight months. The company initiates project F with a feasibility activity authorization of three months. A design phase of five months is authorized for Project G and the team provides a six-month estimate for the subsequent phases (if authorized).

Situation at the start of the seventh month. Project A's feasibility work has been successful and an optimization phase project of four months is authorized. Subsequent phases (if authorized) are estimated to require seventeen additional months. An additional three months of feasibility work is authorized on project C. Projects D, E, F, and G continue with no change. Two new feasibility activity efforts, projects H (fifteen months) and project I (six months), are started, for which the first three months' work on each is authorized.

Situation at the start of the eighth month. There is no change in any program except project E, where, unfortunately, the design phase completion has slipped one month. A decision must be made whether or not to allow it to continue. Since you believe a short time extension is the lesser evil in this case, there is a forecast delay in both the start and completion of the subsequent phases.

Situation at the start of the ninth month. There is no change in projects A, C, D, G, H, and I. Project E is discontinued at the (late) completion of the design phase. A two-month optimization phase is authorized on project F, with subsequent phases (if authorized) estimated to require ten months. A three-month optimization phase for a new program, project J, is authorized and subsequent phases (if authorized) are estimated to require sixteen months.

   Situation at the start of the tenth month. There is no change in projects A and G. A further three months of feasibility work is authorized on project C. The design phase for project D was completed, and a two-month preproduction phase is thus authorized and the production phase (if authorized) is forecast to require six months. The optimization work on project F is completed one month earlier than expected, the four month design phase is authorized, and the forecast for the remaining phases (if authorized) is moved forward. An additional three months feasibility effort is authorized on project H. In the case of project I, a breakthrough occurred, but a little more feasibility work is required, so only two months' more feasibility effort is authorized. Work on project J is also encouraging, focusing on a simple optimized approach, suggesting that the remaining development activity phases (if authorized) will require only twelve months.

   Situation at the start of the twentieth month. Project A continues in the preproduction phase. Project C has been terminated. Project D products are now selling, and the first two maintenance efforts, projects D1 and D2, are authorized for one and two months, respectively. The production phases for projects F and J are now forecast (and authorized) to end two and four months later, respectively, than the forecast at the start of the tenth month. (The breakthrough on project I was rapidly exploited and a new product is already being sold, which is why it does not appear in Exhibit 17-6H.) The second maintenance phase effort for project G, project G2, is authorized for two weeks. (The first, project G1, occurred at some point after the product's introduction, but before the start of the twentieth month.)

HIGHLIGHTS

Stress simplicity and speed as you implement a fast phased approach for new product development.

Install an orderly, thorough approach to the development of new products.

While you can install a phased approach in your company immediately, it is better to do this as you initiate additional new product development programs.

Chapter 18

Special Considerations for New Services

Services are pervasive. They are big business and rapidly growing in total extent. Services differ from products in several ways, but there are enough similarities to use the tools and techniques that have already been described in this book. There are, however, two special considerations to which you must give attention in developing new services rapidly.

THE MAGNITUDE OF SERVICES

Services are diverse as shown in Exhibit 18-1 and contribute approximately twice as much as products to the gross national product. Specifically, private services comprise approximately 60 percent of the gross national product, products are about 30 percent and the remaining 10 percent is government services.

Services are both low (or no) and high technology. There are, for instance, dog walkers and window washers at one end of the technology spectrum and such skills as software development at the other. Providers may have no, or very little, skill (pizza delivery) or a specialized skill (child care). The same provider, for instance, a window washer, may serve both individual consumers and businesses. The scale may be small (an individual value-added reseller) to very large (for instance, Capture, American Airlines' new system to help businesses track travel costs of individuals).

The data are, of course, somewhat blurred. For instance, if you manufacture a product and your company has its own sales force, then the contribution of that sales effort to the gross national product appears within the product segment. However, if you sell your output through

Exhibit 18-1.   Diverse services.

Banking, for which there is a huge proliferation of products and suppliers

Communications of both voice and data

Education

Health care, including dental, medical, nursing, psychological

Professional services, which includes accountants, architects, consulting engineers, insurance, lawyers, management consultants

Protection, which includes private alarm and guard services in addition to conventional police and fire protection

Transportation, which includes airlines and air freight, rail, barge, and roads

---

sales representatives or wholesalers, then the value of that selling effort will show up as a private service under the wholesale trade segment of the gross national product. Similarly, if you perform your own product design, market research, and accounting or other data analysis, those efforts are measured as a part of the manufacturing segment of the product portion of the gross national product. If these services are provided to you by outside independent contractors, then they will show up as other services within the private service sector.

While there is great precision in measuring the segment contributions to the product portion of the gross national product, the same precision is not available within the private services segment, due, in large part, to the fact that the standard industrial classification system used by our government is badly out of date. In fact, perhaps the best definition of private services is that these comprise everything except products (agriculture, forestry, and fishing; mining and construction; and all manufacturing), and government services.

Regardless of measurement detail, everyone agrees that the service segment of the economy is growing more rapidly than the product segment. Currently, there are at least three trends which fuel this growth.

1. Corporate restructuring and downsizing, which has led to reduced internal staffs. Services these staffs traditionally provided, for instance, public relations and advertising, must now be provided by external service providers.

2. The internationalization of business, which has led to a dramatic increase in communications and transportation services. Facsimile (or fax) costs more than boat mail or air mail, but it's justified today by the tremendous need for all business to move faster, with the result that this increases communication costs. Similarly, widespread businesses frequently use small packages for lengthy communications and there is a huge increase in small package express service.

3. The privatization of services traditionally provided by various governmental entities. This leads to an increase in the private service segment of the gross national product, as well as business opportunities for the companies that provide it.

Other factors may be present. For instance, information services, such as on-line electronic data bases, can be expanded almost infinitely and the variety of information provided can be tailored quite specifically to users' needs.

CHARACTERISTICS OF SERVICES

Services are different than tangible products. Products are things, whereas services depend on performance and are thus more ephemeral.

There are three characteristics of services which you should understand to appreciate how they differ from products.

1. Services are intangible. That is, you cannot see or touch the service. To overcome this limitation, one cruise line company shows prospective travelers a videotape to make the food and amenities more tangible. In general, however, a service's intangibility means that you cannot examine a service prior to purchase or use. That is, services are not a product or construction, and frequently, are thus very easy to create.

2. Services are produced and consumed simultaneously and are thus highly perishable. An unsold airplane seat can never produce revenue on that flight and an unsold hotel room cannot be a revenue generator. Services cannot be stored or possessed (although electronic databases would appear to be an exception to this principle). A customer buys the use of an airplane seat or a hotel room, but does not own it. They retain the memory of the total experience encountered in the use of that service. Because services are easy to create, and are produced and consumed simultaneously, there is a danger that you can saturate your operations staff by proliferating your services too widely. I will say more about this point later.

3. Services are heterogeneous. They are produced and consumed at many locations, for instance, every car rental counter. The quality of service is crucially dependent upon the person who provides it to the consumer at the location. Traditional product marketing has the four Ps, namely, product, price, place, and promotion, as key characteristics for marketing. This has led to a fifth P for services, personality.

The three As are perhaps more useful than the fifth P. In this view, service heterogeneity depends upon the ability, affability, and availability of the point of contact. This implies a tremendous need for staff training, which will be discussed later.

In some situations, the availability of the service is reduced because there is a long queue precluding easy access. For example, at one bank in Tennessee, customers had to wait forty minutes to reach a teller. This availability level was unacceptable, and required the service provider, the bank, to rearrange teller work hours. In fact, some queues have irreducible seasonal fluctuations, for instance, at passport offices before the spring and summer travel seasons. This has created another service in which providers will stand in line for you at those locations.

In general, all services have the distinguishing characteristics described above. However, it has been pointed out that service for business and industrial markets differ somewhat from those for individual or consumer markets. Frequently the services are more technically complex, can involve substantial amounts of money, and the provider and user thus, in many situations, work cooperatively on the specification and development. This can lead to much longer term relationships and to services which are unique to a specific user. Some services are sold and provided in conjunction with a product. Car financing is a common example. One paint manufacturer not only provides the paint to a car manufacturer, but also does the application engineering for the paint, and supervises the car manufacturer personnel who apply the paint. Finally, on-going maintenance service on products previously produced by your firm may include periodic maintenance or the provision of spare parts on a timely basis; overnight part delivery is thus a service to augment a previously produced part. In fact, some companies put distribution centers at the hub of overnight air delivery providers (for instance, Memphis, Tennessee, to make use of Federal Express).

Although some services involve no or low technology, others depend quite critically on technology. The technical skill of the paint provider at the car factory is crucial and requires extensive research and development or application laboratories at the paint manufacturer's headquarters. Similarly, when overnight package delivery was just starting, Federal Express chose airplanes as its technology. Purolator, at that time, was using trucks. Trucks as a technology resulted in low cost, so Purolator's advertisements at that time could stress low price and the market was thus those people for whom low price was important, mainly purchasing agents and shipping departments. Conversely, the use of airplanes at Federal Express led to reliability and speed, advertisements that stressed (guaranteed, in fact) 10:30 A.M. delivery, and this service was targeted to executives and their secretaries.

Similarly, one company has built a unique service business repairing automotive and truck windshields. This depends upon unique technology, namely the availability of a virtually invisible acrylic resin that can be cured with ultraviolet light.

A final aspect of services that must always be kept in mind is the extremely high customer dissatisfaction. Hard data are scarce but we can all cite easily, unfortunately, instances in which we received terrible service. The implication of this is that you must stress service quality and its control in both developing and providing services. Normally, this means that you must also have mechanisms for the prompt and courteous resolution of problems which do arise. In some hotels your laundry is returned late; how the hotel handles your unhappiness crucially affects your attitude about how good that hotel is. Handling that kind of problem well today is no assurance that it will be handled by that hotel well the next day. High quality requires that each and every contact and detail be handled well, every time. Adding more supervision in such situations is rarely effective; rather, training, continual reinforcement, and appropriate incentives are some of the elements which are obviously required.

It is important not merely to eradicate dissatisfaction but also to lower the service providers' costs. Every time there is a problem with the service being provided, it takes extra effort to fix that problem and try to smooth ruffled feathers. One approach to consider is to offer an unconditional guarantee of some sort with your service.

One study shows that service quality depends upon reliability, responsiveness, confidence, and empathy of the provider. The most important of these factors is reliability, which means that the service must be dependable and provided both accurately and consistently, time after time. Finally, physical facilities, equipment, and appearance of the personnel are a factor, but virtually insignificant compared to the preceding four.

DEVELOPMENT DISTINCTIONS

While the size of the private services sector of the gross national product is much larger than that of products, and while there are many things that distinguish services from tangible products, there are many similarities in developing new services.

It is rare that it is not feasible to develop a service, although the economics of the service may make it financially unattractive. In that sense, the issues in feasibility activities are more similar to traditional marketing and market research concerns. Indeed, you still have to match a market need with a service solution to have a viable business opportunity.

Assuming plausible feasibility, the development activity might logically entail the same four phases I have previously suggested, namely, optimization, design, preproduction, and production. The maintenance activity will also be required. Services that depend on software will need traditional software maintenance. In other services, much of the maintenance activity will have to do with constantly retraining and reasserting this training with the people who provide the services.

Some services, of course, may require profoundly different marketing efforts than products. For example, professional services entail a substantial effort to educate prospective customers about what realistically can and cannot be expected from a particular service.

Services in general are easy to create. In most cases, however, a service's sales volume cannot increase as rapidly as the most successful tangible products. Conversely, the lifetime of a service may be much longer than that of a product.

The role of a test market for a service is primarily to debug the service provider's delivery chain. This includes verifying that the product can be properly explained by the point of contact. A practical way to do this is to market the service to your own employees first. In one instance, a Los Angeles area bank publicly announced a new loan package before the loan officers knew about it. If employees had first been offered the new service, they might have started to ask the loan officers about it, and that would have identified the lack of start-up information. This demonstrates what was previously stated, that the training of the service's point-of-contact people is, in fact, one of the crucial development distinctions.

In many situations, adding an additional service on top of those you already provide has very low incremental cost. For instance, one bank created a new checking account specifically aimed at recent college graduates.

Finally, it is usually much harder to erect barriers to entry of competition for success. Services cannot be patented, although trademarks to service names can be obtained. There are some exceptions; for instance, a regional hospital in a rural or semi-rural area may not have any significant competition. Similarly, a service depending on a large proprietary database, such as TRW's Credentials Service, will not have any direct competition.

FAST DEVELOPMENT OF NEW SERVICES

The characteristics of new services and the development distinctions lead to two important lessons if you wish to develop new products rapidly:

1. You must train each and every person who will have contact with the recipient of your service. The thoroughness of this training and indoctrination is the limitation on the quality your service will be perceived to have. For some services, such as a new bank product at a large

retail bank, the number of people you must train can be very large. For others, such as the paint specialists at a few car plants, specialized training may involve a much smaller number of people.

2. The operations staff, which is analogous to the manufacturing department for a product, must be involved intensively in the development of the service. Where mainframe computers are an integral element of the service the availability of operations staff time to get the product running, bug free, can be one of the limitations in your ability to provide this service.

HIGHLIGHTS

The distinctions between a tangible product and a more ephemeral service mean that there are some development differences.

Test marketing is required primarily to debug the service's delivery.

Training of all point-of-contact personnel is crucial.

These differences are small enough so that you can still apply the techniques described in this book.

Chapter 19

Where Do You Go From Here?

The purpose of this chapter is to help you improve your skill in practicing the techniques discussed in this book. Because additional tools and techniques to speed new products to the market will undoubtedly be developed, it remains important for you to learn about these as they become known.

CONTINUING TECHNIQUE IMPROVEMENT

Reading this or any other book will not make you an expert in faster new product development immediately. Your company will have to make changes in the way new products are specified and managed during the development and introduction cycle. It takes time (perhaps a few years) and practice for the techniques to become routine.

Furthermore, advances in technology, such as expert systems or computer networks to speed information flow, will continue to provide new timesaving capabilities. You will want to learn of these as they emerge and mature.

In addition, you will have to develop your own style, consistent with your skills, interest, and personality, that works within your company's business environment. There is no substitute for your own experience. What works for one person and one company may not be useful or appropriate in another situation. Thus, you and your company should continue to experiment, read, and seek out other sources for continuing education.

There are three important ways you can continue to improve your own skill and stay abreast of new trends that may be useful in your company: reading; attending executive or management seminars and short courses; and viewing educational television and videocassettes.

Suggested Reading

At the time this manuscript was completed, a few authors have published pertinent articles or books, so literature on faster new product development is beginning to emerge. You may find the following additional reading helpful:

Alsop, R. "Companies Get on Fast Track to Roll Out Hot New Brands." *The Wall Street Journal* (July 10, 1986), p. 25.

Bussey, J., and D. R. Sease. "Manufacturers Strive to Slice Time Needed to Develop New Products." *The Wall Street Journal* (February 22, 1988), pp. 1 ff.

Fraker, S. "High Speed Management for the High-Tech Age." *Fortune* (March 5, 1984), pp. 62 ff.

Gold, B. "Approaches to Accelerating Product and Process Development." *Journal of Product Innovation Management* (June 1987), pp. 81–88.

Goldberg, J. R., and S. Yakatan. "Why Two Can Speed Product to Market Quicker Than One." *Chief Executive* (January/February 1989), pp. 36 ff.

"How Xerox Speeds Up the Birth of New Products," *Business Week* (March 19, 1984), pp. 58–59.

Reiner, G. "Cutting Your Competitor to the Quick." *The Wall Street Journal* (November 21, 1988), p. A14.

Reiner, G. "Getting There First: It Takes Planning to Put Plans Into Action." *The New York Times* (March 12, 1989), p. F3.

Reinertsen, D. G. "Blitzkreig Product Development: Cut Development Times in Half." *Electronic Business* (January 15, 1985).

Rosenau, M. D. "Speeding Your New Product to Market." *Journal of Consumer Marketing* (Spring 1988), pp. 23–36.

Rosenau, M. D. "How to Develop New Products Faster." *Executive Excellence* (April 1988), pp. 8–9.

Rosenau, M. D. "Faster New Product Development." *Journal of Product Innovation Management* (June 1988), pp. 150–153.

Rosenau, M. D. "Phased Approach Speeds Up New Product Development." *Research & Development* (November 1988), pp. 52–55.

Smith, P. G. "Winning the New Product Rat Race." *Machine Design* (May 12, 1988), pp. 95–98.

Stalk, G., Jr. "Time—The Next Source of Competitive Advantage." *Harvard Business Review* (July/August 1988), pp. 41–51.

Takeuchi, H., and I. Nonaka. "The New New Product Development Game." *Harvard Business Review* (January/February 1986), pp. 137–146.

Teresko, J. "Speeding the Product Development Cycle." *Industry Week* (July 18, 1988), pp. 40–42.

Uttal, B. "Speeding New Ideas to Market." *Fortune* (March 2, 1987), pp. 62–66.

Wolff, M. J. "To Innovate Faster, Try the Skunk Works." *Research Management* (September/October 1987), pp. 6–7.

There have also been several recent books and articles that discuss the process of new product development in general. While these lack a special emphasis on accelerating the process, you may also wish to read these:

Cooper, R. G. *Winning New Products*. Reading, MA: Addison-Wesley, 1986.

Hodder, J. E. and H. E. Riggs. "Pitfalls in Evaluating Risky Projects." *Harvard Business Review* (January/February 1985), pp. 128–135.

Kuczmarski, T. D. *Managing New Products*. Englewood Cliffs, NJ: Prentice-Hall, 1988.

Quinn, J. B. Managing Innovation: Controlled Chaos. *Harvard Business Review* (May/June 1985) pp. 73–84.

Rosenau, M. D. *Innovation: Managing the Development of Profitable New Products*. New York: Van Nostrand Reinhold (Lifetime Learning Publications), 1982.

Souder, W. E. *Managing New Product Innovations*. Lexington, MA: Lexington Books, 1987.

Several periodicals have been consistent sources of information on new techniques and trends, so you may also want to read these regularly. The ones that I find most useful are:

> *The New York Times*
> *The Wall Street Journal*
> *Business Week*
> *Fortune*
> *Journal of Product Innovation Management*
> *Harvard Business Review*

Watch for more books and articles as they are published in the future. The source citations at the end of this book can be used to identify publications in which new information may appear.

Management Seminars and Short Courses

Many universities, professional societies and trade associations, and commercial organizations offer management seminars and short courses, typically of one day to one week duration. These vary in quality, teaching method, and subject matter, so you should determine who will lecture and lead these training programs. Then try to check out references by talking with prior participants.

The unique value of attending such sessions is the interaction with other participants. No amount of reading or passive observation of videocassette courses, even if the materials are outstanding, can give you the same opportunity for interactive discussion and sharing.

At the time of this book's publication, three university extension programs were offering periodic seminars on faster new product development:

> Industrial Relation Center (1–90)
> California Institute of Technology
> Pasadena, Calif. 91125
> (818) 356-4041

> Continuing Education Division
> UCSB Extension
> University of California
> Santa Barbara, Calif. 93106
> (805) 961-4200

> Continuing Education Division
> UCB Extension
> University of California
> 2223 Fulton Street
> Berkeley, Calif. 94720
> (415) 642-4231

If you cannot attend a university or commercial seminar, you may want to explore having such a seminar conducted in your own organization. Although you will not obtain the stimulus of interacting with personnel from other, different organizations, you will have a seminar customized to your own specific situation. This may also serve as a workshop to begin to implement some of the techniques described in this book.

Educational Television and Videocassettes

The National Technological University (NTU) is a private, nonprofit institution that offers television courses at multiple sites throughout the United States. These courses can be taken at your company or another site for credit toward a masters' degree in several fields including, for instance, engineering management.

In addition, NTU sponsors many noncredit professional development television programs that are available via satellite. You may wish to obtain more information from NTU:

NTU Satellite Network
P.O. Box 700
Fort Collins, Col. 80522
(303) 484-0565

A consortium of universities, called the Association for Media-based Continuing Education for Engineers (AMCEE) has many video-cassettes that can be leased or purchased. Some of these are single topics and others are multicassette short courses. These can be used to reduce travel cost to external seminars or to augment other training. AMCEE's address is:

AMCEE
c/o Education Extension
Georgia Institute of Technology
Atlanta, Ga.
(404) 894-3362 or (800) 338-9344

Similar materials may also be obtained from the AMA:

American Management Association
135 West 50th Street
New York, N.Y. 10020-1201
(212) 586-8100

PROFESSIONAL GROUPS

There are probably many professional groups which occasionally sponsor meetings or publish information relative to faster new product development. However, there is only one association of which I am aware that consistently deals with the topic of new product development and which has sponsored conferences on faster new product development.

The Product Development and Management Association (PDMA) has a membership of several hundred individuals. PDMA has several regional special topic meetings each year as well as an international conference. In addition, PDMA publishes the *Journal of Product Innovation Management*, mentioned above, which is the only journal that consistently has relevant articles. Additional information about PDMA and the journal can be obtained from:

Product Development & Management Association
c/o Prof. Thomas P. Hustad
Graduate School of Business
Indiana University
801 West Michigan Street
Indianapolis, Ind. 46202-5151
(317) 274-4984

OTHER SOURCES OF HELP

Sometimes you may still find that you are over your head. In such a case, you may wish to retain a management consultant for assistance. The Institute of Management Consultants (IMC) is the one certifying body for management consultants which designates those who meet its standards as a Certified Management Consultant (CMC). For more information:

IMC
Suite 544
230 Park Avenue
New York, N.Y. 10169
(212) 697-8282

There are other management consultants who are not yet certified who are nevertheless superbly qualified. However, if you do not have prior personal experience or a reliable reference from a colleague, you have a better assurance of professional and ethical assistance if you obtain management consulting assistance through IMC.

HIGHLIGHTS

Faster new product development is the new competitive imperative for many companies.

The body of knowledge is still evolving. You and your company will have to continue to follow developments.

Part VI
Summary

Part VI briefly summarizes some of the key points that have been made previously.

Chapter 20
Summary of Some Key Points

This chapter recapitulates a few of the key ideas I have discussed.

Shorter product life cycles, caused by better communications and changing technology, have created an increasing need for faster new product development. Therefore, try to assure that everyone understands that product life cycles are shrinking rapidly and that fast new product development is increasingly important. Stress the benefits of fast new product development:

- The company that is first to market has no competition, which often allows you to charge a premium price;
- You can obtain more sales, which yields more profits;
- You normally will have lower development costs;
- There will be less chance for an unfavorable market or technology change; and
- You can utilize later technology than your competitors who execute more slowly.

Adopt some kind of systematic approach to new product development. Install simple, orderly development procedures that are appropriate for your company's business. Where appropriate, use short phases to improve focus and understanding, increase urgency, and reduce risk. Also, it may be helpful to use external sources (using licensing, joint venture, purchasing, or sub-contracting arrangements), although you may have to share some potential profits.

Specifications are the critical underpinning of a fast new product development effort. Consequently, always start the development activity with a discrete optimization phase in which you establish clear and complete specifications that can be achieved within the desired time. Defer possible enhancements to focus on only these specifications, not others that might be achievable. Do try to consider an entire family of new products—perhaps with less precision—when starting an entirely new effort, with incremental features embodied in later product introductions.

Focus on a few winners and eliminate interruptions of these. Use the phased approach to separate time-critical new product development activities from unpredictable feasibility activities and intrusive maintenance activities. You must recognize that maintenance will be necessary and can delay new product development. A separate feasibility activity can eliminate development delays caused by attempts to invent on schedule, since these attempts are usually unsuccessful.

Devise an organization that separates the new product development activities from the ongoing business. Concentrate your limited resources sequentially on the highest new product priority development efforts for which there are clear market-driven opportunities and assure that these efforts have sufficient human and physical resources to permit their timely completion. Do not hedge your bets by spreading these precious resources over many appealing targets. Necessarily, therefore, stop (either permanently or temporarily) some projects and reject some opportunities.

Accelerate all the work which must be done and complete it quickly by using appropriate tools and techniques, including productivity enhancements. Take advantage of simple project management tools. In particular, use a critical path network diagram schedule and resource forecast, and maintain these with suitable microcomputer project management software. Develop a checklist of tasks that are normally required for your new product development projects to assure these are included in your schedule and that resources will be available when required.

Perform any critical tasks as early as possible. Clearly identify all key decision milestones.

Finally, keep improving your new product development process. Thus, make use of post mortems and continued observation of what others are doing to make incremental new product development process changes that continually improve your company's speed and excellence.

Appendixes

Six appendixes provide some additional detail on issues or techniques that are described briefly in the body of the book.

Appendix A

Some Phased Approach Concepts

There is a variety of proposed phase concepts that differ from mine in detail but are philosophically consistent and thus deserve mention. Many people involved in new product development have proposed phases or sequences of activities to move from the idea stage to the introduction of a product. However, these approaches do not stress speed of execution, perhaps because they were devised when product life cycles were longer. That shortcoming does not invalidate these concepts, and your company may find it useful to use some portions of these concepts to develop your own variation of my phased approach.

Cooper has proposed seven phases (which he calls stages), the first six of which end with go/no-go decisions: idea; preliminary assessment; concept; development; testing; trial; and launch. This is perfectly reasonable. However, I am dealing with the new product development process after the idea exists. I also prefer to lump his next two stages (preliminary assessment and concept) into what I call the feasibility phase. Finally, Cooper's omission of a maintenance phase is important, because there is a need to provide this function on existing products and this will distract people doing development on the current new product unless maintenance work is explicitly relegated elsewhere.

Cooper and Kleinschmidt have enumerated seventeen activities in the new product process: initial screening; preliminary market assessment; preliminary technical assessment; detailed market study/market research; business/financial analysis; product development; in-house product testing; customer tests of product; test market/trial sell; trial production; precommercialization business analysis; production start-up; market launch. While this list of activities is sequential, it is not proposed as a phased approach. Nevertheless, it is a good list of activities to consult when you are planning your own critical path schedule to be certain that you have not omitted any key activities. In common with other activities identified by me and others, these potential activities are consolidated into an activity checklist, which you can review in Appendix C.

Other authors offer still further perspectives. For instance, Merrifield identifies six phases (which, in common with Cooper, he calls stages): (1) idea;

(2) feasibility demonstration; (3) product/process development; (4) pilot plant; (5) semi-commercial; and (6) full-scale production. Merrifield's orientation is toward the development of new chemical processes and is thus a good structure to consider if that is the nature of your business.

Conversely, Butrell lists five phases: (1) concept; (2) production prototype; (3) field testing; (4) marketing development; and (5) field sales. Douglas, Kemp, and Cook have a more narrow focus, concentrating on screening opportunity areas, generating new product ideas, and brand building. Hoo lists five stages: (1) strategic analysis/planning; (2) idea generation/screening; (3) development; (4) test marketing; and (5) national/regional launch. Each of these provides a bit more detail to add to the previously mentioned sources.

Buggie concentrates on the phases preceding the production phase, and identifies many specific activities: product concepts; engineering drawings; secondary market research; primary market research; prototype; operation test; design revision; soft tooling; pilot run; specifications and cost target; marketing plan draft; test market; marketing plan revision; and go. He has portrayed these activities (and some others) in a PERT chart network, which can be helpful. I prefer a time-based critical path network diagram, similar to Exhibits 12-6, 12-8, 12-9, or 12-10, for the reasons I cited in Chapter 12. What Buggie's approach lacks, in my judgment, are clear breaks between smaller increments of activity, with attendant top management approvals to authorize the subsequent phases upon the conclusion of predecessor phases.

McGuire illustrates different new product development flows for a consumer and industrial product company. This is a helpful distinction because you can create markets for some consumer products with effective promotion and advertising; industrial products, conversely, are normally only successful when there is a clear need which the product satisfies. The specific details of the phased approach you adopt for your company obviously depends on whether you produce consumer or industrial products or services.

Bacon and Butler have a still different perspective. They devote much of their thinking to strategic considerations which necessarily precede the idea for a new product. Company strategy is vitally important. While their treatment does not stress carrying out the new product development rapidly, it can help you ensure that your new product efforts support your company's strategy rather than attempt to undermine it.

Crawford provides an integrated view of the total process. He starts with both strategy and staffing and then moves on to concept generation. He then explicitly identifies many activities: concept testing; prescreening; screening; prototype testing; product-use testing; market testing; financial evaluation; prelaunch preparation and control; product announcement; introduction (which he calls beachhead); and growth. In common with the others, however, speed of execution is not explicitly treated and project management techniques, while discussed, are de-emphasized.

Feldman and Page completed a study of eight companies showing how these organizations did (or did not) use a six-phase new product development process that included exploration, screening, concept testing, business analysis, development, and market testing. Only three of the eight firms used the concept testing phase, but all eight of the companies used the other five of these phases.

Appendix B
Conjoint Analysis

The use of conjoint analysis helps set the specifications for a new product (or service). Conjoint analysis is a simple analytic method that you can use to determine the combination of attributes or features your new product (or service) must have to appeal to a specific market or market segment. For example, the technique allows you to determine that combination of attributes for the new product that will allow you to obtain maximum market share or profits.

Products and services have attributes such as price, ease of repair, availability, technical support, and warranty, as well as performance features (for instance, top speed, capacity, frequency response, operating costs, and so on). All potential customers do not value these attributes in the same way. As an example, a user with only one piece of expensive production equipment (such as a computer-controlled milling machine) might value the availability of very fast repair service more highly than a user with many pieces of the production equipment. The user with only one piece of equipment must shut down completely when the production equipment needs service repair. Conversely, with many pieces of equipment, the factory can still maintain production, although its output will be at a reduced level. Thus, it is often important to evaluate the relative importance of each attribute for a representative sample of potential customers. This permits you to produce your new product or service offering with that combination of attributes which is most likely to satisfy your new product development goals.

Subsequent sections will cover the concept of conjoint analysis, how this tool can help you translate market needs into a design specification, an illustration of the technique, means for data reduction, making market share estimates from conjoint analysis data, how conjoint analysis can help you improve your profits, and several practical cautions about the technique.

THE CONCEPT OF CONJOINT ANALYSIS

Conjoint analysis, also called multiattribute utility analysis, is a simple trade-off analysis technique to employ. Its use allows you to:

- Determine which product attributes are most important to specific market segments;

- Clarify which attributes will be most critical to your product's success;
- Estimate what price your prospective product will command for a particular combination of attributes; or
- Estimate the market share your product will obtain.

The basis for this simple, powerful technique is that:

- A product or service is a collection (or bundle) of several attributes (or factors), as illustrated in Exhibit B-1;
- Each of these attributes has a few specified levels, as shown in Exhibit B-2;
- Each level (of each attribute) has a measurable value, its utility, for a person, who may be a customer, user, decision maker, or other participant in the buying process, as shown in Exhibit B-3; and
- The utility of a product or service is the sum of the utilities of its attributes' levels, as illustrated in Exhibit B-4.

In practice, the respondent is given a group of perhaps one or two dozen cards. Each card describes a product embodying a particular combination of attributes at specific levels or values. Then you ask the respondent to rank all the cards: Most attractive (or least *un*attractive) on top; least attractive on bottom; and all the others sorted by preference order in between the top and the bottom.

Exhibit B-1. Some attributes for factory machinery.

- Performance compared to your specifications
- Price
- Delivery time
- Terms

Exhibit B-2. Some levels for the attributes of Exhibit B-1.

Performance Specifications	Delivery Time
• Exceed by 20%	• 6 months
• Exceed by 5%	• 9 months
• Fall short by 5%	• 12 months
• Fall short by 20%	• 15 months

Price	Terms
• $700,000	• Installed, 12-month guarantee
• $800,000	• Installed, 6-month guarantee
• $900,000	• Installed, no guarantee
• $1 million	• FOB seller, no guarantee

Exhibit B-3. Illustrative utilities for the levels of Exhibit B-2.

		Level Utility
Factor A	*Performance Specs*	
A1	Exceed by 20%	.77
A2	Exceed by 5%	.69
A3	Fall short by 5%	.44
A4	Fall short by 20%	.20
Factor B	*Price*	
B1	$700,000	.84
B2	$800,000	.68
B3	$900,000	.41
B4	$1 million	.17
Factor C	*Delivery Time*	
C1	6 months	.64
C2	9 months	.57
C3	12 months	.51
C4	15 months	.38
Factor D	*Terms*	
D1	Installed + 12-month guarantee	1.00
D2	Installed + 6-month guarantee	.88
D3	Installed, no guarantee	.22
D4	FOB seller, no guarantee	.00

Exhibit B-4. Two possible factory machine offerings and their utilities.

PRODUCT/SERVICE A	UTILITY	PRODUCT/SERVICE B	UTILITY
5% above specifications	.69	5% above specifications	.69
$1 million	.17	$700,000	.84
6-month delivery	.64	9-month delivery	.57
Installed, 12-month guarantee	1.00	Installed, no guarantee	.22
Total utility	2.50		2.32

As a simple example, four cards for a possible mail order purchase offer are shown in Exhibit B-5. There are two prices and two locations for the company from which the purchase can be made. Exhibit B-6 shows the actual cost if the purchaser's state imposes a 6 percent sales tax on purchases made within the state. As shown in Exhibit B-7, respondent card rankings will reveal if lowest cost is the most important consideration or if proximity (with implications about delivery time or service availability) is more important. Thus, respondents reveal their preferences by card ranking, which requires them to make trade-offs between different offerings. Each card lists a group of product

Exhibit B-5.   Four cards for two attributes, each with two levels.

Card A

Price	$300
Company location	In state

Card B

Price	$280
Company location	In state

Card C

Price	$300
Company location	Out of state

Card D

Price	$280
Company location	Out of state

Exhibit B-6.   Actual product cost when state sales tax of 6 percent is included.

	Location	
Price	In State	Out of State
$300	$318 (Card A)	$300 (Card C)
$280	$297 (Card B)	$280 (Card D)

Exhibit B-7.   Expected card rankings for two different preferences.

Card Rank Position	Card ranking for respondent with greatest preference for:	
	Lowest Cost	Company Proximity
1st	D	B
2nd	B	A
3rd	C	D
4th	A	C

attributes and values (or levels). The attribute levels themselves may be either qualitative or quantitative.

To analyze the data for a group of respondents, use suitable computer software. This software may be either special purpose software or you may create a spreadsheet program. The rank order data produce measurements of attribute utility, assigning a set of scalar values to each attribute's values. (It is also possible to have respondents put numerical scores on cards, for instance on a scale from 1 to 100, in which case ties between two cards can be accommodated.) The goal is to derive the total utility for each combination so that these provide a best fit with the respondents' rankings. The end result may be a series of scalar plots or tabular data showing the relative utility for each value of each attribute. The power of this simple technique is that these attribute utility values emulate the respondent's behavior when making a purchase choice, because the utility of a product is merely the sum of the utilities of its component attributes.

TRANSLATING MARKET NEEDS INTO A DESIGN SPECIFICATION

Conjoint analysis not only helps answer market research questions, it also provides guidance for design engineers by showing which product attributes should be given serious attention and which deserve less. For example, a conjoint analysis study revealed that easier access to the electrical connectors on the back of a scientific instrument was more important than faster response time or better performance. Naturally, the design engineers would have preferred the challenge of working on the latter aspects rather than mundane connectors.

Most importantly, conjoint analysis provides a link to translate market requirements into a quantitative development specification. Since you may not understand a feature that lacks a numerical specification, this characteristic of conjoint analysis is exceptionally valuable. For instance, in another example, a conjoint analysis study revealed that the need for high reliability did not inherently require a very long time without downtime (that is, a very long mean time between failures); rather, it could more easily be satisfied by providing one-day service after a failure incident rather than the standard two-day service.

CONJOINT ANALYSIS ILLUSTRATION

Imagine a product with three attributes, namely A, B, and C; furthermore, each of these attributes has three values (or levels or characteristics), such as A1, A2, and A3, and so on. It is possible to describe each of the twenty-seven possible combinations on a card and ask potential buyers to rank the twenty-seven cards from most preferred to least preferred. This task might be intimidating and, fortunately, you can reduce it to ranking nine cards with combinations such as those shown in Exhibit B-8 by letters R through Z.

Consider the following specific situation: Suppose you wish to determine the relative importance of three attributes that influence a potential customer's decision to purchase microcomputer software from a direct response advertiser offering discount prices for standard products. The attributes of importance might be price, delivery time, and availability of free technical support. Typical products might be Wordstar, Lotus 1-2-3, dBase II, or similar products. Also we will assume for the example that the retail list price of a typical software product is $500. In this illustration, three possible characteristics or values describe each of the three attributes, as Exhibit B-9 illustrates.

Exhibit B-8.   Nine-card set to cover twenty-seven possible attribute combinations.

CONJOINT ANALYSIS—3x3x3 EXAMPLE SET

	A1	A2	A3	
B1		R		
B2	S			C1
B3			T	
B1			U	
B2		V		C2
B3	W			
B1	X			
B2			Y	C3
B3		Z		

Exhibit B-9.   Example attributes.

Price		Free Technical Support	
$300	(A1)	800 telephone line	(C1)
$325	(A2)	24 hours per day	
$350	(A3)	7 days a week	
		800 telephone line	(C2)
Delivery		Mon.–Fri., 7A.M.–6P.M.	
2 days or less	(B1)	Sat.–Sun., 9A.M.–6P.M.	
3 days to 1 week	(B2)	Toll call	(C3)
1 week to 2 weeks	(B3)	24 hours per day	
		7 days a week	

It is obvious that the potential customer would prefer the lowest price (A1), the quickest delivery (B1), and the most generous level of technical support (C1). However, it may not be possible for you to provide that combination at a profit, and it is not obvious how a real buyer would rank other combinations of these attributes. In practice, therefore, you enter the words from Exhibit B-9 on each of nine cards in accordance with the combinations shown in Exhibit B-8. As a specific example, card W would read as shown in Exhibit B-10.

If low price (A) was of primary importance to a respondent and fast delivery was secondary (which implies technical support is least important), the card ranking is shown in Exhibit B-11. Assuming a respondent makes this ranking, we then determine her values as follows. Since A1 ($300 price) appears on three cards (namely S, W, and X), we first find their ranks and sum these; as we can see, these cards are, respectively, second, third, and first, which yields a sum of 6, as illustrated in Exhibit B-12. The rank sums for the other attributes levels are also shown in Exhibit B-12.

Since this respondent's greatest preference (that is, A1) is the lowest rank sum, we arbitrarily assign this a utility of 1.0; similarly, their least preference (that is, A3) is the highest rank sum, to which we arbitrarily assign a utility of zero. You determine the utilities for other rank sum values by linear interpolation, which Exhibit B-13 illustrates.

A product's utility is the sum of the partial utilities of its component attri-

Exhibit B-10. Example of a single card, namely W in Exhibit B-8.

Price	$300
Delivery	1 week to 2 weeks
Free technical support	800 telephone line
	Mon.–Fri., 7 A.M.–6 P.M.
	Sat.–Sun., 9 A.M.–6 P.M.

Exhibit B-11. Card ranking for respondent with primary preference for A1, then A2, then A3, and secondary preference for B1, then B2, then B3.

Card	Rank
X	1
S	2
W	3
R	4
V	5
Z	6
U	7
Y	8
T	9

Exhibit B-12.   Rank sums for ranking used in Exhibit B-11.

CONJOINT ANALYSIS–3 × 3 × 3 EXAMPLE SCORING

$$
\begin{aligned}
A1 &= S + W + X &=& \ 6\\
A2 &= R + V + Z &=& \ 15\\
A3 &= U + Y + T &=& \ 24\\[6pt]
B1 &= R + U + X &=& \ 12\\
B2 &= S + V + Y &=& \ 15\\
B3 &= T + W + Z &=& \ 18\\[6pt]
C1 &= R + S + T &=& \ 15\\
C2 &= U + V + W &=& \ 15\\
C3 &= X + Y + Z &=& \ 15
\end{aligned}
$$

Exhibit B-13.   Utilities for card ranking in Exhibit B-11.

CONJOINT ANALYSIS–3 × 3 × 3 EXAMPLE UTILITIES

A1 = S + W + X = 6	1.0	
A2 = R + V + Z = 15		.50
A3 = U + Y + T = 24	0	
B1 = R + U + X = 12		.67
B2 = S + V + Y = 15		.50
B3 = T + W + Z = 18		.33
C1 = R + S + T = 15		.50
C2 = U + V + W = 15		.50
C3 = X + Y + Z = 15		.50

butes. For example, the product having the card rankings shown in Exhibit B-11, with the attribute values A1, B1, and C1 shown in Exhibit B-13, has a utility value of 2.17 (that is, 1.00 + 0.67 + 0.50).

Data Reduction

Data reduction for this nine-card illustration can be done very quickly and inexpensively, requiring only the use of a spreadsheet software program. Exhibit B-14 illustrates such software (using SuperCalc, in this instance) for the card rankings illustrated in Exhibit B-11. The column headed "utility range" shows the difference between the maximum and minimum utility for the corresponding variable; the larger the range, the more influential that variable is in the respondent's ranking decision.

The column headed "judgment percent" in Exhibit B-14 is the calculation of what percent importance each variable has for the sample you are analyzing. Judgment percent is that attribute's (or variable's) utility range divided by the sum of all attributes' utility ranges. For example, the respondent's card ranking reveals that variable A represents 75 percent of her judgment (0.75 = 1.00/ [1.00 + 0.33 + 0]).

It should also be clear that some rankings of cards make no sense at all. That is, there are some cards that must always appear ahead of other cards in a "rational" ranking. Thus, if these rational sequence priorities are violated, it is often a signal that the respondent has been careless or indifferent in ranking the cards. When this is the case, perhaps you should discount that respondent's ranking in your analysis. You can arrange to flag such rankings with spreadsheet software, using, for instance, the logic tests at the bottom of Exhibit B-14. (These illustrated tests presume the variables are metric with logical preferences, such as A1 must be preferred over A2, which must be preferred over A3. Metric variables include price, where lower is always presumed to be more preferred. Non-metric variables include brand name or size, even though the latter is quantitative.) Many of the commercially available conjoint analysis software packages will also do this. However, you must be careful in rejecting such flagged data, since your rationality may foreclose consideration of someone's emotional, but still important to them, decision criteria.

This approach is trivial for symmetric orthogonal card arrays; such card arrangements make use of greco-latin square experimental designs. When practical, you can also use these for more elaborate situations, such as those in which there are four attributes, each with four levels, and those with five attributes, each with five levels. More complex situations (for example, six attributes, one with five levels, one with four levels, two with three levels, and two with two levels) require specialized software or use of tabulated experimental designs for the design of the card set; the data reduction can be carried out in analogous fashion, but you must normalize the sum value of each attribute.

As a further example, Exhibits B-15 and B-16 illustrate similar data for an eighteen-card set in which cards number seventeen and number eighteen are so-called holdout cards. These two cards are not used (that is, they are held out) in calculating the utilities, which is accomplished with cards one through sixteen. However, you calculate the least square correlation of the ranks of the holdout cards and their utilities with the data from the other sixteen cards. In the situation illustrated in Exhibit B-16, the regression coefficient (R) is -1.0, indicating a perfect fit; these data are also plotted in Exhibit B-17. If the fit is poor, you may wish to reject the data.

MARKET SHARE ESTIMATES FROM CONJOINT ANALYSIS

Imagine that another company has a product with attributes A2, B2, and C2, and that you are trying to decide which combination of attributes your new
(*text continued on page 250*)

Exhibit B-14. Example of spreadsheet program for data reduction.

	A			B			C			D			E			F			G			H		
1	ORTHOGONAL 3 X 3 (with internal consistency checks in rows 35–48)							
2								
3								
4	Card #	Combination			Sum	Pers 1		
5	R	A2	B1	C1	4	4		
6	S	A1	B2	C1	2	2		
7	T	A3	B3	C1	9	9		
8	U	A3	B1	C2	7	7		
9	V	A2	B2	C2	5	5		
10	W	A1	B3	C2	3	3		
11	X	A1	B1	C3	1	1		
12	Y	A3	B2	C3	8	8		
13	Z	A2	B3	C3	6	6		
14								
15	ILLOGICAL RANK POSITIONS				0			
16								
17					Sum		Utility	Judgment
18					Value	Utility	Range	Percent
19								
20	VARIABLE A							
21	A1	S + W + X			6	1.00	1.00	.75
22	A2	R + V + Z			15	.50		
23	A3	T + U + Y			24	.00		
24								

Line						
25	VARIABLE B					
26	B1	R + U + X	12	.67	.33	.25
27	B2	S + V + Y	15	.50		
28	B3	T + W + Z	18	.33		
29						
30	VARIABLE C					
31	C1	R + S + T	15	.50	.00	.00
32	C2	U + V + W	15	.50		
33	C3	X + Y + Z	15	.50		
34						
35	IF (B5>B7,1,0)	0				
36	IF (B5>B8,1,0)	0				
37	IF (B5>B9,1,0)	0				
38	IF (B5>B12,1,0)	0				
39	IF (B5>B13,1,0)	0				
40	IF (B6>B7,1,0)	0				
41	IF (B6>B9,1,0)	0				
42	IF (B6>B10,1,0)	0				
43	IF (B8>B12,1,0)	0				
44	IF (B9>B12,1,0)	0				
45	IF (B9>B13,1,0)	0				
46	IF (B10>B13,1,0)	0				
47	IF (B11>B12,1,0)	0				
48	IF (B11>B13,1,0)	0				

Exhibit B-15.   Example of respondents' card rankings.

Card #	Acceptable Data			Card Sum
	Pers 1	Pers 2	Pers 3	
1	18	17	9	44
2	17	16	14	47
3	8	8	12	28
4	6	7	7	20
5	1	1	5	7
6	7	5	17	29
7	14	18	18	50
8	10	13	11	34
9	9	9	4	22
10	4	2	10	16
11	15	11	15	41
12	11	14	3	28
13	2	3	1	6
14	5	6	16	27
15	12	10	8	30
16	16	12	2	30
17	3	4	6	13
18	13	15	13	41

competitive product should offer. For simplicity, consider only three options: An identical product; one with attributes A3, B3, and C3; and one with attributes A1, B1, and C1.

To reiterate, a product's utility is the sum of the utilities for each of its attributes at the level that attribute has in the product. Thus, for the card ranking of Exhibit B-11, the product utilities are shown in Exhibit B-18.

The simplest model for market share is to estimate it as being apportioned in proportion to the product utilities, which Exhibit B-19 illustrates for these three options. In fact, academics and other theoreticians are still debating the best way to estimate market share, and many models (for instance, logarithmic, exponential, and so on) have been proposed.

In the simple model, the premium product option (that is, the product with attributes A1, B1, and C1) will have the highest market share, that is 59 percent. However, your costs for this product may not be low enough to provide a satisfactory gross margin; that is, you may be paying to buy relatively unprofitable market share. If this is the case, you may wish to emulate your competitor (that is, produce the product with attributes A2, B2, and C2), which, as you would logically expect, should garner one-half of the market. Or, you may decide to come out with a low-end product (the one with attributes A3, B3, and C3) or, perhaps, devise additional options.

IMPROVING YOUR PROFITS

One of the most frequent problems that new product development managers ask me about is how to determine the best (or highest) price for the new product. To recapitulate, you can do this with conjoint analysis: (1) Describe the choice options; (2) get rankings from appropriate respondents; and (3) determine the utility value that explains the rankings. Conjoint analysis has been used with excellent success in specifying features for a very large array of consumer and industrial products and services; but, curiously, the technique is not in routine use (yet) in all or even most new product development.

As an unfortunate consequence, there are many companies that constantly add features that have little or no utility to prospective customers; the result is products with low gross margins, because the costs are an inherent consequence of the design and customers will not pay for undesired features. You can avoid this situation by using conjoint analysis to decide how much value customers attach to specific attribute values. This can improve your profits.

In general, the more features that a product contains, the more it costs you to produce. Hopefully, of course, the additional features increase its value to a potential customer; thus, while your costs increase as you add features, those additional features often command a higher price. While this trend is generally correct, the real relationship is one with inflection points at which slight increases in costs permit substantial increases in price, as illustrated in Exhibit B-20. This non-linear relationship will exist if you can add useful features that do not cost much and on which customers place substantial value.

Thus, you can first use conjoint analysis to determine the price you can charge for a given combination of product features. Then, the design and manufacturing engineers can estimate the costs you will incur to embody those features in the product. Finally, you can locate the inflection points in the actual price versus cost relationship that are most attractive to you. Sometimes you may produce a family of products, at each (or several) of the attractive inflection points.

CAUTIONS IN USING CONJOINT ANALYSIS

Conjoint analysis requires that you ask people to make judgments about attributes. These must be relevant for them. If you don't ask about an attribute that is important to a respondent, the card ranking you obtain will be flawed. If you ask about the wrong attributes or variables, you will obtain, at best, a meaningless result. This is a classic GIGO—garbage in, garbage out—situation. To be certain you are asking about the relevant attributes, you must have pertinent market knowledge.

If you are in doubt about how solid your market knowledge is, there is a good way to be certain you have the correct attributes and significant levels. Hold a brainstorming session within your company to develop a preliminary attribute list. Some possible non-price attributes to consider are:

(text continued on page 254)

Exhibit B-16. Data reduction for eighteen-card set with two holdout cards.

Card #	Combination	Card Utility	Card Sum	ENTER DATA
1	A4 B2 C2 D4	1.44	44	44
2	A3 B3 C4 D4	1.23	47	47
3	A4 B3 C1 D2	2.13	28	28
4	A3 B2 C3 D2	2.51	20	20
5	A2 B2 C1 D1	3.01	7	7
6	A2 B4 C4 D2	2.11	29	29
7	A4 B4 C3 D3	1.10	50	50
8	A2 B3 C2 D3	1.89	34	34
9	A4 B1 C4 D1	2.42	22	22
10	A1 B3 C3 D1	2.69	16	16
11	A1 B4 C1 D4	1.58	41	41
12	A3 B1 C1 D3	2.16	28	28
13	A1 B1 C2 D2	3.06	6	6
14	A3 B4 C2 D1	2.18	27	27
15	A1 B2 C4 D3	2.04	30	30
16	A2 B1 C3 D4	2.04	30	30
17	A2 B2 C2 D2	2.81	13	13
18	A3 B3 C3 D3	1.59	41	41

Sum Error?   0

Number of logical inconcsistencies   0

R without holdout   -1.00   R Ratio   1.00

R with holdout included   -1.00

		Level's Card Formula	Level Total	Level Utility	Utility Range	Judgment Percent
Factor A	Performance specs				.57	.23
A1	Exceed by 20%	10 + 11 + 13 + 15	93	.77		
A2	Exceed by 5%	5 + 6 + 8 + 16	100	.69		
A3	Fall short by 5%	2 + 4 + 12 + 14	122	.44		
A4	Fall short by 20%	1 + 3 + 7 + 9	144	.20		
Factor B	Price				.68	.27
B1	$700,000	9 + 12 + 13 + 16	86	.84		
B2	$800,000	1 + 4 + 5 + 15	101	.68		
B3	$900,000	2 + 3 + 8 + 10	125	.41		
B4	$1,000,000	6 + 7 + 11 + 14	147	.17		
Factor C	Delivery time				.27	.11
C1	6 months	3 + 5 + 11 + 12	104	.64		
C2	9 months	1 + 8 + 13 + 14	111	.57		
C3	12 months	4 + 7 + 10 + 16	116	.51		
C4	15 months	2 + 6 + 9 + 15	128	.38		
Factor D	Terms				1.00	.40
D1	Inst + 12 mon guar	5 + 9 + 10 + 14	72	1.00		
D2	Inst + 6 mon guar	3 + 4 + 6 + 13	83	.88		
D3	Installed, no guar	7 + 8 + 12 + 15	142	.22		
D4	FOB seller, no guar	1 + 2 + 11 + 16	162	.00		

- Company reputation
- Salesperson's product knowledge
- Ease of use (or user friendliness)
- User training required
- Training provided
- Training site convenience
- Product reliability
- Warranty terms
- Maintenance requirements
- Availability of service technicians
- Availability of spare parts
- Delivery time

You can then use the list you develop with three or four focus groups to determine the most critical attributes. The chosen attributes should be as non-redundant as possible. After that, conduct the conjoint analysis itself.

(*text continued on page 256*)

Exhibit B-17.   Individual attribute utilities, providing an explanation for card rankings.

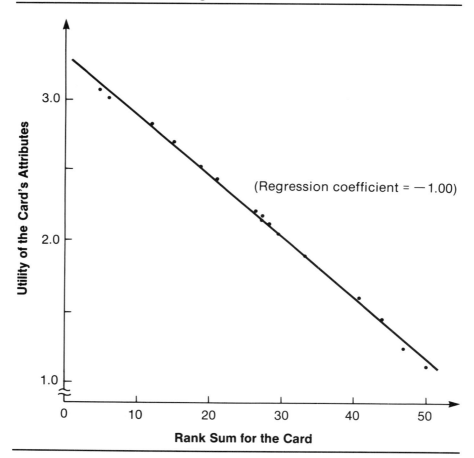

Exhibit B-18. Utilities for three product options.

Competitive Product	Utility
(A2) (B2) (C2) }	1.5

Three Options for Us

(1)	(A3) (B3) (C3) }	0.83

(2) Identical Product	(A2) (B2) (C2) }	1.5

(3)	(A1) (B1) (C1) }	2.17

Exhibit B-19. Estimated market shares for the three product options of Exhibit B-18.

Competitive Product	Utility	Market Share	
(A2) (B2) (C2) }	1.5		

Three Options for Us

(1)	(A3) (B3) (C3) }	0.83	$\dfrac{0.83}{0.83 + 1.5}$	= 38%

(2) Identical Product	(A2) (B2) (C2) }	1.5	$\dfrac{1.5}{1.5 + 1.5}$	= 50%

(3)	(A1) (B1) (C1) }	2.17	$\dfrac{2.17}{2.17 + 1.5}$	= 58%

Exhibit B-20. Price vs. cost relationship.

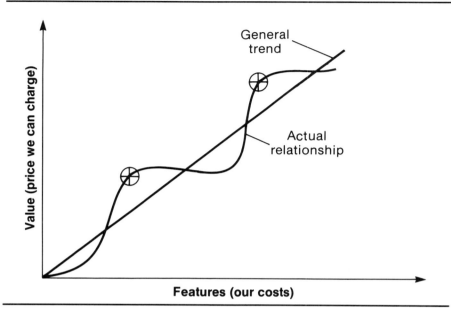

As a practical matter, card sets must be fairly small (three dozen is probably a maximum). I prefer sets with less than twenty cards. Thus, there are practical limits to how many attributes and levels you can sample. If you must evaluate more, you can build linked card sets and sample more people.

However, even at this point there are potential problems of which you should be aware. As with all market research, opinions and intentions change with the passage of time, so you can be misled if the conjoint analysis is performed a long time before the new product reaches the market. In addition, even if the time-to-market is short, point-of-sales displays, advertising, and public relations programs (yours or those of your competition) can alter people's actions. Furthermore, there can still be a problem if your product is not available in a given location at a given time due, for instance, to distribution problems.

Finally, it is extremely difficult to perform any market research if the new product is a totally new-to-the-world type of innovation. In such situations, it is hard to get respondents to imagine such a revolutionary concept.

SUMMARY

Conjoint analysis is a simple analytic technique that will help you specify a product's features. You can use it to guide the product design effort and improve your profits.

FURTHER READING ON CONJOINT ANALYSIS

Nontechnical

Green, P. E., and Wind, Y. "New Way to Measure Consumers' Judgments." *Harvard Business Review* (July-August 1975), pp. 107–117.

Diamond, A. H. "Conjoint Analysis: Ideal Research Technique for Financial Marketers." *Marketing News* (September 17, 1982), pp. 17 ff.

Morton, J., and Devine, H. J., Jr. "How to Diagnose What Buyers Really Want." *Business Marketing* (October 1985), pp. 70 ff.

Gelb, G. M. "Conjoint Analysis Helps Explain the Bid Process." *Marketing News* (March 14, 1988), pp. 1 ff.

Technical

Proceedings of the 1987 Sawtooth Conference on Perceptual Mapping, Conjoint Analysis, and Computer Interviewing. Ketchum, ID: Sawtooth Software, 1987, pp. 237–334.

Proceedings of the 1988 Sawtooth Conference on Perceptual Mapping, Conjoint Analysis, and Computer Interviewing. Ketchum, ID: Sawtooth Software, 1988, pp. 1–149.

Appendix C

Some New Product Development Tasks for Your Checklist

This list is intended to be only a guide to increase the likelihood that you will not omit some required task from your critical path network schedule. No single new product development project will require all of these tasks to be completed. Conversely, the development of almost any new product or service will require some additional tasks that are not included in this list. Your business may require that some of these occur either earlier or later in the development activity; nevertheless, you can use this list as a starting point on your next new product development program. Then, as you modify the list, you will be better prepared for subsequent new product development efforts.

Idea for

Unsolved market problem
New use for old product
New technology to exploit
Unique product
New process

Feasibility

Initial screening
   Fit with strategy
   Fit with culture
   Barriers to entry
      For us
      For competition
      Patent search

Markets
Technology
Manufacturing
Service and support
Timing
Impact on other products
Preliminary market assessment
Preliminary technical assessment
Preliminary manufacturing assessment
Preliminary business assessment
Establishment of proprietary confidentiality policy
Product concept
Concept testing
Feasibility demonstration
Breadboard(s)
Computer simulation
Bench chemistry
Design analyses

Optimization

Formation of triad team
Market research
    Secondary
    Primary
    Names of first three to six buyers
    Ability of customer to assimilate product
    Competitive analysis (in-kind and functional)
    Standards
    Legal and regulatory constraints
    Political constraints
    Social acceptability
Market segmentation
Product positioning
Plan to phase out replaced products
Trade-in plan
Distribution plan
Project schedule and budget plan
    Resource availability
    Facility (e.g., skunk works) or team location
    Priority (compared to alternatives)
Assessment of liability risks
Business analysis
Specifications
    Concept sketches
    Product attributes: musts and wants
        Technical characteristics

User interfaces
Target introduction date
Styles (including shapes, colors, textures)
Sensory features
Sizes
Accessories
Consumables
Adjunct services
Safety
Warranties
Factory cost or sell price and gross margin
Follow-on products and services

Design

System engineering
Block level design
Design and concept reviews
Failure analysis
Power consumption and dissipation analysis
Industrial design and styling
Service access and diagnostics
User controls and interface
Design drawings
Parts list
Accessories
Consumables
Bill of material
Software walk-throughs
Sources of supply
   Long lead time items
   Quantities versus time
   Inventory plan
   Component test plan
   Environmental risks and constraints
Product test procedures
Manufacturing of test equipment
Building of prototype(s)
Prototype testing
   Device characterization
   Qualification life tests
   Endurance tests
   Environmental tests
   Reliability tests
   Maintainability demonstration
Quality assurance plan
In-house product testing

Design revisions
Product name
Public relations plan
Product packaging
Determination of environmental limits
Shelf life tests
Regulatory approvals
    Underwriters Laboratories
    Federal Communications Commission
    Federal Aviation Administration
    Food and Drug Administration
    Environmental Protection Administration
    Premarket notifications
    Material safety data sheets
    Toxic Substances Control Act
Customer tests of product
Labeling requirements
Shipping container design
International distribution plan
Financial evaluation
Obtaining of protection
    Patents
    Copyrights
    Trademarks

Preproduction

Process development
Soft tooling and pilot run
Training of manufacturing personnel
Design verification test
Reliability verification test
Manufacturing verification test
Quality verification test
Software validation test
Documentation releases
Materials requirements plan
Configuration releases
Trial production
Locating second sources of supply
Test marketing
Beta test sites
Pilot plant
Assembly fixtures
Test fixtures
Production cost estimates
Precommercialization business analysis

Tooling
Export license

Production

Production start-up
Sales demonstration samples
Training of
    Trainers
    Salespeople
    Product installation teams
    Product support specialists
    Service personnel
    Users
Training materials
    Demonstration units
    Transparencies
    Programmed instruction
    Videocassettes
    Software data sets
    Accessories
    Consumables
    Handouts
Semi-commercial production
Advertising campaign (all markets)
    Key account preannouncement
    Customer
    Suppliers
    Manufacturers of congruent equipment and supplies
    Trade
    Trade shows
    Influencers
    Financial community
    End user
    Catalog sheets
    Coupons
    Package artwork
    Product tie-ins
    News releases
    Mailing labels
Literature (all languages)
    Installation instructions
    Data sheets
    Brochures
    Warranty cards
    User instructions

Training manuals
Service instructions
Sales tools
Terms and conditions
Trade-in policy
Adjunct services, accessories, supplies, and products
Acceptance test procedure
Giveaways
Contests
Point-of-sale displays
Testimonials
Discount schedule
Sales quotas
User groups

Sales

Market launch
Regional
National
Multinational
Global
Full-scale production
Service spares
Field sales
After-sales support
Brand building
Market growth

Post-introduction appraisal

Post mortem
Lessons learned
Revision of new product development procedures

Appendix D

Examples of Interview Questionnaires

There are some techniques that I have found helpful in conducting face-to-face or telephone interviews, which I illustrate with two disguised examples in Exhibits D-1 and D-2.

The easiest part of constructing an interview is dealing with the mechanical details. I find it helpful to write the questions on the left side of the page, leaving space on the right side to enter the interviewee's answers. The two exhibits illustrate this.

If you store your questionnaire on the computer, you can insert new questions or change the details of the original questions as you begin to collect information. This is mechanically easy to do with a word processor, and permits you to tailor your interviews to each person. It also provides the triad with a clear record of the questions and answers from each interview, presented in such a way that these answers cannot easily be taken out of context.

There are several ingredients that I believe you should include in almost any interview:

1. You should make an introductory statement. This provides a script to open the interview and sets the tone for what follows. It allows the interviewees to say they are not qualified to respond, if that is the case. If they are not qualified, ask if they can suggest someone else to interview.

2. You should determine the personal background of the interviewees, since this establishes their qualifications. (If you are researching a mass market product or service, professional qualifications are normally unimportant. However, in such a case demographics are important, so you may want to get information regarding age, sex, marital status, education, income, and similar factors.) This information allows you to sort the responses by various categories. In the case of industrial products, respondents with marginal qualifications can be discounted and experts can be given greater weight.

3. It is smart to ask if the interviewees are aware of any problems in the general area of the inquiry. They may have a much worse problem in the general area that you are probing than you (or your client) are trying to solve. They

(text continued on page 271)

Exhibit D-1. Noncustomer interview plan and record sheet for common industrial and consumer market product.

Name _____ *Date* _____

Organization _____ *Phone* (_____) _____

[*Introduce self.*] I'm calling because I'm on an assignment to examine the structure of the microcomputer software market. Do you have a few moments? I'd like to ask you a few questions about the role of discount mail order companies.

Do you have a microcomputer, or do you use one at work? Which?

_____

_____

What is the most important factor to you in the selection of a software supplier?

_____

_____

_____

_____

How will telephonic downloading of software programs impact the discount mail order business?

_____

_____

_____

_____

Exhibit D-1. *(continued)*

Do you know about discount mail-order or telephone-order software suppliers (such as Programming International, 800-Software, Microhouse, and Discount Software)?

_____

_____

_____

_____

Other things being equal, would you prefer an in-state or out-of-state supplier?

_____

_____

[*If face-to-face, show ads.*] Here are prices and terms for SuperCalc from six ads. Which would you be most likely to order from? Why?

_____

_____

_____

_____

Have you bought software from such a company?

_____

_____

Which one(s) have you bought from?

_____

_____

_____

_____

[*If yes, continue; if no, go to* **.]

What attracted you to such a company originally?

_____

_____

_____

_____

Were you satisfied with their service?

_____

_____

How could they have served you better?

_____

_____

_____

_____

Do you know of others who have used such suppliers?

_____

_____

_____

_____

Exhibit D-1. (*continued*)

[*If yes*] What was their experience?

_____

_____

_____

_____

[*East only*] Is the three-hour time difference a problem in using West Coast companies?

_____

_____

How is your software procurement budget established?

_____

_____

_____

_____

Which magazines do you read?

_____

_____

_____

_____

What else should I have asked you?

_____

_____

_____

_____

**

Have you seen ads for any of the following discount software suppliers?

☐ Programming International?
☐ Discmail?
☐ 800-SOFTWARE?
☐ Microhouse?
☐ Discount Software?

What is your reaction to them?

_____

_____

_____

_____

Under what conditions would you buy software from one of these companies?

_____

_____

_____

_____

_____

Exhibit D-1. *(continued)*

What would be (or is) most important to you in such a purchase decision?

_____

_____

_____

_____

Do you know anyone who has bought from such a supplier?

_____

_____

_____

_____

What was their experience?

_____

_____

_____

_____

What magazines do you read?

_____

_____

_____

What else should I have asked you?

_____

_____

_____

_____

_____

may thus identify a better opportunity. Or, they may reveal an unexpected aspect that needs priority attention. Several years ago, I was trying to learn about the number of buyers who might have a need for a certain kind of specialized capital equipment my client was considering manufacturing. This line of inquiry elicited frequent complaints about the present cost of this class of equipment and also revealed a reasonably large market. Unfortunately, the estimated selling price of the equipment my client was considering would have been about ten times higher than what was already on the market! Thus, we verified that there was indeed a need, but for a totally different (much lower-priced) solution.

4. It is useful to ask respondents what they know about suppliers or similar products or services. This can be a way to verify their expertise (or lack thereof). I generally list suppliers alphabetically; it is also possible to vary the sequence from one interview to the next. Also, I often insert a completely fictitious, but plausible, supplier name (for example, Discmail, in the Exhibit D-1 interview), which provides a further check of the interviewee's expertise.

5. You want to learn as much as you can about how they currently buy similar products and services. If they buy it all from the boss's brother-in-law (and this kind of purchasing bias does occur), you are not going to sell anything to this company. Other answers indicate how you have to be prepared to sell your product or service.

If you are a market research consultant and if your client has given permission, you can now ask about how familiar they are with your client. It's often helpful to have this permission, since the prospect (early in the interview) that you will later reveal it to the interviewees can provide an inducement for them to continue answering questions. However, in many cases, the client's identity cannot be revealed, and sometimes a person refuses to be interviewed.

It is normally helpful to end with two questions:

1. What else should I have asked you?
2. Can you recommend other experts I might talk with?

(text continued on page 281)

Exhibit D-2.   Interview plan and record sheet for a high-technology industrial product.

Name _____   *Date* _____

Company _____   *Interviewer(s)* _____

Address _____   _____

_____   _____

Telephone _____

[*Introduce self.*] I've been retained by a client to help them better serve their instrumentation customers. I'd like to ask you a few questions before I identify my client; then I'll identify them and conclude by asking you a few more questions about the client specifically. OK?

Personal Background

How long have you been in the test and measurement instrumentation field?

_____

_____

What kind of instrumentation?

_____

_____

_____

_____

What societies are you a member of?

_____

_____

What journals and trade magazines do you read?

_____

_____

_____

_____

Problems

What kind of physical events are you observing (measuring)?

_____

_____

_____

_____

What are the key issues?

_____

_____

_____

_____

What are your impressions of the following seven sensor suppliers:

Bently-Nevada

_____

_____

_____

Exhibit D-2. (*continued*)

CEC—Bell & Howell

_____

_____

_____

Endevco—B&D

_____

_____

_____

Kulite

_____

_____

Rosemount

_____

_____

Statham—Gould

_____

_____

Vibrometer

_____

_____

What kind of information (data) about these events do you require?

_____

_____

_____

_____

What are the key issues?

_____

_____

What dominates your data costs?

_____

_____

What are your impressions of the following seven data display suppliers:

Biomation & Brush-Gould

_____

_____

Datalab—Bell & Howell

_____

_____

Honeywell

_____

_____

Exhibit D-2.   *(continued)*

H-P

_____

_____

Nicolet

_____

_____

Philips

_____

_____

Tektronix

_____

_____

What are major test & measurement problems you now encounter?

_____

_____

_____

_____

_____

_____

What are major test & measurement needs you anticipate in the next five years?

_____

_____

_____

_____

Is there a product or service not now available that you'd like?

_____

_____

Specs?

_____

Key attributes?

_____

Price?

_____

Do you know of anyone at work on this?

_____

Who?

_____

How long?

_____

Exhibit D-2.   *(continued)*

[*If appropriate, probe further about interviewee's needs and wants.*]

☐ Transducers and sensors?

Test/operation duration

_____

Number/kind of sensors

_____

Sensor environment

_____

Accuracy & response

_____

Lifetime

_____

What other sensors used

_____

Technology preference/why

_____

Size/shape importance

_____

☐ Signal processing electronics?

Role of computer?

_____

☐ Readouts and displays?

Environment?

_____

Archival storage need?

_____

Record re-use and why?

_____

Buying Process

Who makes recommendation to buy instrumentation?

_____

Who provides final approval of buying decision?

_____

In buying instrumentation, how important are:

Price?

_____

Quality?

_____

Delivery?

_____

Service?

_____

Exhibit D-2. (*continued*)

Performance specifications?

_____

Other?

_____

Is instrumentation purchase tied to a fiscal year budget?

_____

My client is XYZ. [*If not previously recognized, say*] They supply vibration and pressure sensors, signal processing electronics, transient waveform recorders, and oscillographic chart recorders. Do you know them?

_____

XYZ

What are they best at?

_____

_____

What is their biggest weakness?

_____

_____

Which of their products do you know about?

_____

_____

If there was one thing you could change at XYZ or with their products, what would that be?

_____

_____

Closing

What else should I have asked you?

_____

_____

_____

_____

Can you recommend other experts I might talk with?

_____

_____

_____

_____

THANKS!

The first almost always provides some key insight that leads to modified questions in subsequent interviews. The second can give you entree to other people to interview, and also provides some further calibration of how expert your interviewee is. The second question is obviously inappropriate for a non-technical or mass market product or service.

Appendix E

Audit: Faster New Product Development

These are questions to ask about aspects or elements of your company's new product development performance. Score your company (or individual business unit) with a five-point scale:

5 = Always
4 = Usually
3 = Sometimes
2 = Rarely
1 = Never

Items with scores of 1 or 2 identify areas to which attention should be given promptly, since these offer the greatest opportunity for significant improvement. Items with scores of 3 or 4 also deserve attention, but these can be deferred until the items with lower scores are improved.

This audit is suggestive, not definitive, since no universal mechanical scoring device can accurately diagnose each company's unique and necessarily complex new product development situation.

Specifications

- Are these established and based on well-understood market needs?
- Are musts and wants explicitly differentiated?
- Are all specifications expressed quantitatively?
- Are the specifications frozen and not changed afterwards during the development program?
- Are the specifications established by a triad team?
- Are you the market leader (versus reacting to competitor leadership)?

Market Research

- Is commercial intelligence routinely collected and periodically examined?
- Are quantitative trade-off analysis tools used for market research?
- Is there a systematic analysis of data from returned warranty cards?
- Do you systematically collect data from customer experience (for instance, do you have an 800 telephone number for customers to call with questions or comments, record service needs, reorder frequency, and so on)?
- Do you routinely conduct lost sales analyses? Does the triad jointly conduct some of the field market research?
- Do you have your first few customers for the new product specifically identified?

Timeliness and Schedule Emphasis

- Do your new products reach the market at (or close to) the intended time?
- Are the schedules prepared by the triad?
- Do the schedules have reasonable contingency?
- Do you have lists of the tasks you normally must perform?
- Do your teams routinely seek shortcuts (omit, compress, perform in parallel)?
- Is project management software used for scheduling?
- Do all the significant participants in the new product development effort have current development schedules?
- Have you established mechanisms to avoid inventing on schedule?
- Is a large part of project review time devoted to the development schedule?
- Do you isolate development teams for major development efforts?

Teamwork

- Are there mechanisms in place to actively reduce disharmony?
- Do the rewards for success outweigh the penalties for failure?
- Are there team incentives?
- Is there a well-understood incentive formula?
- Is there a leadership triad for each significant new product development program?

New Product Development Obstacles

- Is top management committed to fast new product development?
- Have you reduced delays for management approvals to a reasonable minimum?

- Are the required resources available in a timely fashion?
- Is project management software used for resource management?
- Have you minimized fire-fighting interruptions?
- Are your new product development teams isolated from the on-going business?
- Does the company have a training program to improve timely development?

Profit Margins

- Does low manufacturing cost receive attention during the optimization and design phases?
- Do you use producibility software to assess your designs?
- Are your new product profit margins close to or above the plan?
- Do you maintain a profit aging chart to routinely calculate the percent of the current year's profits attributable to each of the five prior years' new products?
- Are you able to avoid price concessions for your new products?
- Do users, customers, and buyers value your new products sufficiently so that you can raise your prices?

Procedures

- Are there criteria for desired and acceptable new product ideas that are widely known and clearly understood?
- Are the new product development procedures perceived to be helpful?
- Are the procedures written and available?
- Are the procedures reasonably complete?
- Are the procedures clearly understood?
- Are the procedures followed?
- Were they revised within the last year?
- Do you consistently get successful new products from your new product development procedure?

I have used preliminary versions of this audit with four groups of executives and managers who attended my seminars on faster new product development (approximately 130 people, between December 1988 and March 1989). Not all questions were used with all groups and the wording of some questions was changed to clarify them. Based on this limited sample, some questions have a consistent pattern of scores of 1 or 2. These questions, and my observations for your consideration, are:

Are the specifications frozen and not changed afterwards during the development program?

Set better specifications that are complete and include a simple version of the product family that can be developed quickly.

Are the specifications established by a triad team?

Designate the triad and insist that they set the specifications.

Are quantitative trade-off analysis tools used for market research?

Use conjoint analysis or similar tools.

Is there a systematic analysis of data from returned warranty cards?

This is an inexpensive way to collect customer information and pinpoint emerging needs.

Do you routinely conduct lost sales analyses?

Painful, but an important means to set specifications for later models in a product family.

Does the triad jointly conduct some of the field market research?

This is an easy way to bring the real market need into the new product development activity, and it reduces over-elaboration in the product.

Do your new products reach the market at (or close to) the intended time?

If not, you must try to change the development process.

Are the schedules prepared by the triad?

Schedules set by the development team are more likely to be realistic. The team will also be more motivated and committed to these, because they "own" them.

Do the schedules have reasonable contingency?

A schedule without contingency has infinite risk; a schedule with infinite contingency has zero risk, but will not be approved. You must allow some contingency for the unforcasted surprise, and this is judgmental.

Have you established mechanisms to avoid inventing on schedule?

Devote some proportion of your resources to feasibility activities, to build the foundation for future new product development activities.

Do you isolate development teams for major development efforts?

The isolation may be organizational (a team that is dedicated and has no other assignment) or physical (a separate facility).

Are there team incentives? Is there a well-understood incentive formula?

These two questions suggest an opportunity, but taking advantage of this requires very careful design of the incentive program.

Is there a leadership triad for each significant new product development program?

This is perhaps the easiest way to promote multifunctional teamwork.

Have you minimized fire-fighting interruptions?

Isolation (mentioned above) helps. You also should have separate feasibility and maintenance activities.

Does the company have a training program to improve timely development?

Why not? The points conveyed in this book can be taught in a company setting to stress those that are specifically advantageous in your own situation.

Do you maintain a profit aging chart to routinely calculate the percent of the current year profits attributable to each of the five prior years' new products?

This is a simple tool to indicate when you have to initiate new development activities so there will not be any last minute rushes to fill profit growth holes in your plan.

Are the procedures written and available? Are the procedures reasonably complete? Are the procedures clearly understood? Are the procedures followed?

A training program (mentioned above) can be used to help develop and implement better procedures.

Appendix F

Extracts From Two Companies' Procedures

This appendix contains selected portions of phased approach procedures from two different companies. (I have made some changes and minor omissions to conceal the specific identities.) These might give you some ideas on how to prepare your own procedures, especially if used in conjunction with Exhibit 2-1.

INDUSTRIAL PRODUCT COMPANY
(SEQUENCE OF TASKS AND EVENTS)

Product Research Phase

1. Objectives: To combine a perceived need with a product concept and to establish program priority.

2. Required to Proceed to Next Step: A market potential and a potential technical solution. Also a report outlining the market need and the product concept, assigning a product line manager to assemble the product plan, including a product plan work order, development budget, and schedule.

Product Plan Development Phase

1. Objectives: To establish the program's technical and financial goals, budgets, and capital equipment requirements and schedules to verify the market need, to summarize the company product knowledge, and to state the program implications for all affected departments.

2. Required to Proceed to Next Step: Completed product plan.

3. Responsibility: The product line manager assembles the product plan and authors the marketing and financial sections of the plan. The engineering, manufacturing, quality assurance, and other concerned managers will supply their corresponding sections at the request of the product line manager.

Product Plan Review Meeting

1. Objectives: To analyze the product plan business implications, and to authorize product design if indicated.

2. Required to Proceed to Next Step: Sign-off of product plan by all executives. Sign-off authority is delegated to the vice-presidents of engineering and marketing for programs falling within approved budgets and business plans. Approval initiates product design, which will begin at the specified time approved.

3. Responsibility: Product line manager assembles data, calls and chairs meeting, and publishes minutes.

4. Meeting Attendance: All executives or their representatives, engineering manager, project engineer, product line manager.

5. Documentation: Minutes of meeting, signed product plan including approved capital equipment requests.

Product Design Phase

1. Objectives: To perform product design and development, to generate market introduction plan, to plan for manufacture, and to simultaneously validate the marketing and financial sections of the product plan.

2. Required to Proceed to Next Step: Assembled and tested prototype, completed critical design review, completed manufacturing engineering planning, documented deviations from product plan.

3. Responsibility: Project engineer leads development and chairs critical design review. Product line manager assembles data and updates product plan and is responsible for validating the marketing and financial sections of the product plan.

4. Sample Documentation at Phase Completion: Updated product plan incorporating market introduction section, critical design review minutes, approved capital equipment requirements, project expenditure records, engineering cost of goods estimate, long lead item list, pilot run size and plan, field trial plan, reliability calculation, preliminary specifications and pricing, field trial manual, field experiment results.

Initial Program Review Meeting

1. Objectives: Evaluate product design, review updated product plan, review design phase documentation, and authorize further development or manufacturing introduction.

2. Required to Proceed to Next Step: Minutes of meeting, updated product plan, and preliminary specifications and pricing. The meeting minutes will be co-signed by the engineering manager, manufacturing manager, quality assurance manager, and the product line manager. Sign-off by the vice-presidents of engineering and marketing will constitute an authorization to proceed.

3. Responsibility: Product line manager assembles data, calls and chairs meeting, and publishes minutes.

4. Meeting Attendance: Project engineer, engineering manager, quality assurance manager, manufacturing manager, and materials manager.

5. Documentation: Minutes of meeting.

Engineering Design Release

1. Objectives: Release of engineering documentation package and initiation of transfer of product to the manufacturing department.

2. Required to Proceed to Next Step: Documentation package complete and approved by the engineering manager.

3. Responsibility: Project engineer is responsible for engineering content.

4. Documentation: Completed documentation package.

Manufacturing Introduction Phase

1. Objectives: Validate product manufacturability, verify completeness and accuracy of engineering documentation, develop manufacturing jigs and fixtures, develop final technical manuals.

2. Required to Proceed to the Next Step: Completed pilot run, completed field trial, updated product plan, audit of field trial, and pilot run.

3. Responsibility: Product line manager has overall program, budget, and schedule responsibility; the manufacturing manager is responsible for pilot run completion, the project engineer for field trial completion and pilot run evaluation, the quality assurance manager for field trial and pilot run audit, and the product line manager for field trial customer arrangements and pilot run equipment disposition.

4. Sample Documentation at Phase Completion: Quality assurance audit reports, pilot run report, field trial report, updated product plan, manufacturing plan, factory cost of goods standard, final technical manual, project expenditure records, specification, delivery, application/installation information, disposition of outstanding change requests, and pilot run equipment disposition.

Final Program Review Meeting

1. Objectives: Evaluate pilot run and field trial results, review updated product plan, authorize standard production and release the product to the sales department.

2. Required to Proceed to Next Step: Minutes of meeting, updated product and market plans. The meeting minutes will be co-signed by the engineering manager, the manufacturing manager, the product line manager, and executives, which will then constitute an authorization to proceed.

3. Responsibility: Product line manager assembles data, calls and chairs meeting, and publishes minutes.

4. Documentation: Signed minutes of meeting, final product and market plans.

Standard Production Phase

1. Objective: Profitable production through product life.

2. Required to Proceed: Continuing review of market response, production cost of goods, price, specification, delivery, and competitive products.

CONSUMER PRODUCT COMPANY (PROJECT PLAN CHECKLIST)

Before a project can be undertaken, the first thing is to prepare a concept proposal. This proposal can be initiated by any member of the department. Note that as much information as possible should be provided, even if only ballpark estimates are necessary. Upon completion, approval should be sought from the director.

Once a project concept has been approved, and a team has been assigned, the first order of business is to develop a detailed project plan. As the plan is developed, keep in mind some key points:

- Be sure all team members participate—"If they weren't part of making the plan, they won't be part of implementing the plan."
- Plans basically relate to future events but are based on present knowledge.
- Plans should not be intrinsically inconsistent with other plans.
- Plans involve assumptions, so should include reasonable contingencies.
- The project plan is also a document for monitoring changes in the original plan.

Every project plan must have some key element.

Project File

As soon as a concept has been approved and a project leader assigned, two project files must be created, one file for department use and the other for the project leader. These files must contain all written documentation with reference to the project including project plan, network diagram, communications, and bills. Each team member should also maintain a file for ready reference. Also prepare additional copies for central and chronological files.

Items that need to be included are (1) project title, (2) project number, (3) user, (4) objective, (5) required and desired performance criteria, and (6) date needed.

Detailed List of Activities

Activities should be broken down in sufficient detail to ensure proper estimates of time and cost. For example, an activity might be to evaluate a competitive product. This needs to be broken down to:

1. Determine availability of competitive product.
2. Obtain competitive product.
3. Implement a product evaluation lab test for standard properties (for comparison opposite required/desired criteria).
4. Select products and users for test.
5. Conduct test.
6. Analyze results and issue report.

Network Diagram

When the detailed list of activities is generated, prepare a network diagram and identify critical path(s). This will enable you to visualize interdependencies of activities.

Time Estimates

Every activity requires time to complete. The more detailed the work breakdown structure, the easier it is to estimate time. Recognize that even with the most careful estimates, projects have a way of running longer than anticipated.

Personnel Assignments

Each activity must have a clearly assigned person responsible for accomplishing the activity. The assigned person is responsible for carrying out the activity (or to see that it is carried out, e.g., lab tests) within the agreed time schedule and for reporting at the conclusion of the activity to team members.

Cost Estimates

The project plan should also contain a revised overall cost estimate based on the detailed project plan:

- Labor costs
- Sample costs
- Travel
- Cost of producing samples (outside)
- Miscellaneous (administrative overhead, literature search)

Communication Items

Perhaps the single most important reason why a project fails is poor communication. The project plan should clearly establish tools for communication:

- Within team
- Between team and R&D
- Between team and user
- With resources

The project plan should indicate specific dates for written and oral reviews for the four groups above. The project plan should also clearly identify the person responsible for communication of specific items at the designated times.

Decision Points

The plan must identify key decision points where potential major changes in project direction might occur.

Changes to Plan

The project plan should have a well-devised procedure for changes that occur in time, cost, personnel, and performance criteria.

Project Closure

A clearly identified end point for the project must be shown. Included would be final review for R&D and the user and the issuing of a written final report. Within thirty days of the final report, complete the team member performance appraisal.

Notes on Sources

The source citations are keyed to the text by page number and a short phrase.

CHAPTER 1

Page

3   "actions taken by practitioners": Davis, D. B. "Beating the Clock." *Electronic Business* (May 29, 1989), pp. 21 ff.

3   "Consumer product companies are": Alsop, R. "Companies Get on Fast Track to Roll Out Hot New Brands." *The Wall Street Journal* (July 10, 1986), p. 25.

4   "Eastman Kodak reorganized its": "Kodak Alters Research Setup." *The New York Times* (February 27, 1986).

4   "to get the machines": "How Xerox Speeds up the Birth of New Products." *Business Week* (March 19, 1984), pp. 58–59.

4   "Historically, IBM introduced a": Mulder, J. H. "The Stock Market." *Kidder, Peabody & Company Equity Research* (May 1987), p. 1.

4   "In the current environment": Kelley, D. "A Better Way to Design Products." *High Technology* (December 1986), p. 8.

4   "I can't document it": Fraker, S. "High Speed Management for the High-Tech Age." *Fortune* (March 5, 1984), pp. 62 ff.

4   "The data from one": Qualls, W., Olshavsky, R., and Michaels, R. "Shortening of the PLC—An Empirical Test." *Journal of Marketing* (Vol. 45, pp. 76–80) 1981.

5   "four other research studies": Clark, W., Freeman, H., and Hanssens, D. "Opportunities for Revitalizing Stagnant Markets: An Analysis of Household Appliances." *Journal of Product Innovation Management* (Vol. 4, pp. 242–254) 1984; see also, Onkvisit, S., and Shaw, J. J. "Competition and Product Management: Can the Product Life Cycle Help?" *Business Horizons*, (July/August 1986), pp. 51–62; Ela, J. D., and Irwin, M. R. "Technology Changes at the Boundaries." *Industrial Marketing Management*, (Vol. 12, pp. 153–156) 1983; Cravens, D. W.

Page

"Strategic Forces Affecting Marketing Strategy." *Business Horizons*, September/October 1986, pp. 77–88.

5   "There are several causes": Buggie, F. D. "What Do Product Life Cycles Tell Us?" *Chief Executive* (Spring 1986), pp. 18–20.

5   "Rapid development of new": Cravens, D. W. "Strategic Forces Affecting Marketing Strategy." *Business Horizons* (September/October 1986), pp. 77–88.

5   "The rapid rate of": Fraker, S. "High Speed Management for the High-Tech Age." *Fortune* (March 5, 1984), pp. 62 ff.

5   "The increasing pace of": Onkvisit, S., and Shaw, J. J. "Competition and Product Management: Can the Product Life Cycle Help?" *Business Horizons* (July/August 1986), pp. 51–62.

5   "The ever-increasing pace of": Warren, A. "The Innovation Traps." *Industry Week* (September 17, 1984), pp. 48 ff.

5   "Technology has forced the": Labich, K. "The Innovators." *Fortune* (June 6, 1988), pp. 50 ff.

9   "will earn more money": Reinertsen, D. G. "Whodunit? The Search for the New-Product Killers." *Electronic Business* (July 1983).

13   "Apollo's stock price dropped": Markoff, J. "Word of Apollo Loss Jolts Stock." *The New York Times* (July 8, 1988), p. 23Y.

13   "Fast new product development": Eureka, W. E., and Ryan, N. E. *The Customer-Driven Company*. Dearborn, MI: ASI Press, 1988. See especially p. 10.

14   "The 1987 models of": Mitchell, R. "GM's New Luxury Cars: Why They're Not Selling." *Business Week* (January 19, 1987), pp. 94 ff.

CHAPTER 2

Page

20   "The fact that you": Buttrell, F. *Technology to Payoff: Managing the New Product from Creation to Customer.* Philadelphia: Cresheim Publications, 1984, p. 55.

20   "You might use licensing": Gold, B. "Approaches to Accelerating Product and Process Development." *Journal of Product Innovation Management* (June 1987), pp. 81–88.

21   "the development partner approach": Goldberg, J. R., and Yakatan, S. "Why Two Can Speed Products To Market Quicker Than One." *Chief Executive* (January/February 1989), pp. 36 ff.

21   "overlap of several phases": Takeuchi, H., and Nonaka, I. "The New New Product Development Game." *Harvard Business Review* (January/February 1986), pp. 137–146.

22   "Part of the alleged": Uttal, B. "Speeding New Ideas to Market." *Fortune* (March 2, 1987), pp. 62 ff.

Page
22   "erect unnecessary paperwork hurdles": Wind, Y. and Mahajan. "New Product Development Process: A Perspective for Reexamination." *Journal of Product Innovation Management* (December 1988), pp. 304–310.

39   "no single right way": Duerr, M. G. *The Commercial Development of New Products.* New York: The Conference Board, 1986.

39   "different procedures for different": Krubasik, E. G. "Customize Your Product Development." *Harvard Business Review* (November/December 1988), pp. 46 ff.

CHAPTER 3

Page
46   "checkpoints during the development": Rinholm, B. L. "Formal Process Can Improve Success of New Products." *Marketing News* (September 12, 1988), p. 22.

49   "Compaq reportedly spent two": Uttal, B. "Speeding New Ideas to Market." *Fortune* (March 2, 1987), pp. 62 ff.

50   "real market information to": Bower, J. L., and Hout, T. M. "Fast-Cycle Capability for Competitive Power." *Harvard Business Review* (November-December, 1988), pp. 110–118.

50   "a family can provide": Crawford, C. M. "How Product Innovators Can Foreclose the Options of Adaptive Followers." *Journal of Consumer Marketing* (Fall 1988), pp. 17–24.

50   "The adjunct features (such": Canton, I. D. "Manufacturers Can Be Service Marketers, Too." *Marketing News* (December 19, 1988), p. 12.

57   "some market research techniques": Kornokovich, R. J., and Gross, I. "Consumer Methods Work for Business Marketing." *Marketing News* (November 21, 1988), pp. 4 ff.

59   "In the late 1950s": Example provided by an anonymous AMACOM reviewer.

63   "Carbon composite airliner brake": *The New York Times* (November 23, 1988), p. C6.

63   "a new kind of cement": Port, O. "Why Army Engineers are Stuck on a New Cement." *Business Week* (October 31, 1988), p. 153.

64   "for many years unable": Hammonds, K. H. "Why Polaroid Must Remake Itself—Instantly." *Business Week* (September 19, 1988), pp. 66 ff.

CHAPTER 4

Page
70   "The total production time": Mather, H. "Are You Logistically Effective?" *Chief Executive* (November/December 1987), pp. 32–36.

Page

71   "quality function deployment (the": Hauser, J. R., and Clausing, D. "The House of Quality." *Harvard Business Review* (May/June 1988), pp. 63–73; see also, Eureka, W. E., and Ryan, N. E. *The Customer-Driven Company*. Dearborn, MI: ASI Press, 1988.

72   "rework is rarely required": Whitney, D. E. "Manufacturing by Design." *Harvard Business Review* (July/August 1988), pp. 83–91.

72   "corrosion protection without plating": Sheridan, J. H. "A 'Simultaneous' Success Story." *Industry Week* (August 1, 1988), pp. 73–74.

73   "early arbitrary subsystem partitions": Reinertsen, D. G. "Blitzkrieg Product Development: Cut Development Times in Half." *Electronic Business* (January 15, 1985); see also, Badawy, M. K. "Integration." *Industry Week* (June 19, 1989), pp. 39 ff.

73   "discounted cash flow analysis.": Rosenau, M. D., Jr. *Innovation: Managing the Development of Profitable New Products*. Belmont, CA: Lifetime Learning Publications, 1982.

76   "new software is available": Port, O. "Software That Tells You How Much That New Widget Will Cost." *Business Week* (April 4, 1988), p. 63.

CHAPTER 5

Page

78   "cannot overcome the difficulties": Dixon, J. R., and Duffey, M. R. "Quality is not Accidental—It's Designed." *The New York Times* (June 26, 1988), p. 2F.

79   "key manufacturing department personnel": Dean, J. W., Jr., and Susman, G. I. "Organizing for Manufacturable Design." *Harvard Business Review* (January/February 1989), pp. 28ff; see also, Whitney, D. E. "Manufacturing by Design." *Harvard Business Review* (July/August 1988) pp. 83–91; Langowitz, N. S. "Managing New Product Design and Factory Fit." *Business Horizons* (May/June 1989), pp. 76–79.

80   "product design is robust": Port, O. "How to Make it Right the First Time." *Business Week* (June 8, 1987), pp. 142–143.

80   "Capitalizing upon programmable automation": Hayes, R. H., and Jaikumar, R. "Manufacturing's Crisis: New Technologies, Obsolete Organizations." *Harvard Business Review* (September/October 1988) pp. 77–85.

80   "As a final example": Rohan, T. M. "Factories of the Future." *Industry Week* (March 21, 1988), pp. 33 ff.

81   "plan for these tests": Teresko, J. "Mark it for Success." *Industry Week* (January 4, 1988), pp. 63 ff.

82   "By reducing raw, WIP, and finished inventory levels": McDonald, J. F. "Integrate Manufacturing into Your Strategic Plan." *Chief Executive* (Spring 1987), pp. 26–28.

Page

83   "JIT is a new": I am indebted to the staff at the Industrial Relations Center of California Institute of Technology for much of the material on JIT.

83   "Die changes that used": Holusha, J. "Choreography on a Stamping Line." *The New York Times* (December 2, 1988), pp. Z17 ff.

83   "floor and product flow.": Kuzela, L. "Tracking Product Flow." *Industry Week* (June 20, 1988), p. 98.

84   "you have more labor": Johansson, H. J. "Factories, Services and Speed." *The New York Times* (January 17, 1988), sec. 3, p. 2.

CHAPTER 6

Page

88   "use of Taguchi methods": Holusha, J. "Improving Quality, The Japanese Way." *The New York Times* (July 20, 1988), p. Y35.

CHAPTER 7

Page

91   "Many years ago, 3M": Hinds, M. deC. "A Solution Finds Its Problem: How to Tell if Dinner is Done." *The New York Times* (April 30, 1988), p. 16Y; see also, Siwolop, S. "Why the Heat-and-Eat Market is Really Cooking." *Business Week* (June 27, 1988), pp. 90–91.

91   "Kodak introduced lithium batteries": Ansberry, C. "Kodak 10-Year Battery Has Flaw; Black & Decker Halts Sales of Items." *The Wall Street Journal* (February 22, 1988), p. 24.

91   "Searle may not have": Richards, B. "Monsanto's Searle May Have Misled U.S. On Potential Hazards of IUD, Data Show." *The Wall Street Journal* (March 14, 1988), pp. 2 ff; see also, Richards, B. "Records Raise Question: Did Monsanto Know of IUD Problem in Buying Searle?" *The Wall Street Journal* (March 15, 1988), p. 10; Richards, B. "FDA Says Initial Review Shows Searle Didn't Mislead Agency on IUD's Safety." *The Wall Street Journal* (March 22, 1988), p. 2; Lewin, T. "Searle Documents Unsealed; Early IUD Worry is Implied." *The New York Times* (March 15, 1988), pp. 29Y ff.

92   "Squibb chooses its projects": Benway, S. "Squibb's Rx for Success: Find a Need and Fill It." *Business Week* (October 5, 1987), p. 80.

93   "As I show elsewhere": Rosenau, M. D., Jr. *Innovation: Managing the Development of Profitable New Products.* New York: Van Nostrand Reinhold (Lifetime Learning Publications), 1982, pp. 36–40.

93   "What do you do": Zeldman, M. "Moving Ideas From R&D to the Shop Floor." *Management Review* (December 1986), pp. 24 ff.

97   "There are various ways": Duerr, M. G. *The Commercial Development of New Products.* New York: The Conference Board, 1986.

Page

97   "The National Science Foundation": Siwolop, S. "A Pipeline from the Lab to Industry." *Business Week* (May 4, 1987), p. 126.

97   "contains a representative list": *Technology Applications Bulletin*. Oak Ridge, TN: Martin Marietta Energy Systems, Summer 1988.

97   "your innovative customers may": Goldstin, M. L. "R&D's Source? *Industry Week* (May 2, 1988), pp. 58–59.

98   "research conducted at universities": Uchitelle, L. "U.S. Companies Lift R&D Abroad." *The New York Times* (February 22, 1989), p. C2(Z).

CHAPTER 8

Page

101   "in every conceivable fashion": Bart, C. K. "New Venture Units: Use Them Wisely to Manage Innovation." *Sloan Management Review*, Summer 1988, pp. 35–43.

103   "call for different skills": Bart, C. K. "Implementing 'Growth' and 'Harvest' Product Strategies." *California Management Review*, Summer 1987, pp. 139–156.

104   "there is some evidence": Larson, E. W., and Gobeli, D. H. "Organizing for Product Development Projects." *Journal of Product Innovation Management*, September 1988, pp. 180–190.

105   "Kodak has shifted to": Strong, F. P. "Kodak: Beyond 1990." *Journal of Business and Industrial Marketing* (Fall 1987), pp. 29–36; see also, Helm, L. "Has Kodak Set Itself Up for a Fall?" *Business Week* (February 22, 1988), pp. 134 ff.

105   "has recently been proposed": Dean, J. W., Jr., and Susman, G. I. "Organizing for Manufacturable Design." *Harvard Business Review* (January/February 1989), pp. 28 ff.

CHAPTER 9

Page

108   "priorities for new product": Smith, P. G. "Winning the New Products Rat Race." *Machine Design* (May 12, 1988), pp. 95–98; see also, Davis, D. B. "Beating the Clock." *Electronic Business* (May 29, 1989), pp. 21 ff.

108   "We have to be": *SmithKline Beckman Quarterly Report*. Third Quarter 1988, p. 6.

109   "Bausch and Lomb reportedly": Therrien, L. "Bausch & Lomb Is Correcting Its Vision of Research." *Business Week*, March 30, 1987, p. 91.

111   "Many companies practice intrapreneuring,": DeMott, J . S. "Here Come the Intrapreneurs." *Time* (February 4, 1985), pp. 36–37; see also, Kichell, W. "Managing Innovators." *Fortune* (March 4, 1985), p.

Page

181; Dumaine, B. "What the Leaders of Tomorrow See." *Fortune* (July 3, 1989), pp. 48 ff.

111   "The 3M Corporation is": Fry, A. "The Post-It Note: An Intrapreneurial Success." *SAM Advanced Management Journal* (Summer 1987), pp. 4–9; and "Post-It Notes Clicks Thanks to Entrepreneurial Spirit." *Marketing News* (August 31, 1984), pp. 21–23; see also, Ingrassia, L. "By Improving Scratch Paper, 3M Gets New-Product Winner." *The Wall Street Journal* (March 31, 1983), p. 25.

111   "successes such as microcapsules": Hinds, M. deC. "A Solution Finds Its Problem: How to Tell If Dinner Is Done." *The New York Times* (April 30, 1988) p. 16Y.

111   "the company is investing": Koenig, R. "Money From the Boss." *The Wall Street Journal* (February 24, 1989), pp. R10 ff.

111   "IBM has established many": "How to Start Your Own Company Without Leaving IBM." *Fortune* (June 13, 1983), p. 78.

111   "Kodak has also sponsored": Strong, F. P. "Kodak: Beyond 1990." *Journal of Business and Industrial marketing* (Fall 1987), pp. 29–36; see also, Burdick, A. "New Twist on an Old Idea Moves Kodak Deeper into Electronics." *Electronics* (October 1, 1987), pp. 43 ff; "Kodak Is Trying to Break Out of Its Shell." *Business Week* (June 10, 1985), pp. 92 ff; Helm, L. "Has Kodak Set Itself Up for a Fall?" *Business Week* (February 22, 1988), pp. 134 ff.

111   "Dow has funded hundreds": Dickinson, S. "To Some Entrepreneurial Souls Dow Offers an Irresistible Deal." *The Scientist* (July 11, 1988), pp. 1 ff.

112   "There are significant management": Bart, C. K. "Organizing for New Product Development." *The Journal of Business Strategy* (July/August 1988), pp. 34–38; see also Bart, C. K. "New Venture Units: Use Them Wisely to Manage Innovation." *Sloan Management Review* (Summer 1988), pp. 35–43.

CHAPTER 10

Page

113   "Energy invested in fighting": Patterson, W. P. "Tackling Sacred Cows." *Industry Week* (October 17, 1988), pp. 65 ff; see also, Larson, C. "Team Tactics Can Cut Product Development Costs." *The Journal of Business Strategy* (September/October 1988), pp. 22–25.

113   "Many factors promote disharmony": Barron, C. A. "Silicon Blues." *The New York Times Magazine*, (September 20, 1987), pp. 25 ff.

114   "This inherent cultural difference": Lucas, G. H., Jr., and Bush, A. J. "The Marketing–R&D Interface: Do Personality Factors Have an Impact?" *Journal of Product Innovation Management* (December 1988), pp. 257–268.

Page

114   "in high-tech companies": Gupta, A., Raj, S. P., and Wilemon, D. "R&D and Marketing Managers in High-Tech Companies: Are They Different? *IEEE Transactions on Engineering Management* EM-33 (February 1986), pp. 25–32.

115   "There are data that": Gupta, A., Raj. S. P., and Wilemon, D. "The R&D–Marketing Interface in High-Technology Firms." *Journal of Product Innovation Management* (March 1985), pp. 12–24.

115   "A different study shows": Baker, N., Green, S., and Bean, A. "How Management Can Influence the Generation of Ideas." *Research Management* (November/December 1985), pp. 35–42.

116   "Harmony is not exclusively": Teresko, J. "Speeding the Product Development Cycle." *Industry Week* (July 18, 1988), pp. 40–42.

116   "and purchasing departments, if": Burt, D., and Soukup, W. "Purchasing's Role in New Product Development." *Harvard Business Review* (September/October 1985), pp. 90–97.

116   "such as industrial design": Whitney, D. E. "Manufacturing by Design." *Harvard Business Review* (July/August 1988), pp. 83–91.

116   "One manager has said": Bates, George. June 1, 1988, private communication.

117   "more extensive multifunctional teams": Stalk, G., Jr. "Time—The Next Source of Competitive Advantage." *Harvard Business Review* (July/August 1988), pp. 41–51; see also reports from the Graduate School of Management at Rutgers University by Hull, F. M., and Azumi, K. on "Inventivity and Multifunctional Teamwork in Japanese and U. S. Laboratories."

117   "the work of people": Schopler, J. H. "Interorganizational Groups: Origins, Structure, and Outcomes." *Academy of Management Review* (October 1987), pp. 702–713.

117   "can get better products": Wolff, M. "Overcoming Roadblocks to Commercializing Industrial R&D Projects." *Research Management* (July/August 1986), pp. 9–11.

118   "a project start-up workshop": Ono, D., and Archibald, R. D. *Project Start-Up Workshops: Gateway to Project Success*. Paper presented at the Project Management Seminar/Symposium, September 17–21, 1988.

118   "equitable top management treatment": Gupta, A., Raj, S. P., and Wilemon, D. "R&D and Marketing Managers in High-Tech Companies: Are They Different?" *IEEE Transactions on Engineering Management* EM-33 (February 1986), pp. 25–32.

118   "more harmonious and productive": Goleman, D. "Why Meetings Sometimes Don't Work." *The New York Times* (June 7, 1988), pp. 15Y ff.

118   "Having multifunctional teams responsible": Bower, J. L., and Hout, T. M. "Fast-Cycle Capability for Competitive Power." *Harvard Business Review* (November/December 1988), pp. 110–118.

Page

118   "Xerox has used small": Byrne, J. A. "Culture Shock at Xerox." *Business Week* (June 22, 1987), pp. 106 ff.

118   "Warner Division of Dana": Sheridan, J. H. "A 'Simultaneous' Success Story." *Industry Week*, (August 1, 1988), pp. 73–74.

118   "While it is too": Richman, L. S. "Software Catches the Team Spirit." *Fortune* (June 8, 1987), pp. 125 ff.

119   "Applied Materials relocated some": Applied Materials Annual Report, 1985, p. 10.

120   "Now, the company is": Kapstein, J. "Enough With the Theory— Where's the Thingamajig?" *Business Week* (March 21, 1988), pp. 155 ff.

CHAPTER 11

Page

126   "ensure that no time": Hout, T. M. and Blaxill, M. F. "Make Decisions Like a Fighter Pilot." *The New York Times* (November 15, 1987), p. C3.

126   "to accept the necessity": Bower, J. L. and Hout, T. M. "Fast-Cycle Capability for Competitive Power." *Harvard Business Review* (November/December 1988), pp. 110–118.

127   "the decision to kill": Staw, B. M. and Ross, J. "Knowing When to Pull the Plug." *Harvard Business Review* (March/April 1987), pp. 68–74.

129   "Some companies establish small": Alsop, R. "Consumer Product Giants Relying on 'Intrapreneurs' in New Ventures." *The Wall Street Journal* (April 22, 1988), p. 25.

129   "Some Japanese companies are": Stalk, G., Jr. "Time—The Next Source of Competitive Advantage." *Harvard Business Review* (July/August 1988) pp. 41–51; see especially pp. 49–50.

130   "there are some design": Sheridan, J. H. "Calling in 'Hired Guns'— Contract Design Firms Shorten the Cycle." *Industry Week* (July 4, 1988), p. 61.

130   "NIH (not invented here)": Sheridan, J. H. "State-of-the-Art CIM in 18 Months?" *Industry Week* (December 5, 1988), pp. 76–77.

130   "Both quality function deployment": Holusha, J. "Raising Quality: Consumers Star." *The New York Times* (January 5, 1989), pp. C1 ff.

130   "simultaneous engineering have shortened": Sheridan, J. H. "A 'Simultaneous' Success Story." *Industry Week* (August 1, 1988), pp. 73–74; see also, Smith, E. T. "Defense Trains Its Sights on the Manufacturing Process." *Business Week* (June 5, 1989), p. 98.

131   "Blue Cross of California" Williams, R. *Product/Service Development: A Case Study.* Presentation at PDMA-WEST meeting, March 3, 1989.

131   "You may be able": Alsop, R. "Companies Get on Fast Track to Roll Out Hot New Brands." *The Wall Street Journal* (July 10, 1986), p. 25.

Page

131 "you can substitute concept": Schwartz, D. *Concept Testing: How to Test New Product Ideas Before You Go to Market.* New York: AMA-COM, 1987.

132 "Cincinnati Milacron reportedly built": *Research & Development* (January 1989), pp. 15–16.

CHAPTER 12

Page

135 "Project management is the": Rosenau, M. D., Jr. *Successful Project Management.* New York: Van Nostrand Reinhold (Lifetime Learning Publications), 1981; see also, Rosenau M. D., Jr., and Lewin, M. D. *Software Project Management.* Los Angeles: M. D. Lewin Associates (Lifetime Learning Publications), 1984; Rosenau, M. D., Jr. *Project Management for Engineers.* New York: Van Nostrand Reinhold (Lifetime Learning Publications), 1984.

139 "microcomputer project management software": There are several sources of additional information that you may wish to explore: Rosenau, M. D., Jr. "Software Can Help You Manage R&D Projects." *Research & Development* (November 1985), pp. 86–88; see also, Rosenau, M. D., Jr. "Software Packages That Make Good Managers Better." *Journal of Management Consulting* (Vol. 3, No. 1, 1986), pp. 52–58; Levine, H. *Project Management Using Microcomputers.* Berkeley, CA: Osborne McGraw-Hill, 1986; Rosenau, M. D., Jr. *Project Management, including the use of Microcomputer Software* (videocassette course). Atlanta: The Association for Media-based Continuing Education for Engineers, Inc. (AMCEE), 1988.

143 "manual approaches were proposed": Dusenbury, W. "CPM for New Product Introductions." *Harvard Business Review.* (July/August 1967), pp. 124–139.

149 "ViewPoint provides several different": I am indebted to Hal Miller at Computer Aided Management for providing me the information from which this description of ViewPoint's resource management capabilities was prepared.

CHAPTER 13

Page

158 "many other specialized tools": McLeod, J. "A New Tool Dramatically Cuts VLSI Debugging Time." *Electronics* (April 30, 1987), pp. 51–53.

158 "you can automatically record": Teresko, J. "CAD, CAE, or Chaos?" *Industry Week* (September 19, 1988), pp. 73–74.

158 "computer-controlled laser cutting": McClenahen, J. "Automation's Global Game—Who's Winning?" *Industry Week* (June 20, 1988), pp. 37 ff. See especially p. 41.

Page

158   "Flexible automation may also": Gerwin, D. "Manufacturing Flexibility in the CAM Era." *Business Horizons* (January/February 1989), pp. 78–84.

159   "This emerging field involves": Schuon, M. "Automation That's Flexible." *The New York Times* (October 2, 1986), p. 26.

159   "Because each company has": Zygmont, J. "Manufacturers Move Toward Computer Integration". *High Technology* (February 1987), pp. 28–33; see also, Webster, F. C., Jr. "Computer Integrated Manufacturing Systems: Fact or Fantasy." *Business Horizons* (July/August 1988) pp. 64–68.

159   "a barrier exists because": Feder, B. J. "Test Facility Offers Glimpse of the Factory of Tomorrow." *The New York Times* (December 17, 1986), p. 46Y; see also, "Getting Machines to Communicate." *The New York Times* (May 27, 1987), p. 27Y; and "From Robots to Mainframes." *The New York Times* (June 15, 1988), pp. 31Y ff.

159   "recently some piecemeal steps": Zygmont, J. "Flexible Manufacturing Systems." *High Technology* (October 1986), pp. 22–27; see also, "Automation by Installment Plan." *Industry Week* (June 20, 1988), p. 97.

159   "General Electric's R&D center": Bylinsky G. "The High Tech Race: Who's Ahead?" *Fortune* (October 13, 1986), pp. 26–37.

159   "The paperless factory is": Krouse, J. "Engineering Without Paper." *High Technology* (March 1986), pp. 38–46.

159   "peopleless (fully automated) factory": Holusha, J. "Choreography on a Stamping Line." *The New York Times* (December 2, 1988), pp. Z17 ff; see also, Levin, D. P. "Smart Machines, Smart Workers." *The New York Times* (October 17, 1988), pp. Z1C ff; Hampton, W. J. "GM Bets an Arm and a Leg on a People-Free Plant." *Business Week* (September 12, 1988), pp. 72–73.

159   "the General Electric dishwasher": DeYoung, H. "GE: Dishing Out Efficiency." *High Technology* (May 1985), pp. 32–33.

159   "IBM has a quick": Kinnucan, P. "IBM: Making the Chips Fly." *High Technology* (May 1986), pp. 34–35.

159   "At least one company": Bluestone, M. "Prototype Chips: In by Nine, Out by Five." *Business Week* (July 13, 1987), p. 115; see also, "A Faster Way to Make Chips." *The New York Times* (August 17, 1988), p. 47Y.

159   "to develop a machine": Bluestone, M. "Whipping Up Circuit Boards in No Time at All." *Business Week* (December 19, 1988), p. 95.

159   "many companies offer equipment": Manuel, T. "Mentor Graphics Pulls Away in Electronics CAD/CAE Race." *Electronics* (July 9, 1987), pp. 49–50.

159   "expert systems are now": O'Reilly, B. "Computers That Think Like People." *Fortune* (February 27, 1989), pp. 90–93; see also, Leonard-Barton, D., and Sviokla, J. J. "Putting Expert Systems to Work." *Harvard Business Review* (March/April 1988), pp. 91–98; Port, O. "A Pro-

gram to Cut Elbow Grease in Engineering." *Business Week* (April 18, 1988), p. 73; "Speeding the Design of Some Chips." *The New York Times* (June 24, 1987), p. 32Y.

159   "IBM also has a": Naegele, T. "Laying Out Mixed Chips Takes IBM Days, Not Weeks." *Electronics* (February 18, 1988), p. 75; see also, Joshi, K. C. "IBM's Factory of the Future." Talk presented at the Productivity/Quality Forum at California Institute of Technology, Pasadena, CA (May 1, 1989).

159   "Another useful approach to": Port, O. "Do-It-Yourself Chips Get Easier." *Business Week* (March 30, 1987), p. 92. "Time to Design Custom-Made ICs is Cut to Days." *Research & Development* (April 1987), p. 29.

159   "some vendors sell specialized": Lineback, J. R. "Altera's Speedy Way to Tailor Add-Ons to IBM's PS/2." *Electronics* (February 18, 1988), pp. 99–100.

159   "are still significant obstacles": Brody, H. "Overcoming Barriers to Automation." *High Technology* (May 1985), pp. 41–46; see also, Davis, D. "Renaissance on the Factory Floor." *High Technology* (May 1985), pp. 24–25.

160   "Computer-aided software engineering—CASE": Feder, B. J. "Computer Helper: Software that Writes Software." *The New York Times* (May 8, 1988), p. F5; see also, Port, O. "The Software Trap: Automate—or Else." *Business Week* (May 8, 1988), pp. 142 ff.

160   "If your new product": Harris, C. L. "Office Automation: Making It Pay Off." *Business Week* (October 12, 1987), pp. 142 ff.

160   "Groupware may also prove": Dreyfuss, J. "Catching the Computer Wave." *Fortune* (September 26, 1988), pp. 78 ff; see also, Brandt, R. "'Groupware': Big Breakthrough—Or Big Brother?" *Business Week* (June 5, 1989), pp. 130–131.

160   "Today there are early": "Shortcut to Reality." *High Technology Business* (December 1987), pp. 12–13; see also, "Laser Process Makes Complex 3-D Parts." *Laser Focus/Electro-Optics* (June 1987), pp. 41–42; Lewis, P. H. "Device Quickly Builds Models of a Computer's Designs." *The New York Times* (March 16, 1988), p. 46Y.

161   "However, you may also": "Ardent's Software Package Makes Integrating 3-D Graphics Easy." *Electronics*, January 21, 1988, p. 25; see also, Levine, J. B. "A Quantum Leap in Workstation Wizardry." *Business Week* (March 7, 1988), p. 31; Bluestone, M. "Coming Soon: 3-D Workstations." *Business Week* (August 8, 1988), p. 53; Teresko, J. "Solid Modeling." *Industry Week* (February 6, 1989), pp. 40–44.

161   "there are exciting innovations": P. Villers. "Designing for Predictability: New MCAE Tools." *Harvard Business Review* (July/August 1988), p. 86; see also, Krouse, J. "Engineering Without Paper." *High Technology* (March 1986), pp. 38–46.

161   "software to analyze assembly": Teresko, J. "Speeding the Product Development Cycle." *Industry Week* (July 18, 1988), pp. 40–42.

Page

161   "Apple Computer spent $15": *Business Week* (January 27, 1986), p. 98.

161   "The Zilog Z8000 16-bit": Iversen, W. R. "Relief is on the Way for Documentation Headaches." *Electronics* (February 24, 1986), pp. 76–78.

161   "Electronic publishing systems": Buell, B. "Now the Print Shop Is Just a Few Keystrokes Away." *Business Week* (March 17, 1986), pp. 106–108; see also, Davis, D. "Business Turns to In-house Publishing." *High Technology* (April 1986), pp. 18–26; Iversen, W. "Relief is on the Way for Documentation Headaches." *Electronics* (February 24, 1986), pp. 76–78.

161   "Much of the equipment": Kaplan, R. "Must CIM Be Justified by Faith Alone?" *Harvard Business Review* (March/April 1986), pp. 87–93; see also, Holusha, J. "Cost Accounting's Blind Spot." *The New York Times* (October 14, 1986), pp. 33 ff; Pennar, K. "The Productivity Paradox." *Business Week* (June 6, 1988), pp. 100–102; Port, O. "How the New Math of Productivity Adds Up." *Business Week* (June 6, 1988), pp. 103 ff; Attaran, M. "The Automated Factory." *Business Horizons* (May/June 1989), pp. 80–86.

162   "there may be quality": Teresko, J. "Making CIM Work With People." *Industry Week* (November 2, 1987).

162   "Westinghouse has reportedly improved": Julian, K. "Westinghouse: Building a Better Board." *High Technology* (May 1985), pp. 36–38.

CHAPTER 14

Page

164   "performed a conjoint analysis": Rosenau, M. D., Jr. "From Experience: Schedule Emphasis of New Product Development Personnel." *Journal of Product Innovation Management* (December 1989), pp. 282–288.

172   "usual project review ground rules": Rosenau, M. D., Jr. *Successful Project Management.* New York: Van Nostrand Reinhold (Lifetime Learning Publications), 1981; see also, Rosenau, M. D., Jr., and Lewin, M. D. *Software Project Management.* Los Angeles: M. D. Lewin Associates (Lifetime Learning Publications), 1984; Rosenau, M. D., Jr. *Project Management for Engineers.* New York: Van Nostrand Reinhold (Lifetime Learning Publications), 1984.

173   "at two Japanese companies": Fraker, S. "High Speed Management for the High-Tech Age." *Fortune* (March 5, 1984), pp. 62 ff.

CHAPTER 15

Page

176   "variety of non-monetary recognitions": Rosenau, M. D., Jr. *Successful Project Management.* New York: Van Nostrand Reinhold (Lifetime Learning Publications), 1981, pp. 138–141; see also, Rosenau, M. D.,

Jr. *Project Management for Engineers*. New York: Van Nostrand Reinhold (Lifetime Learning Publications), 1984, pp. 184–189.

176   "install formal incentive plans": Kuczmarski, T. "Success Isn't Always Its Own Reward—Big Bucks Help." *Marketing News* (November 21, 1988), p. 10.

177   "better new product development": Hull, F. "How to Develop Products That Sell." *Summary Excerpts From Management Research at Rutgers* (Winter 1988).

179   "stock or stock options": Therrien, L. "Bausch & Lomb is Correcting Its Vision of Research." *Business Week* (March 30, 1987), p. 91.

179   "Pictel Corporation rewarded a": Gilpin, K., and Schmitt, E. "13 Engineers at Pictel Meet Phone Deadline." *The New York Times* (January 16, 1986), p. 22.

CHAPTER 16

181   "only the necessary people": Whitney, D. E. "Manufacturing by Design." *Harvard Business Review* (July/August 1988), pp. 83–91.

182   "fewest forms and signatures": "Keeping the Fires Lit Under the Innovators." *Fortune* (March 28, 1988), p. 45; see also, Kichell, W. "The Politics of Innovation." *Fortune* (April 11, 1988), pp. 131–132.

183   "Panasonic reportedly separates these": Reiner, G. "Getting There First: It Takes Planning to Put Plans Into Action." *The New York Times* (March 12, 1989), p. F3.

184   "new product risk taking": Power, C. "At Johnson & Johnson, a Mistake Can Be a Badge of Honor." *Business Week* (September 26, 1988), pp. 126–128.

184   "discontinue an existing product": "Linking Different Types of Product Elimination Decisions to Their Performance Outcome: 'Project Dropstat'." *International Journal of Research in Marketing* (No. 4, 1987), pp. 43–57.

185   "for instance, potential liability": Carson-Parker, J. "Who's at Risk?" *Chief Executive* (Summer 1986), pp. 29 ff.

186   "change the organization's climate": Hise, R. T., and McDaniel, S. W. "What is the CEO's Role in New Product Efforts?" *Management Review* (February 1989), pp. 44–48.

CHAPTER 17

200   "Machiavelli produces important cautionary": Machiavelli, N. *The Prince* (1532), Chap. 6.

Page

202 "must allow sufficient time": Bower, J. L., and Hout, T. M. "Fast-Cycle Capability for Competitive Power." *Harvard Business Review* (November/December 1988), pp. 110–118.

CHAPTER 18

Page

217 "contribute approximately twice as": Quinn, J. B., and Gagnon, C. E. "Will Services Follow Manufacturing Into Decline?" *Harvard Business Review* (November/December 1986), pp. 95–103.

217 "American Airlines' new system": Lineback, J. R. "This System Keeps an Eye on T&E Costs," *Electronics* (September 3, 1987), pp. 38–39; see also, Murray, A. "The Service Sector's Productivity Problem." *The Wall Street Journal* (February 9, 1987), p. 1.

218 "the best definition of": Seligman, D. "Failure on the Factory Floor." *Fortune* (May 25, 1987), pp. 135–136.

218 "at least three trends": Taylor, A., III. "What the Sober Spenders Will Buy." *Fortune* (February 2, 1987), pp. 35–38.

219 "on-line electronic data bases": Heskett, J. "Thank Heaven for the Service Sector." *Business Week* (January 26, 1987), p. 22.

219 "three characteristics of services": Berry, L. "Big Ideas in Services Marketing." *Journal of Consumer Marketing* (Spring 1986), pp. 47–50.

220 "a long queue precluding": Kleinfield, N. R. "Conquering Those Killer Queues." *The New York Times* (September 25, 1988), pp. F1 ff.

220 "one bank in Tennessee": Blackiston, G. H. "A Renaissance in Quality." *Executive Excellence* (September 1988), pp. 9–10.

220 "will stand in line": Benway, S. "Presto!" *Business Week* (April 27, 1987), pp. 86 ff.

220 "business and industrial markets": Cooper, P. D., and Jackson, R. W. "Applying a Services Marketing Orientation to the Industrial Services Sector." *Journal of Business and Industrial Marketing* (Summer 1988), pp. 51–54.

220 "One paint manufacturer not": Braham, J. "Marrying Goods and Services." *Industry Week* (November 7, 1988), pp. 69–71.

220 "maintenance service on products": Potts, G. W. "Exploit Your Product's Service Life Cycle." *Harvard Business Review* (September/October 1988), pp. 32 ff.

220 "repairing automotive and truck": "R&D Plus Marketing Equals Success." *Small Business Report* (April 1987), pp. 60–63.

221 "Hard data are scarce": Berger, J. "In the Services Sector, Nothing is 'Free' Anymore." *Business Week* (June 8, 1987), p. 144.

221 "must stress service quality": Uttal, B. "Companies That Serve You Best." *Fortune* (December 7, 1987), pp. 98 ff.

Page

221   "In some hotels your": Greenberg, P. S. "Hotels Taking Steps to Spruce Up Flagging Service." *Los Angeles Times* (March 15, 1987), part VII, p. 7.

221   "High quality requires that": Heskett, J. L. "Lessons in the Service Sector." *Harvard Business Review* (March/April 1987), pp. 118–126.

221   "it takes extra effort": Blackiston, G. H. "A Renaissance in Quality." *Executive Excellence* (September 1988), pp. 9–10.

221   "offer an unconditional guarantee": Hart, G. W. L. "The Power of Unconditional Service Guarantees." *Harvard Business Review* (July/August 1988), pp. 54–62.

221   "One study shows that": Berry, L. L., Parasuraman, A., and Zeithaml, V. A. "The Service–Quality Puzzle." *Business Horizons* (September/October 1988), pp. 35–43.

221   "there are many similarities": Cowell, D. W. "New Service Development." *Journal of Marketing Management* (Spring 1988), pp. 296–312.

222   "professional services entail a": Bloom, P. "Effective Marketing for Professional Services." *Harvard Business Review* (September/October 1984), pp. 102–110.

222   "service's sales volume cannot": Roberts, L. G. "The Nature of Developing and Marketing a Service." *MIT Enterprise Forum: Defining, Developing, and Building Products That Make Money.* Excerpts of the 1986 annual entrepreneurial workshop, pp. 4–12.

222   "market the service to": Ralph, D. *Marketing in a Service Environment.* Talk presented at PDMA-WEST meeting, Los Angeles, March 3, 1989.

222   "one bank created a": "New Bank Product." *The New York Times* (May 12, 1988), p. 29Y.

222   "a regional hospital in": Blackiston, G. H. "A Renaissance in Quality." *Executive Excellence* (September 1988), pp. 9–10.

222   "such as TRW's credentials": Bennett, R. A. "A TRW Twist: Selling a Service That Is Often Free." *The New York Times* (May 10, 1987), p. F9; see also, Sloane, L. "A Service to Keep Tabs on Credit Records." *The New York Times* (February 6, 1988), p. 16Y.

223   "The operations staff": Easingwood, C. J. "New Product Development for Service Companies." *Journal of Product Innovation Management* (December 1986), pp. 264–275.

APPENDIX A

Page

237   "Cooper has proposed seven": Cooper, R. "A Process Model for Industrial New Product Development." *IEEE Transactions on Engineering Management* (February 1983), pp. 2–11; see also, Cooper. R. *Winning at New Products.* Reading, MA: Addison-Wesley, 1986.

Page

237   "Cooper and Kleinschmidt have": Cooper, R., and Kleinschmidt, E. "An Investigation into the New Product Process: Steps, Deficiencies, and Impact." *Journal of Product Innovation Management* (June 1986), pp. 71–85.

237   "Merrifield identifies six phases": Merrifield, D. *Strategic Analysis, Selection, and Management of R&D Projects.* New York: AMACOM, 1977.

238   "Butrell lists five phases": Buttrell, F. *Technology to Payoff: Managing the New Product from Creation to Customer.* Philadelphia: Cresheim Publications, 1984.

238   "Douglas, Kemp, and Cook": Douglas, G., Kemp, P., and Cook, J. *Systematic New Product Development.* New York: John Wiley & Sons, 1978.

238   "Hoo lists five stages": Hoo., D., (ed.) *How to Develop and Market New Products . . . Better and Faster.* New York: Association of National Advertisers, Inc., 1985.

238   "Buggie concentrates on the": Buggie, F. D. *New Product Development Strategies.* New York: AMACOM, 1981.

238   "McGuire illustrates different new": McGuire, E. *Evaluating New-Product Proposals* (Conference Board Report 604). New York: Conference Board, 1973.

238   "Bacon and Butler have": Bacon, F. R., Jr., and Butler, Thomas W., Jr. *Planned Innovation.* Ann Arbor: University of Michigan, 1981.

238   "Crawford provides an integrated": Crawford, C. M. *New Products Management.* Homewood, IL: Richard D. Irwin, Inc., 1983.

238   "Feldman and Page completed": Feldman, L., and Page, A. "Principles vs. Practice in New Product Planning." *Journal of Product Innovation Management*, January 1984, pp. 43–55.

Index